What Mean
These Bones?

What Mean These Bones?

 Studies in Southeastern Bioarchaeology

Edited by

Mary Lucas Powell,
Patricia S. Bridges,
Ann Marie Wagner Mires

A DAN JOSSELYN MEMORIAL PUBLICATION

The University of Alabama Press
Tuscaloosa and London

Copyright © 1991 by
The University of Alabama Press
Tuscaloosa, Alabama 35487–0380
All rights reserved
Manufactured in the United States of America

The paper on which this book is printed meets the minimum requirements of American
National Standard for Information Science-Permanence of Paper for Printed Library Materials, ANSI A39.48-1984.

Library of Congress Cataloging-in-Publication Data

What mean these bones? : studies in southeastern bioarchaeology /
    edited by Mary Lucas Powell, Patricia S. Bridges, and Ann Marie Wagner
    Mires.
        p. cm.
    Includes bibliographical references.
    ISBN-0-8173-0484-3 (alk. paper)
    1. Indians of North America—Southern States—Anthropometry.
    2. Anthropometry—Southern States. 3. Indians of North America—
    Southern States—Antiquities. 4. Southern States—Antiquities.
    I. Powell, Mary Lucas. II. Bridges, Patricia S. III. Mires, Ann
    Marie Wagner.
    E78.S65W43   1991   89-20455
    975'.01—dc20   CIP

British Library Cataloguing-in-Publication Data available

❋ Contents

✳ Figures and Tables

Figures

Tables

✳ Acknowledgments

We would like to thank Richard W. Jefferies, Henry T. Wright, John H. Blitz, Bruce D. Smith, and Jane E. Buikstra for their valuable advice and encouragement during the production of this volume. Victoria Horwitz and Jo Stone prepared the figure and table in the introductory chapter, and Wanda Smith and Betsy R. Davis provided expert secretarial assistance throughout the project. We commend the authors for their timely and courteous responses to our queries; the care with which they prepared their manuscripts made our tasks much easier. And finally, our deep and sincere gratitude to Judith Knight, Marketing Manager and Editor at The University of Alabama Press, who guided the three fledgling editors through the lengthy transition from symposium to published volume with admirable patience, knowledge, and persistence.

What Mean
These Bones?

＊ 1

Introduction

Mary Lucas Powell, Patricia S. Bridges, and Ann Marie Wagner Mires

Despite the number of ongoing archaeological projects that include research on human skeletal remains, few are characterized by active collaboration between archaeologists and physical anthropologists from the planning stages onward. An unfortunate lack of coordination in research goals, sampling strategies, and recovery methods is the common result, with neither group realizing the maximum return for their efforts. To address this critical problem, a symposium entitled "What Mean These Bones? The Dynamic Integration of Physical Anthropology and Archaeology in the Southeastern United States" was organized by Mary Lucas Powell, Patricia S. Bridges, and Ann Marie Wagner Mires for the 42d Southeastern Archaeological Conference. The primary goal of the symposium was to encourage communication between the two subdisciplines in regard to analysis of human skeletal remains from archaeological contexts. This volume includes nine papers presented in the symposium, all representative of the intrinsically integrative bioarchaeological approach.

As symposium discussants Bruce D. Smith and Jane E. Buikstra note in their comments (Chapters 11 and 12), skeletal analyses have in the past often been relegated to small-print appendixes in archaeological reports. Physical anthropologists who work with excavated collections regularly publish additional reports of general and specific aspects of their research in the *American Journal of Physical Anthropology* and other journals, but these are seldom read by their archaeological colleagues. This lack of synthesis is especially distressing given the number of recent theoretical and methodological advances in anthropology that enhance investigations of critical biocultural determinants of such phenomena as differential health levels within populations. Physical anthropologists today address an array of questions inaccessible to earlier generations of researchers, who concentrated primarily upon descriptive studies of populations or the identification of unique cases of syphilis or scalping. Even today, many archaeologists do not realize the extent to which data from human burials can shed light upon key questions of cultural development, such as the effect of population growth on the rise of complex societies in the late prehistoric Southeast. The explicit goal of this symposium was to heighten awareness of the tremendous potential for creative collaboration, and the nine papers included in this volume clearly illustrate the benefits of such interaction.

Figure 1-1 shows the locations of the nine case studies reported here, representing eight southeastern states. Table 1-1 provides the chronological data for each study, reflecting more than 4,000 years of prehistoric and historic occupation. The first four papers focus upon one of the most active areas of contemporary bioarchaeological research, the study of biological changes accompanying the cultural transition from food collection to food production. In the Midwest and Southeast, particular attention has been paid to the adoption of maize agriculture by Mississippian populations in a variety of ecological and social contexts. In Chapter 2, Jerome C. Rose, Murray K. Marks, and Larry L. Tieszen discuss articulations between archaeological and biological evidence for the introduction of maize into the lower and central Mississippi Valley, and they develop a compelling argument that maize became a dietary staple only in Middle Mississippian times despite its earlier appearance in the region. In the paramount community of the complex Mississippian chiefdom at Moundville, Alabama, Mary Lucas Powell (Chapter 3) found no significant differences in health between elite and nonelite individuals, with the population as a whole appearing reasonably well adapted relative to more northern agricultural groups. George R. Milner examined changes in mortality, health, and population density during the Mississippian period in the American Bottom. In Chapter 4 he notes that while the regional population gradually decreased in size, increases in mortality and infectious disease rates were not evident, suggesting that poor health was not a factor in population decline. Leslie E. Eisenberg describes in Chapter 5 a quite different pattern at Averbuch, a Late Mississippian site in central Tennessee, where infectious disease rates were so high as to suggest a major cause for the disappearance of Middle Cumberland populations in that area. Collectively, these case studies clearly delineate different regional patterns of biocultural adaptation as well as present well-reasoned discussions of the factors underlying such diversity.

The cultural shift from casual cultivation to substantial reliance upon maize and other tropical cultigens during the Mississippian period not only produced major changes in demography and health but also occasioned new patterns of physical activity, with resultant changes in skeletal morphology. Two papers included in this volume focus upon this

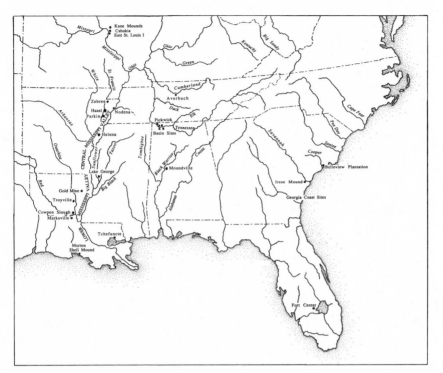

Figure 1-1
Geographical Location of Sites

particular aspect of biological adaptation. Patricia S. Bridges (Chapter 6), documents increases in both arm and leg strength in a Mississippian group from northwest Alabama, relative to their late Archaic predecessors. Clark Spencer Larsen and Christopher B. Ruff (Chapter 7), on the other hand, attribute an observed decrease in leg strength from Woodland to Mississippian times on the Georgia coast to a reduction in levels of mechanical stress upon the human body in the later time period. These contrasting findings indicate, once again, significant regional variations in patterned activities associated not only with subsistence (specifically with methods of cultivation and food preparation) but also with ceremonial activities related to warfare.

The remaining three papers cover a variety of topics and time periods. Ann Marie Wagner Mires (Chapter 8) analyzes the complex mortuary program at a Late Archaic site in northeast Louisiana that included both primary and secondary interments and cremations. Patricia Miller-Shaivitz and Mehmet Yaşar İşcan (Chapter 9) describe the health and

Table 1-1
Chronology of Sites

			B.C.						A.D.	
3000	2500	2000	1500	1000	500	0			0	200
LOWER MISSISSIPPI RIVER VALLEY							–1– Arkansas			
		Poverty Point		Tchefuncte						
		Late Archaic					–1-9– Louisiana			Marksville
							–2– Illinois			
							–3– Tennessee			
Pickwick Basin		Terminal Archaic					–4-5– Alabama			
		Preagricultural Populations					–6– Georgia			
							–7– Florida			
							–8– South Carolina			

–1– Rose et al.
–2– Milner
–3– Eisenberg
–4– Bridges
–5– Powell
–6– Larsen and Ruff
–7– Miller-Shaivitz and İşcan
–8– Rathbun and Scurry
–9– Mires

physical characteristics of a skeletal sample from the Fort Center site, an enigmatic ceremonial center in southern Florida. In a case study from Colonial South Carolina, Ted A. Rathbun and James D. Scurry (Chapter 10) discuss similarities and differences in health, nutrition, and physical activity between white masters and black slaves at Belleview Plantation.

In the two concluding chapters of the volume, the symposium discussants provide trenchant comments on the papers and on bio-archaeological method and theory. We are indeed fortunate to have these contributions by two anthropologists who have worked vigorously for many years to encourage communication and cooperation between archaeologists and physical anthropologists. Bruce D. Smith presents an archaeologist's perspective on the recent trend toward granting "data parity" to various categories of biological materials (including botanical, faunal, and human remains) formerly considered as "peripheral" rather

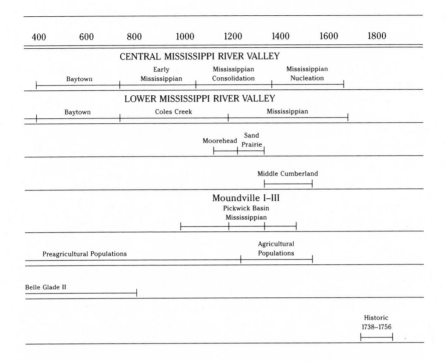

than "core" sources of information on prehistoric life. He stresses the substantive contributions of the analyses presented here toward understanding the biological consequences of major cultural transformations, in particular the Mississippian emergence. Smith concludes his discussion with an example of productive interaction between bioarchaeological and archaeobotanical investigations of a major step in this transition in the late prehistoric Southeast, that is, "the shift to heavy reliance upon indigenous starchy seeds [which] preceded the transition to maize-based agriculture" in the lower Mississippi Valley.

Jane E. Buikstra places the 1985 symposium in historical perspective within the mainstream of American anthropological development through a detailed comparison with a similar symposium organized in 1976 by Robert Blakely for the Southern Anthropological Society, published the following year as *Biocultural Adaptation in Prehistoric America*. In her contribution to that volume, Buikstra introduced the conjunctive term "bio-archeology" into the scientific literature. As the title of her chapter in the present volume indicates, she continues to encourage the promotion of human burial data from peripheral to core status in the planning and execution of archaeological research.

By presenting the specific conclusions and the broader anthropological implications of these case studies, we wish both to illustrate the wide variety of problem-oriented projects encompassed by the term "bioarchaeology" and to emphasize its active role in the advancement of anthropological inquiry. One of the major emphases of bioarchaeological research over the past ten years (and one that is well illustrated in this collection of papers) has been the documentation of regional and developmental diversity in biocultural adaptations. The variety and complexity of these adaptations have overturned earlier assumptions that all populations who adopt maize agriculture will display exactly the same degree of biological perturbation as, for example, the Middle Mississippian population at Dickson Mounds reported by Lallo (1973) in one of the earliest diachronic studies of changing patterns of health from preagricultural to agricultural times in eastern North America.

In the conjunctive analysis of archaeological and human biological data sets, anthropologists now have the necessary theoretical and methodological tools to advance beyond simple description to address truly complex variations on the eternal questions, "What happened in prehistory?" and "Why?" The future promises to be an exciting one for bioarchaeology. Through creative coordination at all levels of planning, excavation, and analysis, archaeologists and physical anthropologists should integrate their research to enhance achievement of their mutual goals. The stimulus for producing this volume is the hope that by demonstrating the substantial benefits of conjunctive studies, we will foster a greater spirit of cooperation between the two subdisciplines for the ultimate benefit of anthropology.

✳ 2

Bioarchaeology and Subsistence in the Central and Lower Portions of the Mississippi Valley

Jerome C. Rose, Murray K. Marks, and Larry L. Tieszen

During the past two decades archaeologists have demonstrated a great interest in establishing both the timing of the origins of agricultural dependency and the cultural-ecological mechanisms that stimulated this mode of human adaptation (e.g., Cohen 1977; Rindos 1984; among others). A more recent development has been the use of bioarchaeological data derived from the analysis of prehistoric skeletal remains to provide supporting evidence for this dietary transition (e.g., Gilbert and Mielke 1985; Wing and Brown 1979; among others). In addition, bioarchaeological data have been employed to assess the impact of the adoption of maize horticulture upon prehistoric human populations (e.g., Cohen and Armelagos 1984). Despite this interest, the date for the adoption of agriculture as the major subsistence strategy in the central and lower portions of the Mississippi Valley remains undetermined and clouded by conflicting evidence. This chapter uses published bioarchaeological data from prehistoric human skeletons to interpret the available archaeological information and provide a scenario of subsistence change over time.

Four major lines of archaeological evidence (settlement patterns, monumental earthworks, artifacts, and botanical remains) have been used to postulate dependency upon tropical cultigens (primarily maize) throughout the Neo-Indian era (after Williams and Brain 1983) in the lower Mississippi Valley. Both settlement patterns (Webb 1968) and the presence of polished hoes (Webb 1970) have been used to suggest that the Poverty Point culture of the lower valley (2000–400 B.C.) was dependent upon maize horticulture. This conclusion is not widely accepted (Neuman 1984), and the earliest actual remains of cultigens, squash, and bottle gourd (Byrd and Neuman 1978) presently date only to the Tchefuncte culture (400 B.C.–A.D. 1). Site location, settlement patterns, and earthworks have been used to postulate maize utilization by Marksville peoples (A.D. 1–350) (Belmont 1967; Brain 1976). This contention is supported by isolated finds of maize at Marksville sites (Byrd and Neuman 1978; Haag 1978). Many archaeologists have suggested that the settlement patterns, site locations, monumental earthworks, and presence of shell hoes establish maize dependency by the Coles Creek peoples (A.D. 800–1200) (Belmont 1967; Brain 1971; Haag 1978; Williams and Brain 1983). This conclusion is drawn despite the fact that there is "no hard evidence in the form of the cultigens themselves" (Williams and Brain 1983:408). Neuman (1984:213) concludes: "the fact that not a single specimen of corn, beans, or squash has been reported from all the thousands of cubic feet of dirt excavated at Troyville–Coles Creek sites would seem to indicate that these foodstuffs were as yet relatively unimportant items in the people's diet." The one possible exception to this statement is a single kernel of maize from the Coles Creek St. Gabriel site, which has been dated to A.D. 1000 (Woodiel 1980). One specimen of maize at a Plaquemine site has been reported (Neuman 1984:262), while they are very numerous at Mississippian sites (Byrd and Neuman 1978).

For the purposes of this chapter, the lower Mississippi Valley is divided into two portions. The central valley (Figure 1-1) as defined by Morse and Morse (1983) extends from just north of the mouth of the Ohio River to the mouth of the Arkansas River. The lower valley extends from the Arkansas River to the Mississippi Delta. In the central valley, the absence of a widespread early cultural florescence has inhibited speculation concerning early maize horticulture. Morse and Morse (1983) suggest that the location of Marksville sites in the meander-belt region of the valley, where agriculturally productive soils are plentiful, could indicate that horticulture was important. The assumption that the appearance of Mississippian cultural traits and maize agriculture were contemporaneous is commonly held (Lynott et al. 1986; Morse and Morse 1983). This idea is supported by the fact that the earliest remains of maize are from Baytown (A.D. 400–700) and Early Period Mississippian sites (A.D. 700–1000; after Morse and Morse 1983), and Mississippian sites are consistently found adjacent to easily worked, well-drained, and agriculturally productive soils (Morse and Morse 1983). Central valley Baytown sites where maize has been found include Hoecake (Byrd and Neuman 1978), Zebree (Morse and Morse 1976), Brougham Lake (Klinger et al. 1983), and Little Cypress Bayou (Shea 1985). In fact, Klinger et al. (1983) suggest that 31.8 percent of the edible plants utilized at the Brougham Lake site derived from tropical cultigens. Despite the evidence of plant remains, settlement location, and cultural development, maize dependency by Terminal Baytown and Early Mississippian peoples is subject to question.

This brief summary of the archaeological evidence demonstrates that the earliest dates for dependency upon maize horticulture in the central and lower portions of the Mississippi Valley have not been firmly established. Following Gibson's (1970) advice to employ multiple lines of evidence, we turn to the bioarchaeological data for indications of maize dependency.

Methodology and Rationale

In accordance with the bioarchaeological research design adopted for Arkansas (Rose and Marks 1985), this chapter constitutes the first step in the design and provides a synthesis and interpretation of the extant osteological data. Osteological data, interpretations, and conclusions were collected from publications, cultural resource management contract reports, unpublished master's and honors theses, manuscript reports on file in various locations, and student papers. All data were reduced to raw scores and subsequently transformed into percentages using only documented observables as the denominators. The paucity of subadults in the majority of the skeletal collections required that the data reported here be restricted to adults over the age of eighteen years. Use of this heterogeneous data base, which has been collected by numerous researchers over a period of more than forty years, required two major methodological concessions. First, none of the rates could be age adjusted because ages at death were not consistently reported and they often could not be associated with the individuals displaying the skeletal lesions. Second, skeletal lesions (i.e., infections and porotic hyperostosis) could not be reported as either healed or active because this information was not consistently reported by the various investigators. As a consequence of these limitations and in order to maximize the available data, all the information had to be reduced to the lowest common denominator.

As will be demonstrated in the discussion, the bioarchaeological data are not distributed equitably over time, cultures, or geographic areas; thus, significant gaps in the sequences hinder comparison. In many cases the sample sizes are very small and render statistical evaluation meaningless. Consequently, the bioarchaeological data are examined for directional frequency trends whether they be increasing, decreasing, or stable. Within the context of our research design the literature synthesis presented here represents the problem definition stage. The interpretations derived from this synthesis are considered tentative hypotheses and, in conjunction with the overall scenario, are envisioned as forming the framework for structuring a long-term research program. Thus, the inherent goals of this chapter are to identify the time periods, cultures, and geographic areas on which future research can and should focus, and to provide interpretations of the extant bioarchaeological data that can be developed into testable hypotheses. This chapter is not a completed research project but an initial step in a long-term research program and an attempt to provide a guide to a literature that is not easily accessible and is often overlooked.

Bioarchaeological Evidence from the Lower Valley

Bioarchaeological data from the early part of the Neo-Indian era are relatively scarce and can provide only hints of subsistence practices. The poorly preserved human skeletal remains from the Poverty Point Cowpen Slough site have produced no evidence that supports dependency on domesticated plants (Mires, Chapter 8 of this volume). No dental caries (Table 2-1) was reported in the analysis of seven Marksville individuals from the Womack Mound site (Heckel 1966), which is located just to the east of the lower Mississippi Valley. Following the interpretation that a rate of 2 carious lesions per person is the dividing point between high- and low-carbohydrate diets (Rose et al. 1984; Turner 1979), this absence of caries suggests a low-carbohydrate nonhorticultural diet. However, the rate from Helena Mounds, another Marksville site, exceeds 1.5 carious lesions per person (Ford 1963) and suggests a somewhat higher proportion of carbohydrates in the diet. Examination of the published burial descriptions suggests that the true rate would not exceed 2 lesions per person.

At present, the Marksville data do not indicate any extensive use of domesticated plant foods. The absence of maize consumption at a number of midwestern Hopewell sites has been confirmed with stable carbon isotope analysis (Bender et al. 1981). Further discussion of these early cultural traditions must await publication of recently collected data from Tchefuncte and Marksville sites located in Louisiana (Manhein 1985).

A more detailed discussion of this biological feature should begin with the Baytown period cultures in both the lower and the central portions of the valley. Examination of Table 2-2 shows that Baytown dental wear scores are consistently higher than scores from Mississippian sites.

Table 2-1
Dental Caries in Adults in the
Central and Lower Mississippi Valley

Culture and Site	Reference	N	X̄ Lesions Per Dentition
Late Mississippian-Central Valley			
Campbell	Spier 1955	27	1.8*
Hazel	Powell 1989	33	2.6
Middle Nodena	Powell 1989	52	2.7
Parkin	Murray 1985	8	5.9
Turner	Black 1979	52	1.4*
Upper Nodena	Powell 1989	103	3.9
Wapanocca	Harmon 1984	13	3.9
Total**		209	3.5
Middle Mississippian-Central Valley			
Bay Village	Rose et al. 1984	1	9.0
Burris	Condon and Rose 1979	1	1.0
Floodway	Rose et al. 1984	1	3.0
John Wilson	Rose et al. 1984	7	2.6
Mangrum	Sperber 1982	1	2.0
Zebree	Powell 1977	2	0.0
Total		13	2.6
Early Mississippian-Central Valley			
Owls Bend	Rose and Burnett 1985	1	1.0
Zebree	Powell 1977	13	2.4
Total		14	2.3
Baytown (Late)-Central Valley			
Banks	Rose, Marks, and Tieszen 1985	7	0.9
Hyneman 2	Rose et al. 1984	1	0.0
Little Cypress Bayou	Rose, Marks, and Tieszen 1985	3	2.7
Total		11	1.3
Coles Creek-Lower Valley			
Lage George	Egnatz 1983	11	1.6*
Mount Nebo	Giardino 1977	86	8.1
Total**		86	8.1
Baytown-Lower Valley			
Gold Mine	Walker 1980	89	1.1
Powell Canal	Blaeuer and Rose 1982	4	0.5
Total		93	1.1
Marksville-Lower Valley			
Helena Mounds	Ford 1963	13	1.5*
Womack Mound	Heckel 1966	7	0.0
Total**		7	0.0

*Caries rates probably underestimated

**Total rates $= \dfrac{\text{observed dentitions}}{\text{carious lesions}}$. The underestimated site specific rates are not included in these calculations.

Dental wear scores clearly differentiate Baytown and Mississippian teeth and indicate that the Baytown diets were far more coarse and abrasive than those of later cultures. Studies of broader scope than the present chapter have indicated that horticultural dependency is usually associated with a more refined diet and decreased dental wear (Powell 1985a; Rose et al. 1984).

Examination of molar occlusal surfaces with a scanning electron microscope corroborates this interpretation. Baytown molars from the lower valley Gold Mine and Powell Canal sites have rough surfaces with large striations, numerous microstriations, a variable frequency of compression fractures, and variable amounts of polishing (Blaeuer and Rose 1982). Blaeuer and Rose (1982) interpret these features to suggest that Baytown diets in the lower valley were composed of foods coarsely processed with stone implements and containing minor amounts of minimally altered vegetable fiber and large quantities of seasonally available hickory nuts. The average dental caries rate of 1.1 (Table 2-1) indicates low carbohydrate consumption and the absence of high-carbohydrate domesticates. These bioarchaeological data, although derived from only two sites, support the archaeological interpretation of Baytown period subsistence that emphasizes aquatic resources and the collection of wild plants, fruits, and nuts (House 1982; Springer 1980).

Table 2-2
Adult First Molar Mean Wear Scores in the Central and Lower Mississippi Valley

Culture and Site	Reference	Mean (N) Maxillary		Mean (N) Mandibular	
Late Mississippian-Central Valley					
Campbell	Scott 1979b	19.3	(64)	17.6	(68)
Middle Nodena	Powell 1989	17.9	(54)	16.4	(57)
Parkin	Murray 1985	22.0	(4)	22.5	(4)
Upper Nodena	Powell 1989	17.3	(125)	16.5	(102)
Wapanocca	Harmon 1984	19.4	(16)	18.5	(22)
Mean Score		18.1	(263)	17.0	(253)
Baytown-Central Valley					
Banks	Rose, Marks, and Tieszen 1985	34.7	(3)	28.8	(5)
Little Cypress Bayou	Rose, Marks, and Tieszen 1985	18.5	(2)	21.5	(2)
Mean Score		28.2	(5)	26.7	(7)
Baytown-Lower Valley					
Gold Mine	Walker 1980	23.0	(89)	24.0	(89)
Powell Canal	Blaeuer and Rose 1982	20.5	(4)	23.4	(4)
Mean Score		22.9	(93)	24.0	(93)

Molar scoring system described in Scott 1979a.

The first major change in the dentition is found among skeletons associated with the Coles Creek culture of the lower valley. Molars from the major Coles Creek sites exhibit very rapid attrition, which produced an angled and cupped occlusal surface on the molars (Giardino 1977; personal observation by Rose). Although no lower valley molars have been examined with a scanning electron microscope, there are data from the Coles Creek period component of the Alexander site, which is located north of Little Rock adjacent to the Arkansas River. Although well outside the lower valley culture area, this site may provide a useful analogy for interpreting lower valley Coles Creek period diets. These molars exhibit the same cupped wear observed on the lower valley teeth. As observed with a scanning electron microscope, the Alexander molars have numerous compression fractures, large sharp striations, numerous intermediate and microstriations, and intermittent areas of polished enamel (Rose and Marks 1985). The striation size distribution and pattern, in conjunction with excessive molar attrition, indicate a heavy grit load, which implies increased processing with stone utensils (Rose and Marks 1985).

This change in dental attrition is accompanied by a significant increase in dental caries (Table 2-1): the mean rate of 8.1 lesions per person is well past the mean frequency of agriculturalists (Giardino 1977; Rose and Marks 1985; Rose et al. 1984). Personal observation by Rose confirmed that Egnatz (1983) radically underestimated the caries rate at Lake George, which in reality should be virtually identical to that found at Mount Nebo by Giardino (1977). Without having stable carbon isotope data, we originally thought that the caries rates indicated that the Coles Creek peoples were dependent upon maize horticulture. However, the absence of maize in the archaeological deposits was bothersome (Byrd and Neuman 1978; House 1982; Neuman 1984). A clue was provided by King (1985), who reported that the Coles Creek period occupation at the Alexander site contained no maize but instead numerous starchy seeds: maygrass, knotweed, and goosefoot. The small size of these seeds and their hard seed coats would require extensive grinding. The grit in the flour from the grinding implements and seed coat particles would produce a very abrasive food, which could explain the extensive tooth wear and the unusual microwear observed with the scanning electron microscope. The high carbohydrate content of these seeds could also account for the high Coles Creek culture caries rate in the lower valley. Paleobotanical studies of Coles Creek culture sites in the lower valley are rare (Neuman 1984), and only knotweed has been reported from the Troyville site (Byrd and Neuman 1978). Although all of these starchy seed species have been domesticated in the eastern United States, there is as yet no evidence that this was true in the lower valley.

Table 2-3
Percentages of Adult Infections and Porotic Hyperostosis in the Lower Mississippi Valley

Culture and Site	Reference	Infection		Porotic Hyperostosis	
		%	(N)	%	(N)
Plaquemine-Mississippian					
Boytt's Field	Hrdlička 1909	36.0	(25)	4.0	(25)
Gordon	Rose et al. 1984	18.7	(16)	31.2	(16)
McArthur	Rose et al. 1984	66.7	(3)	33.3	(3)
Myatt Landing	Hrdlička 1909	11.1	(18)	0.0	(18)
Ward Place	Hrdlička 1909	25.0	(20)	0.0	(25)
Total*		25.6	(82)	8.0	(87)
Coles Creek					
Lake George	Egnatz 1983	7.5	(80)		
Mount Nebo (A)	Giardino 1977	16.7	(24)	0.0	(24)
Mount Nebo (F)	Giardino 1977	3.3	(30)	0.0	(30)
St. Gabriel	Woodiel 1980	42.8	(7)		
Total*		9.9	(141)	0.0	(54)
Baytown					
Gold Mine	Berg 1984	25.8	(31)		
Powell Canal	Blaeuer and Rose 1982	25.0	(4)	0.0	(4)
Total*		25.7	(35)	0.0	(4)
Marksville					
Womack Mound	Heckel 1966	0.0	(7)		
Tchefuncte					
Tchefuncte	Manhein 1985	20.0+	(?)		

N = Number of individuals observed.

Total* = Total percentage = $\dfrac{\text{total affected individuals}}{\text{total individuals observed}}$.

Paleopathology provides an additional source of data for indirectly establishing maize dependency, because this dietary regimen is associated with increases in skeletal lesions indicative of dietary iron deficiency. No cases of porotic hyperostosis, a condition frequently associated with maize-induced iron-deficiency anemia, have been reported from Coles Creek or Baytown skeletal series (Table 2-3). It is not until the appearance of the Mississippian cultural tradition in the lower valley that consistent increases in porotic hyperostosis are observed. Increased infection rates are attributed to the adoption of larger sedentary residential units.

These bioarchaeological data suggest the following interpretation for dietary change in the lower valley. The Baytown period subsistence pattern appears to emphasize aquatic resources with a lesser reliance upon both large and small mammals (House 1982), while plant utilization includes a large variety of seeds, fruits, nuts, and other vegetable foods. The Coles Creek culture participated in a subsistence shift that included large quantities of carbohydrates (high caries rates) and grit (high dental attrition rates) in the diet. The bioarchaeological and archaeological evidence suggests that this shift might be characterized by a reliance upon native starchy seeds and not maize. Until additional data from stable carbon isotope and flotation analyses are available, this reconstruction must be considered a hypothesis to be tested. Thorough bioarchaeological analyses of Plaquemine and Mississippian skeletal series must be performed before any dietary reconstructions can be offered for these later cultural traditions.

Bioarchaeological Evidence from the Central Valley

Within the central Mississippi Valley, understanding of subsistence and dietary change is limited by the absence of good bioarchaeological data prior to the Baytown period. Archaeologists working in northeast Arkansas and southeast Missouri have cited paleobotanical evidence to suggest that initial maize dependency occurred during the terminal Baytown to Early Mississippian transition. Morse and Morse (1976) point to the abundant remains of maize at the Early Mississippian component (ca. A.D. 900) of the Zebree site to infer that the appearance of the Mississippian culture and maize horticulture were contemporaneous. Klinger and co-workers' (1983) interpretation of the paleobotanical remains from the Terminal Baytown (ca. A.D. 800) component of the Brougham Lake site is that maize made up 28.7 percent of the edible flora. They conclude that "these people gained the vast bulk of their vegetable diet from cultivated sources" (Klinger et al. 1983:461). Similarly, maize was found at the Baytown component (ca. A.D. 800) of the Little Cypress Bayou site, but its frequency is surprisingly lower than at the Brougham Lake site (Shea 1985). Other Baytown sites from the same time period, such as DeRossitt, have produced no maize despite the use of flotation (Spears 1978).

Examination of the bioarchaeological data suggests that although maize may have been grown in some unknown quantity, it was not a dietary staple. As was true in the lower valley, the molar attrition rates are much higher for Baytown individuals than for the later Mississippian peoples (Table 2-2), which implies a coarse non-maize-dependent diet. It should be pointed out that the two individuals from Little Cypress

Bayou are young adults and therefore have relatively lower mean wear scores.

The scanning electron microscope reveals that the Early Mississippian component molars from the Zebree site display numerous large sharp striations, numerous intermediate and microstriations, a rough enamel surface with no polishing, and a variable occurrence of compression fractures (Rose, Marks, and Tieszen 1985). This pattern indi-

Table 2-4
Percentages of Adult Infections and Porotic Hyperostosis in the Central Mississippi Valley

Culture and Site	Reference	Infection % (N)		Porotic Hyperostosis % (N)	
Late Mississippian					
Campbell	Spier 1955	0.0	(29)	0.0	(29)
Hazel	Rose et al. 1984	87.5	(72)		
Middle Nodena	Powell 1989	56.2	(16)	1.9	(53)
Parkin	Murray 1985	41.7	(12)	16.7	(6)
Upper Nodena	Powell 1989	86.0	(43)	3.4	(118)
Wapanocca	Harmon 1984	55.5	(9)	0.0	(9)
Total*		65.7	(181)	2.8	(215)
Middle Mississippian					
Bay Village	Rose et al. 1984	0.0	(1)	0.0	(1)
Burris	Condon and Rose 1979	100.0	(1)	0.0	(1)
Floodway	Rose et al. 1984	0.0	(1)	0.0	(1)
John Wilson	Rose et al. 1984	33.3	(15)	0.0	(2)
Mangrum	Sperber 1982	0.0	(2)	0.0	(2)
Zebree	Powell 1977	100.0	(1)	0.0	(1)
Total*		33.3	(21)	0.0	(8)
Early Mississippian					
Owls Bend	Rose and Burnett 1985	0.0	(1)	0.0	(1)
Zebree	Powell 1977	25.0	(8)	11.1	(9)
Total*		22.2	(9)	10.0	(10)
Baytown					
Banks	Rose, Marks, and Tieszen 1985	24.0	(25)	0.0	(25)
Hyneman 1	Rose et al. 1984	0.0	(4)	0.0	(4)
Hyneman 2	Rose et al. 1984	100.0	(1)	0.0	(1)
Little Cypress Bayou	Rose, Marks, and Tieszen 1985	0.0	(2)	0.0	(2)
Total*		21.9	(32)	0.0	(32)

N = Number of individuals observed.

Total* = Total percentage = $\dfrac{\text{total affected individuals}}{\text{total individuals observed}}$.

cates coarsely prepared foods and variable use of hickory nuts (Rose, Marks, and Tieszen 1985). Comparison of microwear patterns from Zebree (Early Mississippian) and Little Cypress Bayou (Baytown) with those from lower valley Baytown sites (Gold Mine and Powell Canal) indicates that they are remarkably similar (Rose, Marks, and Tieszen 1985). Compression fractures (nut consumption) and polishing (vegetable fiber consumption) are the only variable microwear features within and between the samples from these sites, and this variability has been attributed to seasonal dietary shifts (Rose, Marks, and Tieszen 1985). The Middle Mississippian molars from the Zebree and John Wilson sites reflect a major change in the physical consistency of the diet from the previous Early Mississippian samples. A greater than 50 percent reduction in large striations occurs, and large patches of smooth enamel are produced by numerous microstriations (Rose and Harmon 1986). This pattern change indicates a radical reduction in abrasive particles associated with changes in both food content and preparation.

A dietary shift between Baytown and Mississippian sites is indicated by an increase in the caries rates (Table 2-1). The caries rates increase from a Baytown average of 1.3 to 2.3 in the Early Mississippian to 2.6 in the Middle Mississippian and to 3.5 in the Late Mississippian. These data suggest a gradual increase in carbohydrate consumption from the Baytown to Late Mississippian cultures.

Porotic hyperostosis, associated with maize-induced iron-deficiency anemia, is found at Early Mississippian Zebree (11.1 percent) and the Terminal Late Mississippian Parkin site (16.7 percent) (Table 2-4). The values do not approach the elevated levels common at other prehistoric maize-dependent sites in the eastern United States (Cohen and Armelagos 1984). The absence of a clear-cut pattern of increased porotic hyperostosis prevents the determination of a date for maize dependency, but it does indicate well-balanced diets throughout this cultural sequence, at least with respect to iron intake.

The adult infection rates increase from approximately 22 percent in the Baytown and Early Mississippian sites to 33 percent in the Middle Mississippian and 66 percent in the Late Mississippian. This increase in infections appears to be associated not with a decline in dietary quality but with the adoption of a nucleated settlement pattern (Morse and Morse 1983), which promotes the transmission of infectious pathogens (Rose et al. 1984). None of these bioarchaeological data sources clearly indicates the data of maize dependency, but fortunately stable carbon isotope ratios are available from the central valley.

Stable carbon isotope values reported by Lynott et al. (1986) and Rose, Marks, and Tieszen (1985) indicate that maize consumption was

Table 2-5
Stable Carbon Isotope Values from the Ozark
Highlands and Central Mississippi Valley

Culture and Site	Reference	Burial No.	Value
Late Mississippian			
Berry	Lynott et al. 1986	22	− 13.5
Campbell	Lynott et al. 1986	52	− 10.4
Hazel	Lynott et al. 1986	56	− 12.9
Average		($N=3$)	− 12.3
Middle Mississippian			
Lilbourn	Lynott et al. 1986	16D	− 14.9
Turner	Lynott et al. 1986	21A	− 15.8
		28	− 13.2
		36B	− 14.1
Zebree	Lynott et al. 1986	4	− 13.0
Average		($N=5$)	− 14.2
Early Mississippian			
Zebree	Lynott et al. 1986	3F	− 21.2
		3G	− 21.2
		6	− 20.5
Average		($N=3$)	− 21.0
Late Baytown			
Banks	Rose, Marks, and Tieszen 1985	1	− 21.2
		6	− 21.5
Little Cypress Bayou	Rose, Marks, and Tieszen 1985	1	− 22.3
		2	− 21.1
		3	− 15.7
Average		($N=5$)	− 20.4
Ozark Highlands Archaic and Woodland			
Average	Lynott et al. 1986	($N=6$)	− 20.7

not significant at either Late Baytown or Early Mississippian sites, despite the presence of maize in the archaeological deposits (Table 2-5). The average stable carbon isotope values from the Late Baytown (− 20.4) and Early Mississippian (− 21.0) cultural components are not different from the non-maize-consuming Archaic and Woodland samples, which average − 20.7. Values indicating maize consumption appear during the Middle Mississippian (− 14.2) and increase still further in the Late Mississippian (− 12.3). These data prompted Lynott et al. (1986:61) to conclude that maize dependency was not present during the Early Mississippian period and did not develop until the appearance of sedentary villages and major civic-ceremonial centers. This establishment of a late date (i.e., A.D. 1200) for maize dependency is also supported by the previously described caries, dental attrition, and molar microwear data. It is also significant that high infection rates (Table 2-4) are not found until the Late Mississippian when population nucleation was at its greatest (Rose et al. 1984) and the carbon isotope values indicate the greatest reliance upon maize. Thus, we postulate that maize dependency did not occur until population nucleation resulted in localized stress upon the bountiful natural food resources of the central Mississippi Valley. These data lead to the inescapable conclusion that Mississippianization and maize dependency were not contemporaneous in the central Mississippi Valley. However, these data do not explain the presence of maize in the Baytown and Early Mississippian archaeological deposits.

The presence of one individual (Burial 3 from the Little Cypress Bayou site) with a maize-dependent stable carbon isotope value of -15.7 (Rose, Marks, and Tieszen 1985) may offer a clue to the use of maize prior to the Middle Mississippian in the central valley. This twelve-year-old individual, interred within an elaborate grave with four corner posts, is associated with a single Mississippian sherd and a wood charcoal radiocarbon date of A.D. 1000 (Dicks and Weed 1985). This unusual burial mode can reasonably be interpreted to represent a mortuary context of some significance to the inhabitants. The unusual nature of this burial with its atypically high stable carbon isotope value, considered with data from the American Bottom region to the north, indicates that at least some individuals were consuming high-maize diets in some special contexts before the Middle Mississippian period in the central valley.

It has been clearly demonstrated that the development of Mississippian culture and maize dependency are contemporaneous in the lower Illinois Valley and, by extrapolation, in the American Bottom (Buikstra 1984; Cook 1984). In addition, stable carbon isotope analysis of skeletal material from the Terminal Late Woodland Ledders site (lower Illinois Valley) and the Fairmont phase at Cahokia (American Bottom) indicates that maize may have been originally consumed as a high-status food (Bender et al. 1981). Cross-cultural studies of modern societies have clearly demonstrated that the staple carbohydrate crop becomes so embedded within the ideology of agriculturally dependent cultures that its presence at meals and religious events and its consumption by the sick becomes ideologically mandatory as well as necessary for cultural identification (Mead 1955:198–217; see also Swanton 1911:80, 113). We suggest that the adoption of Mississippian social and ideological behaviors by the central valley inhabitants required the cultivation and occasional consumption of maize. However, the abundant natural resources and dispersed settlement pattern of the central valley (Morse and Morse 1983) did not require the adoption of maize as a dietary staple. Thus, maize was grown to be used in religious ceremonies and social events and to be eaten by certain designated individuals. A similar interpretation has been offered by Beavers (1982) to explain the presence of maize in the Mississippi Delta. This scenario would explain the large quantities of maize found in storage features (i.e., Brougham Lake, Klinger et al. 1983; Zebree, Morse and Morse 1976) where it was kept until needed during special events. The single individual from Little Cypress Bayou with a maize-dependent stable carbon isotope value (Rose, Marks, and Tieszen 1985) is also the only nontypical burial analyzed to date and may represent one of these special individuals who, for any one of the previously postulated reasons, consumed significant quantities of maize. Once population nucleation reached a critical level during the Middle Mississippian period, maize was consumed regularly by all segments of society as a dietary staple (Lynott et al. 1986).

This scenario leaves only the increase in dental caries during the Early Mississippian period to be explained. The similarity in dental attrition and microwear patterns of the central valley Baytown and Early Mississippian samples with the lower valley Baytown and, to some extent, Coles Creek samples suggests a dietary similarity. We postulate an increased dependency upon starchy seeds over time in the central valley. This hypothesis is further supported by the presence of such seeds at Brougham Lake (Klinger et al. 1983), DeRossitt (Spears 1978), Little Cypress Bayou (Shea 1985), and Zebree (Morse and Morse 1976). Although Klinger and co-workers (1983) suggest that these are domesticated varieties, further confirmation from other sites is required.

Conclusions

When considered together, the archaeological and bioarchaeological data indicate that the changes in subsistence patterns in both the lower and central portions of the Mississippi River Valley are extremely complex and not well understood. The data presented in this chapter are used to construct a scenario (one of several that are possible) of dietary change that can be used as a hypothesis to be tested with additional archaeological and bioarchaeological data, especially stable carbon isotope assays of large skeletal series.

Bioarchaeological data from the Poverty Point and Marksville cultural traditions are sparse, but no evidence exists for dependency upon domesticated plants. Stable carbon isotope data from elsewhere in the Midwest indicate that the Hopewell culture was not maize dependent, despite the occasional presence of maize (Bender et al. 1981). The bioarchaeological data all indicate the absence of evidence for regular maize consumption during the Baytown period in both the central and the lower portions of the Mississippi Valley. These data are compatible with the archaeologically established dietary reconstruction that suggests an emphasis upon aquatic resources, small and large mammals, and the collection of wild plants, fruits, and nuts.

An increase in caries associated with a dramatic change in the dental attrition pattern suggests that the first major change in subsistence occurred with the advent of the Coles Creek culture in the lower valley. It is suggested here that the Coles Creek adaptation was partly based upon the exploitation of starchy seeds, such as knotweed, maygrass, and goosefoot.

Mississippianization of the indigenous Baytown peoples began as early as A.D. 700 in the central Mississippi Valley (Lynott et al. 1986). As these people adopted the technological, social, and ideological trappings of the Mississippian culture, which was developing further north in the valley, they also began to grow maize. It is hypothesized that participation in the Mississippian way of life required the growing of maize, but the abundance of the natural resources, in particular starchy seeds, and the relatively low population density made the adoption of maize as a dietary staple unnecessary. It is further suggested that maize was regularly eaten only by special individuals and only in conjunction with rituals by the general population. This scenario explains the abundance of maize in the archaeological deposits as well as the absence of bioarchaeological indicators of maize consumption. As continuing population nucleation resulted in stress upon local natural resources, maize became a dietary staple during the Middle Mississippian period in the central valley.

Acknowledgments

Funds for original research that led to many of the conclusions contained within this chapter were made available to the authors by New World Research under terms of a contract with the Memphis District U.S. Army Corps of Engineers. Additional research incorporated within this chapter was funded by numerous small grants to Rose by the Arkansas Archaeological Survey, U.S. Army Corps of Engineers, and the National Park Service. We thank these organizations for their support of this research, but they are in no way responsible for any errors or misconceptions that might be contained within this work; these must remain the responsibility of the authors. Rose wishes to thank Dr. Michael P. Hoffman for useful suggestions and vocal criticisms throughout several years of bioarchaeological research in the Mississippi Valley.

✳ 3

Ranked Status and Health in the Mississippian Chiefdom at Moundville

Mary Lucas Powell

A dominant theme in the archaeology of the southeastern United States over the past fifty years has been exploration of Mississippian sites of the late prehistoric and protohistoric periods. This interest was sparked in part by early discoveries of spectacular artifacts of stone, copper, marine shell, and other exotic materials deposited with burials in earthen mounds. Analyses of settlement patterns and ceramic, lithic, and other technologies have delineated the complexity of regional adaptations to a variety of ecological settings (Smith 1978). The social organization of these societies has also been investigated (Brown 1981; Goldstein 1980; Hatch 1976; Larson 1971; Peebles 1971, 1974, 1978, 1983; Peebles and Kus 1977) by examination of patterned variations in demography, burial location, associated artifacts, interment facilities, and the mortuary processing of human remains, with reference to models developed by Saxe (1970) and Binford (1971) to elucidate systems of hierarchically ranked ascribed status that crosscut age and sex.

The research summarized in this chapter forms part of a broader assessment of the biological and social dimensions of health at Moundville, the paramount center of a regional chiefdom located in the central Black Warrior River Valley in west-central Alabama (Powell 1988). Data on skeletal metrics, developmental and diet-related dental features, and skeletal evidence of iron-deficiency anemia, trauma, and infectious disease experience were analyzed by age, sex, and ranked status, the latter classification derived from the mortuary analysis of a large sample of Moundville burials by Christopher S. Peebles (1971, 1974, 1978, 1983; Peebles and Kus 1977). The patterns of association between health and ranked status in this community were then compared with similar data reported for Mississippian communities in Georgia (Etowah) and Tennessee (Dallas, Hixon, and Chucalissa).

The Mississippian Community at Moundville

Moundville is located on the south bank of the Black Warrior River thirteen miles southeast of Tuscaloosa (Figure 1-1). Our present knowledge of the development and dimensions of this impressive site are derived from more than 140 years of investigation, ranging from casual examinations of eroded mound slopes to a large, multidisciplinary project under National Science Foundation sponsorship (Steponaitis 1983).

A small Late Woodland (West Jefferson phase) village in the western area of the site preceded the Mississippian occupation. The earliest mound (Mound O) was constructed near this locale during the Moundville I subphase (A.D. 1050–1250). During the next two centuries (Moundville II, A.D. 1250–1400, and Moundville III, A.D. 1400–1550) the community increased in size and organizational complexity. By the mid-fifteenth century it included at least twenty mounds ringing a 40-ha plaza, several large multiroom structures that were perhaps the habitations of highly ranked families, and scores of wattle-and-daub houses clustered near nonmound cemeteries. A wooden palisade enclosed the site on the sides unprotected by the river, flanked by residential areas. The identification of facilities (i.e., large hearths that probably were kilns) and debris associated with the manufacture of ceramics and marine-shell and copper items in restricted areas of the site suggests the localization of specialized crafts production.

The peak population in the mid-fourteenth century probably approached 3,000 individuals, making Moundville the second largest known prehistoric community north of Mexico, surpassed only by the American Bottom site of Cahokia (Peebles 1978). Smaller villages with single mounds lay to the north and south along the Black Warrior River Valley. They were bound to the paramount center by sociopolitical ties, as indicated in the archaeological record by artifacts of nonlocal origin in mound burials at these secondary sites. Numerous hamlets and farmsteads scattered throughout the floodplain evidently served as provisioning centers for the larger centers, as suggested by the differential representation of faunal remains in the different types of communities (Welch 1990).

In the late fifteenth century, Moundville began to decline in size and magnitude of extraregional relations, for poorly understood reasons (Peebles 1983). It was apparently bypassed by the de Soto expedition in 1540 en route to the cacique Tascaluca's realm along the Alabama River to the southeast. During the succeeding protohistoric period (the Alabama River phase, A.D. 1550–1700), mound construction ceased and the centralized Black Warrior population gradually dispersed southward to settle in small villages characterized by more egalitarian forms of social organization.

Ranked Status at Moundville:
Social Dimensions and Biological Expectations

Excavations at Moundville in 1905 and 1906 by Clarence B. Moore uncovered approximately 800 human burials within and around the mounds (Moore 1906, 1907). The Alabama Museum of Natural History (AMNH) uncovered some 2,400 additional interments from 1929 to 1941, all from nonmound locales, for a total of 3,200 reported burials at the site (Peebles 1979). Peebles's analysis of mortuary data (Peebles 1974; Peebles and Kus 1977) from the Moore and AMNH excavations divided a sample of the 2,000 best-documented burials into a series of clusters on the basis of associated grave goods and burial location (Table 3-1). He interpreted these groupings as representing different sociopolitical aggregates: (1) an elite sector, distinguished by access to certain artifacts, design motifs, exotic materials, and special burial locales primarily in mounds (Segment A); and (2) a nonelite sector interred near mounds or village areas (Segments B and C), with the majority of individuals (Cluster XI) lacking any reported associated artifacts. The association of elite items with both sexes and all ages (including infants) suggested to Peebles that social rank was to some degree ascribed at birth, although achievements in adult life probably played an additional role.

Ethnographic evidence from historic southeastern chiefdoms indicates that, in some circumstances, elite individuals enjoyed varying degrees of preferential access to selected foods as well as to other material items and ceremonial privileges (Bourne 1904; Du Pratz 1972; Swanton 1911, 1946; Garcilaso de la Vega 1951). If critical subsistence resources, particularly animal protein of high nutritional value, were in short supply, the biological consequences of such preferential access could be significant. Normal growth and development depend heavily upon nutritional adequacy (Acheson 1960; Albanese and Orto 1964; Dubos 1965; Garn 1966). Differential exposure to pathogens provides initial possibilities for differential infection rates within populations, but the nutritional status of the threatened hosts determines to a large extent the strength of immunoresistance to pathological stress and therefore the ultimate success or failure of adaptation to prevalent stresses (Deo 1978;

Table 3-1
Mortuary Analysis of Moundville Burials

Cluster	Ages	Characteristic Artifacts	Burial Locations	Segment	% of Sample
Ia	A	Copper axes Pearl beads	Mounds	A	5.92
Ib	A, C	Copper earspools Bear teeth Stone disks Pigments	Mounds, cemeteries near mounds	A	
II	A, C, I	Shell beads Galena cubes Oblong copper gorgets	Mounds, cemeteries near mounds	A	
III	A, C, I	Effigy vessels Animal bone Shell gorgets Freshwater shell	Cemeteries near mounds	B	13.21
IV	A, C, I	Discoidals Bone awls Projectile points	Cemeteries near mounds	B	
V, VI	A, C, I	Bowls Jars	Cemeteries near mounds, village areas	C	80.87
VII, VIII IX	A, C	Water bottles	Cemeteries near mounds, village areas	C	
X	A, C, I	Sherds	Village areas	C	
XI	A, C, I	No artifacts	All locations	C	

After Peebles and Kus 1977.
Key: I = infants, C = children, A = adults.

Hoeprich 1977; Scrimshaw et al. 1968). Poorly nourished individuals grow more slowly and unevenly and resist disease less effectively than do well-nourished individuals.

Preliminary analysis of strontium levels in human bone samples from Moundville suggested that elite diets included more meat than nonelite diets and that within both groups males consumed more meat than females did (Schoeninger and Peebles 1981). Such dietary differences, however, may not have produced significant differences in actual physical health, if general levels of nutrition were adequate to buffer prevalent stresses.

Table 3-2
Modeled Expectations of Variability in Biological Dimensions of Ranked Status at Moundville

Biological Dimensions	Modeled Expectations
Demography	Elite mortality should be lower than nonelite mortality at all ages.
Adult body size	Elite individuals should be larger than nonelite individuals, particularly males.
Dental health	Elite dentitions might show less caries and wear than nonelite dentitions.
Growth and development	Elite individuals should display smoother growth trajectories than nonelite individuals.
Nutritional status	Elite individuals should display less evidence of deficiency than nonelite individuals.
Trauma	Elite males should display more war-related trauma than nonelite males.
	Elite females should display less trauma from ordinary tasks than nonelite females.
Infectious disease	Members of the elite population segment should display evidence of stronger immune response and exposure to fewer types of pathogens than nonelite individuals.

Table 3-2 presents in summary form a set of modeled expectations of variability in the biological dimensions of ranked status at Moundville. Inasmuch as the ultimate test of successful adaptation is avoidance of death, differences in mortality experience in age-matched population segments are particularly reliable indicators of differential health.

Adult body size reflects not only the potential for growth regulated by the genetic substrate but also the adequacy of nutrition during critical growth stages. Nutritional stress may cause chronic or acute growth disruption that is evident in developmental defects of bone and teeth. Dental caries and wear reflect the cariogenic nature of the diet as well as its texture, which may be inversely related if starchy plant foods such as maize and squash are dietary staples. Nutritional disorders such as iron-deficiency anemia may result from diets deficient in meat, if other foods are also inadequate.

Trauma and infectious disease experience reflect both behavioral and dietary constraints within populations. Given the important role of warfare as a means for social advancement for males in the late prehistoric southeastern chiefdoms (Brown 1976), it seems reasonable to expect more evidence of trauma among elite compared to nonelite males. If elite females were exempt from tasks such as the cultivation of agricultural fields that entailed considerable physical stress, they, too, might display less evidence of trauma. The nonparticipation of elite adults in hunting and the dressing of carcasses would tend to minimize their contacts with a variety of potentially dangerous zoonotic diseases. If the elite diet was significantly richer than the nonelite diet in protein, the superior elite disease resistance resulting from this crucial dietary difference could be evidenced in intrapopulation differences in patterns of skeletal pathology.

The Skeletal Sample

Approximately 1,500 individuals from Moundville are presently represented by skeletal material curated at the Laboratory for Human Osteology at The University of Alabama in Tuscaloosa. When Clarence B. Moore's archaeological collections from southeastern sites were transferred in the late 1920s from the Philadelphia Academy of Natural Sciences to the Museum of the American Indian (Heye Foundation) in New York, the human skeletal remains were apparently deaccessioned. Attempts to locate these skeletons for study have been unsuccessful (C. S. Peebles, M. J. Schoeninger, personal communications, 1980). Because skeletal material from Moore's excavations at Moundville is unavailable, only material from the AMNH excavations could be examined in the present study.

The skeletal sample selected for analysis consists of 140 subadults (24.8 percent) and 424 adults (75.2 percent) (Table 3-3), reflecting the proportion of these two broad age categories in the total available series (Peebles 1971). Only those individuals with well-documented intrasite provenience were included to minimize the probability of including individuals from the pre-Mississippian West Jefferson phase occupation (Figure 3-1). Of the 564 individuals, 81 (14.4 percent) meet Peebles's criteria for elite burials (Peebles and Kus 1977). This group unfortunately does not, for reasons stated above, include any elite individuals interred in mounds. Of the remainder, 190 (33.7 percent of the total) were interred with nonelite grave goods. The final 293 (52.0 percent of the total) had no artifacts. This last group is placed in a residual category (Peebles's and Kus's Cluster XI, Table 3-1) to differentiate them from the other nonelite burials. However, no assumptions are made concerning the relative social rank of these two nonelite groups. The respective proportions of these three skeletal subsamples, termed "elite," "subelite," and "residual" in the present study, do not correspond with the proportions reported in Peebles's analysis (Table 3-1) because for analytic purposes the "elite" subsample has been deliberately increased in size relative to the two other groups.

Each individual has been scored for degree of skeletal completeness. Of the 564, 144 (25.5 percent) are represented solely by cranial elements and 99 (17.5 percent) solely by postcranial elements (Table 3-3). One-fifth (119, or 21.1 percent) are scored as "poorly represented" (by less than one-fourth of the skeleton), leaving only 202 (35.8 percent) rated as "fair to good" (more than one-fourth of the skeleton). Subadult skeletons are generally more complete than are adult skeletons (chi-square significance, $p < .05$), but no significant differences in skeletal representation by sex or status are indicated. Examination of burial records suggests that policies of burial recovery contributed more strongly to these patterns of unequal representation than did aboriginal mortuary practices, as the great majority of burials were apparently primary interments of extended, articulated individuals (Peebles 1979).

Table 3-3
Demography, Status, and Skeletal Representation at Moundville

	Elite		Subelite		Residual		Total	
	N	R%	N	R%	N	R%	N	R%
Demography								
Subadults	20	14.3	50	35.7	70	50.0	140	24.8
Adults	61	14.4	140	33.0	223	52.6	424	75.2
Females	23	10.4	72	32.4	127	57.2	222	39.4
Males	29	16.8	54	31.2	90	52.0	173	30.7
Unknown	9	31.0	14	48.3	6	20.7	29	5.1
Total	81	14.4	190	33.7	293	52.0	564	100.0
Skeletal Representation								
Cranial only	27	18.8	50	34.7	67	46.5	144	25.5
Postcranial only	13	13.1	33	33.3	53	53.5	99	17.5
Both: poor	21	17.6	34	28.6	64	53.8	119	21.1
Both: fair to good	20	9.9	73	36.1	109	54.0	202	35.8
Total	81	14.4	190	33.7	293	52.0	564	100.0

R% = percentage of row total N.

Results of Analysis

Demography

Subadults were seriously underrepresented in the total burial sample, according to available field records. The present skeletal sample reflects this deficiency (Table 3-2). Individuals fifteen years old or younger constitute only 19.5 percent (110/564), in contrast to 30 to 50 percent in the anthropological population samples utilized by Weiss (1973) in his construction of model life tables. In particular, infant mortality (subadults aged less than one year) at 4.4 percent (25/564) is well below expectations when compared with proportions reported for other Amerindian samples (e.g., 21.9 percent [48/219] for Dickson Mounds Middle Mississippians [Lallo 1973], 20.3 percent [165/813] for the Indian Knoll Archaic series, and 38.1 percent [193/506] for the Mobridge Arikara [Kelley 1980]). The next oldest portion of the sample, however, does approximate "the general shape of human juvenile mortality . . . declining from ages 1 to 5, then decreasing steadily until those from 10 to 15 years have the lowest mortality" (Weiss 1973:26).

Adult females outnumber males 222 to 173. The sex estimates reported here match in almost all cases those made in 1977 by Margaret J. Schoeninger and Clark Spencer Larsen (personal communication 1981) based on identical osteological criteria, and thus it seems unlikely that observer error is responsible for the large discrepancy between expected and observed sex ratios. Possible contributing factors are disproportionate representation of younger males and older females in mound burials not available for analysis and/or additional loss of younger males to the sample through mortality in warring raids and hunting accidents.

Age and sex differences among the three sample segments designated by status were assessed by chi-square analysis as not significant (p > .05). No conclusions regarding differential mortality experience, and, by extension, differential adaptive success, of the two sexes or of elite and nonelite at Moundville could be reached, however, because of the substantial deviations from "normal" age and sex profiles noted above.

Adult Body Size

Data on six skeletal measurements (maximum diameter of humerus and femur head, femur midshaft circumference and anterior-posterior diameter, and maximum length of femur and tibia) were collected from complete bones of adult females and males (Table 3-4). Statistical analysis of sexual dimorphism by Student's t-test and one-way analysis of variance indicated significant differences ($p < .001$) within each status subgroup. Separate comparisons by sex across status boundaries using the same analytic methods, however, revealed no significant differences ($p > .05$). On the average, elite males were slightly larger than nonelite males in all but humerus head diameter, while elite females slightly exceeded nonelite females for only that measurement.

Table 3-4
Moundville Postcranial Skeletal Metrics

		Females			Males	
Measurement	N	X̄	SD	N	X̄	SD
Humerus Head Diameter						
Elite	2	41.25	3.89	10	46.70	3.06
Subelite	13	39.53	1.43	17	45.59	2.82
Residual	21	40.92	2.63	14	49.93	10.08
TOTAL	36	40.12	2.12	41	47.34	6.49
Femur Head Diameter						
Elite	5	40.30	0.67	10	46.80	2.21
Subelite	24	40.64	2.18	21	46.50	2.65
Residual	39	41.37	1.55	24	46.02	2.66
TOTAL	68	40.88	1.92	55	46.35	2.56
Femur Midshaft Circumference						
Elite	8	77.06	4.30	13	89.35	4.17
Subelite	26	79.21	4.81	28	89.00	4.93
Residual	61	77.48	4.72	37	89.17	5.37
TOTAL	95	77.92	4.73	78	89.14	4.97
Femur Midshaft Anterior-Posterior Diameter						
Elite	8	26.00	2.42	14	31.14	2.58
Subelite	27	26.94	3.39	29	30.50	2.73
Residual	65	25.85	1.86	40	30.30	2.50
TOTAL	100	26.16	2.43	83	30.51	2.63
Femur Maximum Length						
Elite	4	407.10	13.45	9	456.22	18.67
Subelite	15	412.53	18.04	18	447.61	23.69
Residual	31	415.52	20.55	25	442.88	22.47
TOTAL	50	413.95	19.20	52	446.83	22.42
Tibia Maximum Length						
Elite	3	336.00	4.58	7	371.14	16.51
Subelite	12	334.58	15.72	12	369.29	20.67
Residual	19	342.55	19.45	13	363.50	18.52
TOTAL	34	339.26	27.46	32	367.34	18.66

All measurements in mm.

Table 3-5
Maxillary First Molar: Mean Wear Scores

		Females			Males	
	N	X̄	SD	N	X̄	SD
20–30 Years						
Elite	6	14.33	3.14	0	—	—
Subelite	11	13.45	3.04	6	13.33	3.20
Residual	23	12.65	2.93	7	14.86	3.08
TOTAL	40	13.12	2.98	13	14.15	3.10
30–40 Years						
Elite	5	16.40	3.58	2	19.00	4.24
Subelite	15	15.93	3.65	8	18.50	3.50
Residual	20	17.35	4.42	14	15.93	4.21
TOTAL	40	16.70	4.01	24	17.04	4.05
+40 Years						
Elite	4	10.00	3.92	8	20.62	9.09
Subelite	7	22.71	7.99	2	27.00	11.31
Residual	3	12.33	0.58	6	24.17	6.76
TOTAL	14	19.71	7.11	16	22.75	8.24
All Ages Combined						
Elite	15	16.53	4.00	10	20.30	8.17
Subelite	33	16.54	5.70	16	17.62	6.10
Residual	46	14.67	4.25	27	17.48	5.77
TOTAL	94	15.63	4.82	53	18.06	6.33

Dental Wear and Caries

Dental wear is not a pathological condition per se, but dietary features that produce occlusal abrasion (e.g., grit or rough-textured foods) may also influence other aspects of dental health through irritation of adjacent soft tissues. Scott's (1979a) quantification system for scoring occlusal molar wear was employed on all intact molars in adult dentitions. Observed wear was moderate (Tables 3-5 through 3-8), with little dentine exposure evident prior to the fourth decade. This pattern agrees well with archaeological evidence from the site and ethnohistoric data from the Southeast in general indicating that plant foods were processed in wooden rather than in stone utensils (Powell 1988). Within each group, males display slightly heavier occlusal wear than females, but breakdown of mean wear scores indicates a strong age effect. Statistical analysis of molar wear across status boundaries for age-controlled samples of females and males revealed no consistent significant patterns of

Table 3-6
Maxillary Second Molar: Mean Wear Scores

	Females			Males		
	N	X̄	SD	N	X̄	SD
20–30 Years						
Elite	5	12.40	1.82	0	—	—
Subelite	14	10.64	3.20	7	10.00	2.52
Residual	22	10.50	2.82	8	9.12	2.42
TOTAL	41	10.78	2.87	15	9.53	2.42
30–40 Years						
Elite	4	12.00	1.83	2	11.00	2.83
Subelite	13	12.08	4.27	9	14.89	3.44
Residual	20	13.10	2.77	12	14.00	2.63
TOTAL	37	12.62	3.27	23	14.09	3.04
+40 Years						
Elite	4	15.75	2.63	4	13.25	3.20
Subelite	5	18.60	8.68	1	23.00	0.00
Residual	1	13.00	0.00	5	22.20	5.07
TOTAL	10	16.40	6.30	10	18.70	6.07
All Ages Combined						
Elite	13	13.31	2.56	6	12.50	3.02
Subelite	32	12.47	5.36	17	13.35	4.51
Residual	43	11.77	3.03	25	14.08	5.57
TOTAL	88	12.25	3.98	48	13.62	4.91

differences between the three groups ($p > .05$), whether assessed by Student's t-test or one-way analysis of variance.

The prevalence and patterning of dental caries provide a valuable index to the proportionate representation of soft-textured high-carbohydrate foods in a population's diet (Powell 1985a; Turner 1979). Comparisons of caries prevalence by ranked-status classification in samples controlled for age, sex, and tooth type (Table 3-9) by the statistical tests listed above paralleled the patterns of molar wear: no consistent pattern of significant differences by status ($p > .05$). Inter- and intragroup comparisons revealed almost identical mean caries rates for both sexes, controlled for age, between and within status subgroups. The majority of carious lesions (65 percent) were located in occlusal pits and fissures of the premolars and molars. These patterns of prevalence and location more closely resemble those reported for other Mississippian populations and for traditional agriculturalists in general (Turner 1979) than patterns observed in nonagriculturalists.

Table 3-7
Mandibular First Molar: Mean Wear Scores

	Females			Males		
	N	X̄	SD	N	X̄	SD
20–30 Years						
Elite	6	16.00	2.90	0	—	—
Subelite	11	15.09	3.27	5	12.40	3.36
Residual	24	13.08	3.17	6	12.33	6.35
TOTAL	41	14.05	3.31	11	12.36	4.96
30–40 Years						
Elite	2	13.50	3.54	3	18.00	2.65
Subelite	7	15.71	0.95	8	19.12	4.88
Residual	14	16.36	2.79	17	17.12	3.44
TOTAL	23	15.91	2.47	28	17.78	3.81
+40 Years						
Elite	2	20.50	6.36	5	24.00	4.64
Subelite	5	22.20	6.50	4	23.00	7.79
Residual	3	18.00	5.29	8	26.75	6.06
TOTAL	10	20.60	5.76	17	25.06	5.97
All Ages Combined						
Elite	10	16.40	4.03	8	21.75	4.89
Subelite	23	16.83	4.61	17	18.06	6.43
Residual*	42	14.45	3.64	31	18.68	6.96
TOTAL	75	15.44	4.11	56	18.93	6.55

*Includes one unaged adult.

Linear Enamel Hypoplasia

The patterning of nonspecific developmental stress experienced by the Moundville Mississippians was assessed through observation of linear enamel hypoplasia. This condition results from short-term episodes of arrested enamel development initiated by a variety of stimuli, including infection and psychological stress (Goodman et al. 1980). Although determination of the specific etiology of any particular lesion-forming episode is not possible, the developmental age of the affected individual at the time of the lesion's formation may be calculated by comparison of the lesion location on the tooth crown with standardized charts of enamel development. Enamel lesions visible at 10x magnification were scored on all undamaged permanent incisors and canines in the series. To eliminate "false positive" scores from idiosyncratic developmental

Table 3-8
Mandibular Second Molar: Mean Wear Scores

	Females			Males		
	N	X̄	SD	N	X̄	SD
20–30 Years						
Elite	6	10.83	2.32	0	—	—
Subelite	13	10.92	3.47	6	8.50	1.22
Residual	28	10.71	3.31	7	9.14	3.16
TOTAL	47	10.79	3.19	13	8.85	3.16
30–40 Years						
Elite	3	11.00	2.65	1	14.00	0.00
Subelite	10	13.10	2.08	9	16.55	4.47
Residual	18	13.17	5.11	20	14.45	5.07
TOTAL	31	12.93	4.12	30	15.07	4.83
+40 Years						
Elite	1	20.00	0.00	5	19.20	5.07
Subelite	4	21.00	10.68	5	19.20	4.97
Residual	4	15.00	4.08	8	23.37	3.54
TOTAL	9	18.22	7.64	18	21.05	4.65
All Ages Combined						
Elite	10	11.80	3.58	6	18.33	5.01
Subelite*	28	13.82	6.41	20	14.80	5.75
Residual*	51	11.86	4.27	35	15.43	6.62
TOTAL	89	12.47	5.01	61	15.51	6.19

*Includes two unaged adults.

errors on single teeth, only cases in which synchronous lesions were observed on two or more teeth in a dentition were scored as positive instances of systemic developmental disturbance.

The prevalence of this developmental defect was calculated as the proportion of hypoplastic to nonhypoplastic enamel segments formed during each of the twelve six-month periods during the first six years of postnatal life. The great majority of lesions reflect acute growth arrest episodes during the third and fourth years of postnatal life. Similar patterns are reported by other researchers of Mississippian health for an American Bottom series (Milner 1982), in Middle Mississippians from Dickson Mounds (Goodman et al. 1980), in a Late Mississippian population sample from Nodena in northeast Arkansas (Powell 1989), and in the Lubbub Creek population from the Tombigbee River in west Alabama that was contemporaneous with Moundville (Powell 1983). Contributory factors undoubtedly include weaning from a protein-rich diet to one less able to meet the physiological needs of the developing organism and greater exposure to environmental pathogens (including parasites) due to increased mobility of the child. The role of differential sensitivity to systemic insults of the certain portions of the dental enamel during development has yet to be accurately assessed (Condon 1981). Chi-square analysis of both the absolute and the age-associated prevalence of hypoplasia by age, sex, and ranked status revealed no significant differences (p > .05) (Table 3-10).

Skeletal Pathology

All skeletal remains were examined for macroscopic lesions. All lesions were initially described as "resorptive" or "proliferative," according to whether focal bone loss or bone increase resulted. Statistical comparisons of prevalence by age, sex, and ranked status were performed for lesions representing nutritional deficiencies, traumatic injuries, or infectious reaction. Differential diagnosis of specific infectious diseases followed the initial stage of analysis.

Iron-Deficiency Anemia

Skeletal evidence of anemia was rarely observed. No cases of porotic hyperostosis were noted, but ten young children (10/47 observable, 21.3 percent) and five adults (5/115, 4.3 percent) exhibit remodeled lesions of cribra orbitalia (Table 3-11), a condition generally considered to represent a mild skeletal response to iron-deficiency anemia (Hengen 1971; Ortner and Putschar 1981; Steinbock 1976). The overall prevalence rate of 9.3 percent is slightly higher than the 7 percent reported by Powell (1983) for the combined Mississippian and protohistoric samples at Lubbub Creek, but it is much lower than those reported by Hill-Clark (1981) for two protohistoric samples (24 percent at 1Tu4, 62 percent at 1Ha19) along the Alabama River to the south or the prevalence rate of 45 percent reported by Lallo (1973) for subadults (0–15 years) from the Middle Mississippian population at Dickson Mounds. No evidence of rickets or other nutritional disorders was observed.

Prevalence of cribra orbitalia was lowest among elite individuals (2.5 percent, 1/40 of observed orbits), intermediate among individuals in the

Table 3-9
Teeth Carious or Lost Antemortem in Adults
(Maxilla and Mandible Combined)

Age Category*	Elite			Subelite		
	1	2	3	1	2	3
Anterior Teeth						
N Teeth observed	23	63	57	145	147	62
N Teeth carious	0	3	4	0	6	2
% Carious teeth	0	4.8	7.0	0	4.1	3.2
N Teeth lost						
antemortem	0	0	3	0	5	3
% Teeth affected	0	4.8	12.3	0	7.5	8.1
Posterior Region						
N Teeth observed	76	102	128	321	348	145
N Carious teeth	25	17	41	71	82	44
% Carious teeth	32.9	16.7	32.0	22.1	23.6	30.3
N Teeth lost						
antemortem	12	17	33	17	70	25
% Teeth affected	48.7	33.3	57.8	27.4	43.7	47.6
Total Teeth						
N Teeth observed	99	165	185	466	495	207
N Carious teeth	25	20	45	71	88	46
% Carious teeth	25.2	12.1	24.3	15.2	17.8	22.2
N Teeth lost						
antemortem	12	17	36	17	75	28
% Teeth affected	37.4	22.4	43.8	18.9	32.9	35.7

*Age categories: 1 = 20–30 years, 2 = 30–40 years, 3 = +40 years.

residual category (6.5 percent, 11/169), and highest among subelite individuals (9.9 percent, 10/101). This distribution suggests that chronic anemia may have been a less common health problem among the elite than among the nonelite at Moundville, perhaps as a result of higher meat consumption as suggested by bone strontium assay (Schoeninger and Peebles 1981). Chi-square analysis revealed no statistically significant differences ($p > .05$) in prevalence by ranked status, but this result may have been skewed by the extreme inequality of the sample sizes.

	Residual			Total		Grand Total
1	2	3	1	2	3	All
174	251	89	342	461	208	1011
2	8	10	2	17	16	35
1.1	3.2	11.2	0.6	3.7	7.7	3.5
0	6	3	0	11	9	20
1.1	5.6	14.6	0.6	6.1	12.0	5.4
470	595	179	867	1045	452	2364
128	145	42	224	244	127	595
27.2	24.4	23.5	25.8	23.3	28.1	25.2
45	114	96	74	201	154	429
36.8	43.5	77.1	34.4	42.6	62.2	43.3
644	846	268	1209	1506	660	3375
130	153	52	226	261	143	630
20.2	18.1	19.4	18.7	17.3	21.7	18.7
45	120	99	74	212	163	449
27.2	32.3	56.3	24.8	31.4	46.4	32.0

Trauma

Reparative proliferation of bone at fracture sites was the most common traumatic injury observed, noted in thirty-four adults but no subadults. Ribs, hands, feet, sterna, radii, clavicles, and ulnae were most often broken (Table 3-12). Moundville male prevalence (1.0 percent of observed individuals) is double that of females (0.5 percent). The greatest differences by sex are noted in the rates for fractured ribs (9.4 percent of males vs. 1.4 percent of females) and hands (4.1 percent of males vs. 2.2 percent of females). Elite males display fewer fractures than non-

Table 3-10
Prevalence of Enamel Hypoplasia by Ranked Status

		Ranked Status Categories	
Tooth Type	Elite	Subelite	Residual
Incisors			
N units observed	21	55	71
N units affected	3	13	18
% units affected	14.3	23.6	25.4
		Chi-square = 1.12901	
		p = .5686	
Canines			
N units observed	21	57	79
N units affected	13	25	46
% units affected	61.9	43.9	58.2
		Chi-square = 3.43553	
		p = .1795	

Only units that displayed 10 percent or higher prevalence were considered in these statistical comparisons.

Table 3-11
Skeletal Evidence of Anemia

Burial Number	Age	Status	Sex	Porotic Hyperostosis	Cribra Orbitalia	
Subadults						
1008	1–4.9	S	0	No	R*	Unhealed
1028	1–4.9	R	0	No	L+R	Healed
1455	5–9.9	S	0	No	L+R	Unhealed
1522	5–9.9	S	0	No	L*	Healed
1724	5–9.9	S	0	No	L	Healed
1791	1–4.9	S	0	No	L+R	Unhealed
2028	1–4.9	R	0	No	L+R	Healed
2034	1–4.9	R	0	No	L+R	Healed
2064	0–1.0	R	0	No	L+R	Unhealed
2690	1–4.9	S	0	No	L+R	Unhealed
Adults						
1539	45–49.9	S	F	No	R*	Healed
1560	25–29.9	R	F	No	R*	Healed
1603	30–34.9	S	F	No	L+R	Healed
1921	20–24.9	R	?	No	L*	Healed
1979	20–24.9	E	F	No	R*	Healed

*Antimere missing.
Status designations: R = residual,   S = subelite,   E = elite.

Table 3-12
Anatomical Distribution of Fractures by Sex
(Left and Right Sides Combined)

Skeletal Element	Females			Males			Totals		
	N Fractures	N Observed	%	N Fractures	N Observed	%	N Fractures	N Observed	%
Cranium*	0	252	0	0	202	0	0	454	0
Mandible	0	286	0	0	202	0	0	488	0
Sternum	0	41	0	1	22	4.5	1	63	1.6
Clavicle	2	178	1.1	1	144	0.7	3	322	0.9
Scapula	0	98	0	0	79	0	0	177	0
Rib	1	72	1.4	6	64	9.4	7	136	5.1
Vertebra*	0	99	0	1	74	1.4	1	173	0.6
Humerus	0	216	0	0	156	0	0	372	0
Radius	3	182	1.6	2	144	1.4	5	326	1.5
Ulna	1	189	0.5	2	145	1.4	3	334	0.9
Hand*	2	93	2.2	3	74	4.1	5	167	3.0
Innominate	0	172	0	0	132	0	0	304	0
Femur	0	237	0	0	182	0	0	419	0
Patella	0	158	0	0	141	0	0	299	0
Tibia	0	242	0	0	192	0	0	434	0
Fibula	0	189	0	2	146	1.4	2	335	0.6
Foot*	4	133	3.0	4	118	3.4	8	251	3.2
Total	13	2837	0.5	22	2217	1.0	35	5054	0.7

*All bones considered together as a unit.

Table 3-13
Trauma Cases by Age, Sex, and Status

Age Category	Elite			Subelite			Residual			Total		
	F	M	?	F	M	?	F	M	?	F	M	?
20–24.9	0	0	0	0	0	0	0	0	0	0	0	0
25–29.9	0	0	0	2	0	0	2	0	0	4	0	0
30–34.9	0	0	0	3	6	0	1	5	0	4	11	0
35–39.9	0	0	0	0	1	1	0	2	0	0	3	1
40–44.9	0	2	0	1	1	0	0	0	0	0	3	0
45–49.9	0	0	0	0	0	0	1	1	1	2	1	1
+50	0	0	0	0	0	1	0	1	0	0	1	0
Unaged	0	0	0	0	0	0	0	0	1	0	0	1
Totals	2	2	0	6	8	2	4	9	1	10	19	3
N	0/23	2/29	0/9	6/72	8/54	2/14	4/127	9/90	1/6	10/222	19/173	3/29
%	0	6.9	0	8.3	14.8	14.3	3.1	10.0	16.7	4.5	11.0	10.3

elite males (Table 3-13), and elite females exhibit no trauma, unlike non-elite females. This difference may owe in part to the absence of the highest stratum of elite burials from this sample and to the generally less complete representation by long bones (the site of most fractures in the sample as a whole) of elite than nonelite individuals. At the Mississippian site of Chucalissa in Tennessee, adult elite males displayed *more* fractures than did nonelite males, possibly a reflection of their prowess in warfare that earned them elite burial (Robinson 1976), and a similar pattern was predicted for Moundville (Table 3-2).

Infectious Disease

A young adult male of the subelite subgroup exhibited severe anterior kyphosis (forward curvature of the spine) resulting from extensive destruction of numerous vertebral bodies by a chronic infectious process (Figure 3-1). This condition is suggestive of a mycobacterial disease, tuberculosis, which has been documented in other prehistoric Amerindian populations (Buikstra 1981; Kelley and Eisenberg 1987; Ortner and Putschar 1981; Steinbock 1976). A more common type of focal resorptive lesion was a small circular or oval concavity in the cranial vault, affecting almost exclusively the outer table and appearing well remodeled at death. These were noted in twenty-three individuals of all ages. Chi-square analysis of the prevalence of focal resorptive lesions in the three ranked status groups (matched for age and sex) indicated no significant differences ($p > .05$).

Proliferative osseous reaction (periostitis) affecting the subperiosteal surface of lower long bone shafts and, more rarely, appearing on flat bones, the mandible, or the vertebrae, was far more abundant in the series. This condition results from a nonspecific inflammatory response to pathological insults that may be provoked by infection or by trauma and is not, in itself, diagnostic for any particular disease (Hoeprich 1977; Ortner and Putschar 1981; Steinbock 1976). The anterior tibia shaft was the bony area most often affected (Table 3-14), with an overall prevalence rate of 50.7 percent, followed by the fibula shaft (26.2 percent) and the shafts of the femur (14.7 percent), patella (9.1 percent), ribs (6.6 percent), humerus (4.9 percent), clavicle (4.4 percent), radius (3.7 percent), and ulna (3.5 percent). Analysis by chi-square of associations between presence of proliferative reaction and age, sex, or status indicated no significant differences ($p > .05$). Rates of prevalence and anatomical patterns of involvement are almost identical for adult females and males and for the members of all three status subgroups (controlled for age, sex, and differences in skeletal representation).

Table 3-14
Age Distribution of Proliferative Skeletal Reaction (Left and Right Sides Combined)

Skeletal Region	0–4.9 Years N	%	5–9.9 Years N	%	10–19.9 Years N	%	+20 Years N	%	Total N	%
Cranial										
Calvarium	2/105	1.9	0/33	0.0	2/30	6.7	7/469	1.5	11/637	1.7
Orbit	9/56	6.1	0/15	0.0	2/20	10.0	2/219	0.9	13/310	4.2
Frontal	0/72	0.0	2/24	8.3	2/28	7.1	0/392	0.0	4/516	0.8
Face	0/16	0.0	0/11	0.0	2/21	9.5	7/232	3.0	9/280	3.2
Basicranium	4/20	20.0	0/3	0.0	0/7	0.0	0/133	0.0	4/163	2.5
Endocranium	17/99	17.2	0/34	0.0	4/34	11.8	5/463	1.1	26/630	4.1
Mastoid area	0/61	0.0	0/23	0.0	0/35	0.0	0/439	0.0	0/558	0.0
Mandible	4/77	5.2	0/27	0.0	4/43	9.3	13/530	2.5	21/667	3.1
Postcranial										
Sternum	0/0	0.0	0/1	0.0	1/7	14.3	1/63	1.6	2/71	2.8
Ribs*	2/29	6.9	1/9	11.1	1/16	6.3	8/129	6.2	12/183	6.6
Cervical vertebra*	0/16	0.0	0/7	0.0	0/18	0.0	0/155	0.0	0/196	0.0
Thoracic vertebra*	0/22	0.0	0/9	0.0	0/17	0.0	1/167	0.6	1/215	0.5
Lumbar vertebra*	0/14	0.0	0/6	0.0	0/15	0.0	2/137	1.5	2/172	1.2
Sacrum	0/6	0.0	0/5	0.0	0/13	0.0	2/118	1.7	2/142	1.4
Clavicle	1/46	2.2	0/14	0.0	2/30	6.7	15/318	4.7	18/408	4.4
Scapula	1/26	3.8	0/26	0.0	1/20	5.0	1/171	0.6	3/243	1.2
Humerus	2/62	3.2	0/10	0.0	5/41	12.2	16/360	4.4	23/473	4.9
Radius	0/43	0.0	0/19	0.0	2/32	6.3	13/311	4.2	15/405	3.7

Ulna	0/43	0.0	2/18	11.1	5/39	12.8	8/325	2.5	15/425	3.5
Hand*	0/4	0.0	0/0	0.0	2/14	14.3	0/160	0.0	2/178	1.1
Innominate	4/53	7.5	0/17	0.0	2/33	6.1	6/285	2.1	12/388	3.1
Femur	0/77	0.0	0/21	0.0	12/49	24.5	71/416	17.1	83/563	14.7
Patella	0/2	0.0	0/1	0.0	0/26	0.0	30/299	10.0	30/328	9.1
Tibia	10/69	14.5	5/15	33.3	20/44	45.5	250/434	57.6	285/562	50.7
Fibula	1/47	2.1	2/11	18.2	12/40	30.0	98/333	29.4	113/431	26.2
Foot*	0/6	0.0	0/4	0.0	1/21	4.8	7/256	2.7	8/287	2.8

*Region considered as a unit, rather than as separate bones.

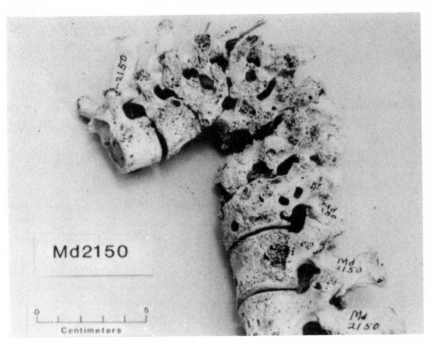

Figure 3-1
Spinal Tuberculosis (Pott's Disease)

The high prevalence of well-healed periosteal lesions suggests that the majority of affected individuals survived the pathologic or traumatic insults responsible for this response. The majority of affected elements display localized involvement, typically affecting only a small area of cortex. These factors, along with the lack of association with early mortality and the nonrandom anatomical distribution, suggest an endemic pathological entity that afflicted many members of each generation but was rarely a direct cause of death.

Careful comparison of the recorded anatomical and demographic patterning of the observed lesions with disease models that feature a high prevalence of postcranial periostitis and a low prevalence of resorptive cranial lesions suggests that the Moundville pattern of skeletal involvement resulted from an endemic treponematosis (Powell 1988). Speculation concerning the presence of syphilis among prehistoric eastern U.S. Indians was initiated by Joseph Jones's (1876) diagnosis of pathological skeletal material from Tennessee stone-box graves. Clarence B. Moore sent a sampling of Moundville pathological specimens to the Army Medical Museum in 1906 and received an identification of syphilis for the

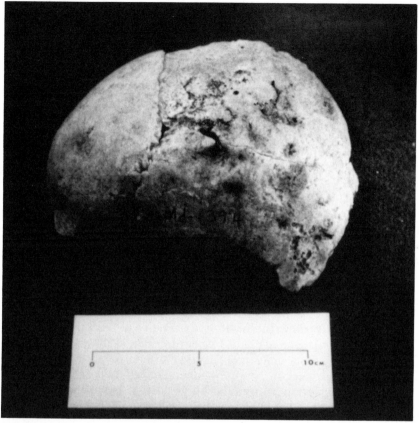

Figure 3-2
Caries Sicca of Endemic Treponematosis

majority of them (Moore 1907). Haltom and Shands (1938) noted that
this earlier diagnosis matched their own for other pathologic specimens
excavated at Moundville in the 1930s. In the present sample, three adult
crania display the characteristic stellate lesions of healed caries sicca,
considered to be strongly pathognomonic of treponemal infection
(Hackett 1976). The most complete of these specimens is illustrated in
Figure 3-2 and closely resembles those illustrated by Haltom and
Shands. Other diagnoses of treponematosis in pre-Columbian skeletal
material from the Southeast include Bullen's (1972) analysis of Weeden
Island period burials from Florida, Cassidy's (1972) description of bone
lesions at Hardin Village in Kentucky, Cook's (1976) explicitly epidemiological evaluation of skeletal pathology in lower Illinois River Val-

ley samples, and Robbins's (1978) discussion of a "yawslike" disease at Morton Shell Mound, Louisiana.

Summary

The overall impression gained from this study is of an aboriginal agricultural population that was generally well adapted to its natural and social environment. The skeletal record documents minor developmental disturbances in early childhood and the inevitable encounters with minor trauma and endogenous pathogens, but infectious reaction was usually restricted to localized, non-life-threatening involvement. Nutritional deficiencies are not widely evident, although the high-carbohydrate Mississippian diet may have promoted anemia in some young children. This diet produced moderate dental wear and substantial dental decay, similar to patterns reported for other comparable Amerindian agriculturalists. The age-associated distribution of linear enamel hypoplasia closely matches patterns reported for other Mississippian populations.

Comparisons of prevalence of the biological features selected for observation clearly show the basic homogeneity of the three status-defined population segments with respect to these features (Table 3-15). Subadults and adults differ more markedly than do adult females and males. Analyses of occlusal molar wear and dental caries suggest that all three status subgroups consumed foods similar in texture and in cariogenic properties. The lack of statistically significant differences in skeletal metrics by status may be due, in part, to the absence in the sample of the most highly ranked individuals, those buried in mounds. However, no consistent differences were evident among the nonelite population segments that are presumably completely represented, suggesting that status differentiation at Moundville brought no substantial biological benefits nor levied any heavy penalties.

Table 3-16 summarizes comparisons of the biological dimensions of ranked status at Moundville with available data from four other Mississippian communities, Etowah in Georgia and Dallas, Hixon, and Chucalissa in Tennessee. Peebles (1974) noted that subadults were underrepresented in mound burials as reported by Moore (1906, 1907) and suspected, from the available field notes, that adult males were also overrepresented in those locales. This pattern of greater elite male stature has been reported in numerous population samples from the prehistoric Eastern Woodlands (e.g., the Illinois Hopewell [Buikstra 1976c]). A percentage of these taller males probably represents individuals

Table 3-15
Biological Dimensions of Ranked Status at Moundville: Modeled Expectations vs. Observations

Biological Dimensions	Modeled Expectations	Observations
Demography	Lower elite mortality at all ages.	Sample unsuitable for assessment.
Adult body size	Elite individuals should be larger than nonelite individuals.	Elite males slightly larger, but difference not significant at .05.
Dental health	Elite dentitions may show less caries and wear than nonelite dentitions.	No differences significant at .05.
Growth and development	Elite individuals would display smoother trajectories than nonelite individuals.	No differences significant at .05.
Nutritional status	Elite individuals should show less evidence of deficiencies than nonelite.	Elites show less cribra orbitalia but difference is not significant at .05.
Trauma	Elite males should show more trauma from warfare, and elite females should show less trauma from ordinary activities.	Elites show less trauma but sample bias suspected.
Infectious disease experience	Members of the elite population segment should display stronger response and exposure to fewer diseases than nonelite individuals.	No differences significant at .05.

whose status-mediated superior nutrition in childhood promoted full realization of their genetically determined growth potential, but others probably were accorded elite burial because of prowess in warfare related to their greater size. This emphasis upon warfare as an avenue for male status advancement probably accounts for the higher prevalence of fractures among elite males at Chucalissa and Etowah. The almost complete absence of this form of skeletal pathology at Moundville suggests that the elite males represented in the present skeletal sample may have been primarily identified with roles and duties unconnected with warfare.

Table 3-16
Ranked Status, Diet, and Health at Chucalissa, Dallas/Hixon, Etowah, and Moundville

	Chucalissa	Dallas/Hixon	Etowah	Moundville
Sample Composition	Elite mound burials, elite and nonelite burials from other sectors. Boxtown (A.D. 1400–1500) and Walls (A.D. 1500–1600 phase.[1]	Elite mound burials, elite and nonelite burials perimound and in village. Dallas phase (A.D. 1300–1550).[3]	Elite mound burials, Wilbanks phase (A.D. 950–1440), nonelite village burials (post-A.D. 1400).[7]	No elite mound burials, elite and nonelite burials from perimound and village sectors. Moundville phase (A.D. 1050–1550).[11]
Demographic structure	Children absent, adult males overrepresented in mound burials. More infants in nonelite than in elite sector.[1]	Subadults underrepresented in mound and perimound burials, adult males overrepresented in mounds.[3]	Children underrepresented in mound, adult males overrepresented. Village sample shows normal distribution.[8]	Subadults underrepresented in mounds. No significant differences by age or sex in present subsamples.
Adult stature	Tallest males in mound burials, but nonelite taller than elite in nonmound sectors. No difference for females.[1]	Elite males significantly taller than nonelite males. No such pattern for females.[3,4]	No significant differences between mound and village adults, matched for sex.[9]	Elite males slightly taller but not significantly so. No such pattern for females.
Traumatic injuries	Elite males display significantly more fractures than anyone else.[1,2]	No data reported.	Mound burials display more fractures than village burials but difference is not significant.[9]	Males display more fractures than females, but elite individuals display fewer than any others.
Other skeletal pathology	Mound burials display less cranial	No data reported on pathology of infectious	No significant differences by status	No significant differences by status for

	osteoporosis and more degenerative joint disease than other sectors. Little difference in bone inflammation rate between sectors.[1]	or nutritional etiology. Adult femur cortex is thickest in perimound burials, thinnest in mound burials. Mound male burials display more transverse lines formed at 10–14 years than any other group.[6]	for periostitis, osteomyelitis, gerontal osteoporosis, vertebral osteoarthritis, or porotic hyperostosis.[9]	pathology of infectious or nutritional etiology.
Dental pathology	No differences by status for dental caries, abscesses, or antemortem tooth loss.[1]	No data reported.	More periodontal disease in village than in mound burials.[9]	No significant differences by status for dental wear, caries, antemortem tooth loss, or enamel hypoplasia. Lower strontium levels in elite adults suggest a diet richer in meat, but differences are not significant.[12]
Trace element levels	No data reported.	Levels of strontium, manganese, and vanadium differ significantly for mound and nonmound subadults. Difference is less for adult males, and adult females do not differ consistently.[5]	No significant differences by status in levels of magnesium, strontium, zinc or copper.[10]	

[1]Robinson 1976.
[2]Lahren and Berryman 1984.
[3]Hatch 1976.
[4]Hatch and Willey 1974
[5]Hatch and Geidel 1983.
[6]Hatch et al. 1983.
[7]Larson 1971.
[8]Blakely 1977.
[9]Blakely 1980.
[10]Blakely and Beck 1981.
[11]Peebles 1974.
[12]Schoeninger and Peebles 1981.

The absence of patterned differences in infectious disease experience between mound and nonmound population segments at these sites suggests that whatever status-mediated behavioral and dietary constraints were present in these societies did not have a strong effect upon health. No dental evidence indicates significant dietary differences, but differential elite/nonelite consumption of meat would not be easily detectable from such features. The evidence from bone chemistry assay of strontium levels for patterned dietary differences by status, and possibly also by sex, at Moundville may be biologically correlated with the almost complete absence of evidence of iron-deficiency anemia in elite individuals. The Dallas and Hixon samples also show patterned differences for mound and nonmound individuals in levels of several trace elements in bone. With regard to Etowah, the absence of such differences raises the possibility that the lack of contemporaneity between the mound and nonmound samples may entail dietary differences not strictly determined by ranked status.

The lack of patterned significant correspondence between the social and biological dimensions of ranked status at Moundville is intriguing but not mysterious. Given the sophisticated technological and organizational nature of this chiefdom and its beneficent environment, the elite sector may have been somewhat *over*nourished but not at any real expense to everyone else. Ranked status may have mandated certain behavioral and dietary differences within the community, but general health seems to have been little affected. European accounts of African and Polynesian chiefdoms often comment upon striking physical differences between chiefly families and commoners, differences deliberately manipulated through diet and patterns of activities to give visual emphasis to key dimensions of social inequality (Powell 1988). Equivalent accounts of protohistoric southeastern chiefdoms do not mention such literal "personifications of power" as a general pattern, though they do mention distinctions of dress, dwelling location and form, and activities. A major contribution of the present study, then, is the bioarchaeological corroboration of the powers of observation of the New World explorers who led the conquest of the Southeast.

Acknowledgments

I would like to thank the Alabama State Museum of Natural History for permission to present these data, and the Department of Anthropology, University of Alabama, for support and encouragement throughout the project. Donald J. Ortner, Gillian R. Bentley, George R. Milner, Henry T. Wright, Bruce D. Smith, and Ann Marie Wagner Mires provided valuable comments for improving the manuscript.

✳ 4

Health and Cultural Change
in the Late Prehistoric
American Bottom, Illinois

George R. Milner

The development of organizationally complex Mississippian cultures and their later decline were significant events in the prehistoric and protohistoric cultural trajectories of North America. The Mississippian cultural tradition in Illinois is particularly well represented by habitation sites, mounds, and cemeteries in a segment of the central Mississippi River Valley known as the American Bottom.

Hierarchically organized societies in this region had their origins during the Emergent Mississippian (A.D. 800–1000) and Early Mississippian periods (Kelly et al. 1984; Milner et al. 1984). They reached a climax in the Stirling phase (A.D. 1050–1150), only to collapse during the following 250 years. By the end of that time, the American Bottom was largely depopulated.

Archaeological research conducted over many years in the American Bottom has begun to delineate the nature of changes in intrasite organization, settlement distribution, intersite relationships, and social organization, as well as fluctuations in regional population density (review in Milner 1987). Complementary research focusing on human skeletal biology provides an additional perspective on the complex, relatively rapid, and presumably interrelated processes of cultural and demographic change that occurred during the late prehistoric era.

Archaeological Background

Cahokia, the largest site in eastern North America, reached its peak of development and influence during the Stirling phase. The material culture of the American Bottom at this time can be considered fully Mississippian in nature. Shell-tempered pottery and wall-trench construction buildings, long considered Mississippian hallmarks, were innovations that had become firmly established by the Stirling phase, although both appeared somewhat earlier in the region. Appreciable quantities of shell-tempered pottery occur first in terminal Emergent Mississippian Edelhardt phase assemblages (A.D. 950–1000) (Emerson and Jackson 1984; Kelly 1980), whereas wall-trench structures often occur in the Lohmann phase (A.D. 1000–1050), the earliest of the Mississippian phases (Esarey and Good 1981; Mehrer 1982; Milner 1983c). More importantly in terms of the adaptive stance of Mississippian populations, the subsistence practices throughout this period were strongly oriented toward the diverse, resource-rich habitats of the Mississippi River floodplain. Hunting, fishing, and collecting strategies were combined with the cultivation of native and introduced tropical cultigens, particularly maize (Johannessen 1984; Kelly and Cross 1984).

There is also considerable evidence for the existence of a hierarchically organized society at this time. Mississippian sites throughout the American Bottom varied considerably in terms of overall size, number of associated mounds, and density of occupational debris. They were part of a settlement system that included the paramount site of Cahokia, subsidiary sites with one or more mounds, and settlements lacking evidence of associated mounds (Fowler 1974, 1978). Individual town-and-mound complexes had somewhat different occupational histories and presumably controlled, at least for a time, territories that encompassed numerous farmsteads. These farmsteads apparently formed dispersed communities that were distributed across high parts of the floodplain.

A significant reorganization of society at the beginning of the Mississippian period is indicated by a shift in the internal organization of the outlying habitation sites that lacked mounds. Nucleated villages typical of the Emergent Mississippian period (Kelly et al. 1984) were supplanted in the Mississippian period by communities consisting of widely dispersed farmsteads (Milner 1987; Milner et al. 1984). The farmstead community arrangement proved to be remarkably stable, lasting for hundreds of years despite the changing fortunes of nearby town-and-mound centers.

Early in the Mississippian period, if not before, there developed social inequalities that are most clearly expressed in the differential treatment of the dead (Fowler 1974; Milner 1984; Winters 1974b). At least two social strata are represented—the elite of the mound centers and the nonelite who occupied mound complexes as well as peripheral settlements. While an elite versus nonelite dichotomy is as exacting a model as is possible with existing archaeological data, it simplifies a more sophisticated social structure. Mortuary remains indicate that gradations occurred in wealth and prestige-denoting artifacts within the two macrocategories (Milner 1984), and similar patterns of social differentiation are known to have occurred in Mississippian societies elsewhere (Goldstein 1980; Hatch 1976; Peebles and Kus 1977). For a historical analogue, archaeologists can look to the early eighteenth century Natchez where the principal social strata displayed internal distinctions of rank (Du Pratz 1972; White et al. 1971).

Interaction with distant regions is indicated by the presence of exotic raw materials, much of which occurs as the funerary accompaniments of an elite stratum who occupied the town-and-mound centers (Fowler 1974; Milner 1984; Winters 1974b). The residents of outlying sites also had access to exotic materials. These items included utilitarian objects, such as hoes made from Mill Creek and Kaolin chert, as well as generally small and often ornamental objects fashioned from hematite, galena, and whelk shell, among other materials (Milner et al. 1984).

The American Bottom Mississippian culture's dissolution probably began as early as the Moorehead phase (A.D. 1150–1250), if population size is considered a reliable indicator of the continued viability of an elaborated and centralized social organization. Occupation of the Mississippi River floodplain had increased until the Stirling phase; thereafter, it declined. While the most adequately controlled information on population history comes from dated farmstead structures south of Cahokia (Milner 1986), the Stirling phase population peak and subsequent decline seem to have occurred at Cahokia as well (Gregg 1975). A reduction of the floodplain population appears to have resulted in part from a dispersal of people to the tributary creek valleys in the surrounding uplands. Archaeological investigations of areas to the east of the main river valley have found an uneven distribution of late prehistoric sites, but most known settlements belong to the early or late ends of the period that encompassed the development and dissolution of an organizationally complex cultural system centered on Cahokia (Bareis 1976; Denny et al. 1983; Woods 1986:72).

It was not until the Sand Prairie phase (A.D. 1250–1400), however, that there is appreciable evidence for major structural changes in American Bottom society. At Cahokia significant alterations occurred in the internal configuration of the site, and by the end of the Sand Prairie phase the elite stratum apparently had lost their ability to enforce adherence to a site plan featuring a sizable functionally differentiated core area. A palisade screening Cahokia's center, which was rebuilt on several occasions during the Stirling and Moorehead phases, was not in existence during the terminal Mississippian phase (Fowler 1974). Residential structures were built and people were buried in what previously had been a specialized precinct near Monks Mound that was dominated by large, public architecture (Fowler 1974; Fowler and Hall 1972; Wittry and Vogel 1962). In addition, members of the nonelite social stratum were buried in at least one mound in the central portion of the site, which represented a departure from the mound's original function (Milner 1984).

The Sand Prairie phase also seems to have been a period of increasing local autonomy for the farmstead communities scattered across the floodplain. Increased social segmentation may account for a shift from large, prominently located, presumably multicommunity cemeteries to the small, single-community cemeteries that are typical of the Sand Prairie phase (Milner 1984). A reduction in the number of communities using a particular cemetery may have contributed to the Sand Prairie phase preference for floodplain burial locations—these cemeteries were located on the same ridges that were inhabited—instead of the earlier emphasis on relatively inaccessible, but highly visible, bluff crests for the development of extensive mortuary areas.

Late Mississippian social fragmentation, however, had little effect on the extent to which the farmstead occupants enjoyed access to a variety of exotic raw materials (Milner et al. 1984). The exchange networks providing much of the nonlocal materials used by the residents of the peripheral Mississippian settlements seem to have been maintained despite a breakdown in the level of regional integration needed to support an elite social stratum and to construct the massive earthen mounds at superordinate centers.

Skeletal Series

Given this clear record of cultural change, it is reasonable to ask whether the relatively rapid cultural and demographic transformations in the region were accompanied by equally pervasive alterations in community health. Although many cemeteries dating to the Mississippian period have been found in the American Bottom (Milner 1982:256–88, 1984; Illinois Archaeological Survey site files), there are unfortunately few reasonably well-preserved and sizable skeletal collections available for study. The most well-known American Bottom skeletal series is from Mound 72 at Cahokia, but it is composed largely of sacrificial victims whose ultimate origin is unknown (Fowler 1974). The two largest skeletal collections representing local populations date to the last half of the Mississippian period. One is from the Moorehead phase Kane Mounds site ($N = 140$) (Milner 1982), and the other is from the Sand Prairie phase East St. Louis Stone Quarry site ($N = 120$) (Milner

1983b). Both cemeteries are thought to contain the remains of individuals from one or more farmstead communities. Therefore, they represent the nonelite segment of Mississippian society.

Paleodemography

Population Change

The number of dated structures in extensive excavations is one reasonably straightforward means of establishing the direction and magnitude of shifts over time in American Bottom population size. Population estimates, therefore, have been derived from a count of farmstead structures at eleven extensively excavated sites distributed along a segment of floodplain south of Cahokia that is 15 km long. A temporally sequential series of population estimates for this portion of bottomland is provided in Table 4-1, standardized for different phase lengths and based on the number of structures and an average occupancy of five years. Additional data manipulation and computation details are provided in Milner (1986), and the formula used to calculate the growth rate (r) is found in Hassan (1981:139).

Estimates of absolute population size in this particular example depend on a series of assumptions, including phase duration, the amount of land that was potentially habitable, the number of individuals who occupied a building, and the longevity of structure occupancy. While higher or lower absolute estimates are obtained by substituting other values for each variable, the figures in Table 4-1 provide one means of assessing relative population change from one phase to the next. The estimates probably best approximate the number of people alive at the middle of each phase, for there appear to have been directional trends in population size that spanned multiple generations. The period of Late Mississippian demographic decline is especially apparent from available data. Therefore, phase midpoints were used when determining the time elapsed between population estimates.

The population estimates indicate an increase early in the Mississippian sequence, a peak in the Stirling phase, and a decrease in numbers late in the period. Calculations of the rate of increase or decrease show that population change from one phase to the next was less than 1 percent per year. The Stirling to Sand Prairie phase reduction in the Cahokia-area population, with its overall value of r = -0.0085, would have been difficult for the widely dispersed farmstead residents to perceive, assuming that the decline was a more or less gradual process instead of

Table 4-1
American Bottom Mississippian Phases and
Population Change Over Time

Phase	Duration	Midpoint	Population	r
Sand Prairie	A.D. 1250–1400	1325	435.9	− 0.0079
Moorehead	A.D. 1150–1250	1200	1,175.9	− 0.0093
Stirling	A.D. 1050–1150	1100	2,981.3	+ 0.0057
Lohmann	A.D. 1000–1050	1025	1,943.3	—

Midpoint: Midpoint of phase duration.
Population: Population estimates are from Milner 1986: Table 4, Column 8.

a series of catastrophic events. Nevertheless, the cumulative effect of this process was dramatic—the floodplain was only sparsely populated by the end of the Mississippian period.

Mortality

Certain demographic characteristics pertaining to the American Bottom populations can be derived from life tables based on the age structure of skeletal series from mortuary contexts (Milner 1982:317, Table 19, 1983b:85, Table 8). Life table figures derived from age-at-death information, assuming a stationary population, differ somewhat between the two temporally sequential skeletal series. These figures include the probability of dying (q_x) and life expectancy (e_x) that are largely unaffected by the underenumeration of preceding age intervals, particularly infants (Moore et al. 1975). For example, in most age groups the probability of dying values are greater for the Moorehead sample than for the Sand Prairie phase skeletons (Figure 4-1). Nevertheless, several problems, including the effects of an unknown birth rate, are associated with the conventional paleodemographic derivation and interpretation of life table statistics calculated on the basis of only age-at-death data (Johansson and Horowitz 1986; Sattenspiel and Harpending 1983).

Paleodemographers usually develop life tables as if the population was stationary as well as stable. Both requirements are usually assumed to be met when generating life tables for prehistoric skeletal series because it is rarely possible to control a number of critical variables, including shifts over time in population composition and size (see Acsadi and Nemeskeri 1970; Buikstra and Mielke 1985; Palkovich 1978; Ubelaker 1974; and Weiss 1973 for discussions of these and other issues that affect

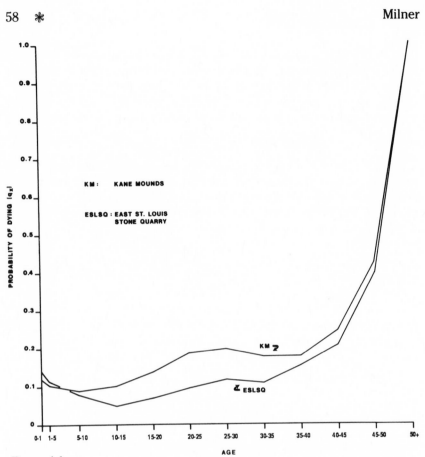

Figure 4-1
The Probability of Dying (q_x) for the Moorehead Phase Kane Mounds (KM) Population and the Sand Prairie Phase East St. Louis Stone Quarry (ESLSQ) Population

the precision of paleodemographic estimates). An estimated rate of change could be derived, however, for the American Bottom through an independent data set (i.e., the number of residential structures belonging to different periods of time), although the relative contributions of shifts in birth and death rates and almost certainly migration remain unknown. An overall Stirling to Sand Prairie figure of $r = -0.0085$ modifies life table values calculated from the distribution of deaths (see Bennett 1973b; Carrier 1958; Moore et al. 1975). Life expectancy estimates at birth and at fifteen years, for example, are changed by several years for the two archaeological samples when the accumulations of skeletons are not treated as coming from stationary populations. The American

Bottom example where the rate of population change can be estimated from archaeological data highlights only one of the several significant problems in the comparison of life table values derived from separate skeletal series, especially when there is unambiguous evidence for population growth or decline and when the available samples are as small as those typically found at archaeological sites (for a discussion of these issues see Moore et al. 1975, among others).

Despite the problems with interpreting age-at-death information from prehistoric skeletal series, the American Bottom mortality-related figures depart in several important ways from model life tables developed by Weiss (1973) for anthropological populations. First, infants are underrepresented in the archaeological samples. This underrepresentation is undoubtedly a function of poor preservation and the practice of secondary burial at both sites, both of which contribute to the loss and destruction of small, fragile bones (this archaeological sampling problem is quite common and has been recognized for over 200 years [Jefferson 1954:99]). Second, the probability of dying (q_x) for both archaeological samples rises more rapidly than expected at the upper end of the age distributions. This rapid increase is an artifact of the skeletal age-estimating process, because all individuals older than fifty years were combined in a single +50 category. Third, there is an anomalous peak in young adult mortality in the Kane Mounds population where female deaths exceeded those of males during these years. Discrepancies in the two ends of the archaeological mortality distributions are attributable to biases in sampling and the grouping of old individuals in a single +50 category. Elevated mortality among Moorehead phase young females may be a sampling artifact or it may have some biological significance. It could reflect the rigors of bearing and rearing children coupled with an already stressful way of life involving strenuous labor during the annual subsistence cycle (see Wells 1975).

One possible difference between these two populations lies in the patterns of juvenile mortality (Figure 4–2). Although many infants in both populations died, any discrepancy in these figures is insignificant given the likelihood of differential bone preservation and, hence, the incomplete recovery of small skeletons. Figures for children in archaeological samples tend to have greater biological significance because it is more likely that the skeletal total is representative of the patterning of deaths occurring during the juvenile years. The bones of children are larger and more durable than those of infants, reducing sampling error introduced by vagaries of preservation and excavation procedures.

Mortality during the first five years in the Moorehead phase population seems to consist of three stages. High first-year mortality dimin-

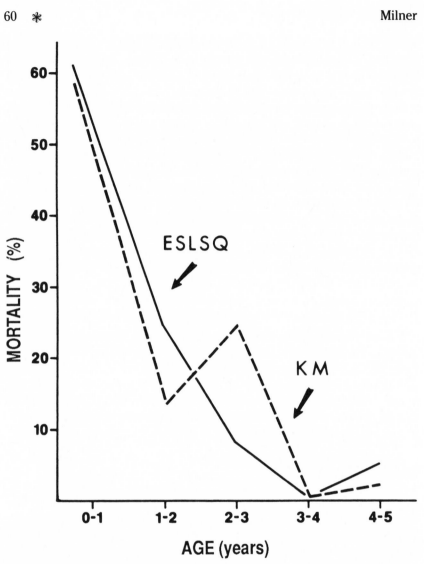

Figure 4-2
Distribution of Mortality Between the Ages of 0 to 5 Years in the Moorehead
Phase Kane Mounds (KM) Population and the Sand Prairie Phase East St. Louis
Stone Quarry (ESLSQ) Population

ished to an intermediate level spanning the second and third years. This
plateau was followed by a further drop to the low levels associated with
the fourth and fifth years. Many Sand Prairie phase infants also died, and
comparatively few children, like their earlier counterparts, died during

their fourth or fifth years. It is the mortality pattern for the second and third years that differentiates the two populations. In the Sand Prairie phase, a decline in mortality, instead of a plateau, occurred during this period.

Juvenile mortality, especially that associated with the first several years of life, is considered a sensitive measure of community health for modern populations, particularly in societies where children experience a high risk of succumbing to diseases encouraged by poor diets and contaminated environments (Gordon et al. 1967; Puffer and Serrano 1973). The prolongation of breast-feeding and the use of nutritionally incomplete supplemental foods dominated by starchy gruels commonly occur in societies from underdeveloped parts of the modern world that experience major public health problems (Behar 1968; Popkin et al. 1982; Scrimshaw et al. 1968). Many of these same populations experience elevated mortality rates for several years beyond infancy.

Paleopathology

It is always difficult to identify specific diseases when only dry bones are available. Nevertheless, it is possible to identify and count various types of lesions that affect hard tissues. This information can serve as a useful, albeit crude, measure of community health, although the frequency of bone lesions in a skeletal collection, which is a mortality sample, should not be confused with the prevalence of a particular condition in a living population.

Infectious Diseases

Lesions classified as periostitis are the predominant forms of pathological bony involvement in both skeletal series. The pathological proliferation of bone frequently contributed to an irregular elevation of bone surfaces, including a fusiform expansion of long bone shafts. Periostitis in both series was often localized, had healed, and displayed a smooth, undulating appearance. Infections in some individuals, however, resulted in chronic conditions that had spread throughout the skeleton. This more severe form of pathological involvement often included marked alterations of bone cortices and a filling of medullary cavities with coarse, disorganized trabeculae, in addition to an exuberant proliferation of new periosteal bone (osteomyelitis). These lesions were occasionally accompanied by the drainage sinuses characteristic of suppurative osteomyelitis, infections caused by pyogenic bacteria

(Aegerter and Kirkpatrick 1975; Ortner and Putschar 1981; Steinbock 1976).

The proportions of adults (> 15 years) from the two populations with postcranial skeletons exhibiting predominately proliferative forms of pathological bony involvement were similar: 27 percent and 25 percent of the adults in the series representing the Moorehead (94 observable individuals) and Sand Prairie phases (49 observable individuals), respectively. Many skeletons in both collections, however, were incomplete and the bones displayed postmortem damage. The nature of the collections raises the distinct possibility of biases attributable to differential preservation and the unequal representation of skeletal elements.

Comparisons of single skeletal elements avoid problems attributable to incomplete skeletons. The reliance on single bones, however, entails a considerable loss of information, particularly the patterning required for the differential diagnosis of diseases. Tibiae were used for the single-bone comparisons of the predominately proliferative forms of pathological bony involvement because these bones were the most frequently affected skeletal elements. The numbers of affected adult (>15 years) tibiae were similar: 26 percent and 29 percent of the bones in the Moorehead (145 observable tibiae) and Sand Prairie (63 observable tibiae) collections, respectively. Again, the frequency figures for the two skeletal series are similar, although comparability problems attributable to bone preservation are not eliminated because of the condition of much of the skeletal material.

Juvenile figures are not provided here because of the poor preservation of bone coupled with the unequal representation of children of different ages. In addition, it often proved difficult to distinguish the rapidly remodeling, hypervascular bone of infants from a response of bone to infection, particularly when the bones also displayed postmortem surface erosion.

Some examples of periostitis and osteomyelitis in the American Bottom series presumably had a treponemal origin, as has been suggested for other prehistoric North American skeletal series. The possibility that pre-Columbian skeletons display evidence of a treponemal infection was first recognized in the nineteenth century, when lesions attributed to venereal syphilis were described in Tennessee skeletons that were much later recognized as dating to the Mississippian period (Jones 1876). Since that time, many specimens have been found supporting the interpretation that a treponematosis was present in the New World prior to European contact (reviews in El-Najjar 1979; Hackett 1976; Ortner and Putschar 1981; Steinbock 1976), but population-based studies of the specific nature of this disease in American Indian skeletons have only recently begun to appear in the literature (Powell 1988).

Several American Bottom skeletons display lytic lesions resembling those found in individuals with skeletal tuberculosis. While the pre-Columbian existence of tuberculosis has been debated for many years, the identification over a decade ago of distinctive lesions in prehistoric Peruvian mummified remains indicates that the disease was indeed present in the prehistoric Americas (Allison et al. 1973). Recent studies have provided strong support for a tuberculosis-like disease in prehistoric North America as well (recent reviews of this topic by several authors can be found in Buikstra 1981). Moreover, distinctive osteolytic lesions occur in Mississippian and Oneota skeletons from the Illinois River Valley, which is immediately north of the American Bottom (Buikstra and Cook 1978, 1981; Milner and Smith 1990).

One of the American Bottom specimens, a Moorehead phase adult's sacrum and fifth lumbar vertebra, is shown in Figure 4–3. A lesion had destroyed much of the inferior surface of the fifth lumbar vertebra and had spread to the anterior surface of the body as well as to the first two sacral elements. Trabeculae at the borders of this lesion are somewhat thickened, and there is limited surrounding proliferation of reactive bone. Lytic lesions displayed by several additional American Bottom skeletons, including others from the Kane Mounds and East St. Louis Stone Quarry cemeteries, are probably attributable to the same disease process, which closely approximates modern skeletal tuberculosis. Nevertheless, alternative diagnoses, including blastomycosis, should always be considered in these cases (see Buikstra 1976a; Kelley and Eisenberg 1987; Ortner and Putschar 1981).

Nutritional Deficiency

Orbital and cranial lesions known as cribra orbitalia and porotic hyperostosis, respectively, are exhibited by a number of American Bottom skeletons. These distinctive lesions result from erythropoietic tissue hyperplasia and are associated with several forms of anemia (Angel 1966b; El-Najjar et al. 1976; Hengen 1971; Mensforth et al. 1978; Ortner and Putschar 1981; Palkovich 1987; Steinbock 1976; Stuart-Macadam 1985, 1987). The conditions are usually attributed to iron-deficiency anemia when found in pre-Columbian New World skeletons, and they tend to occur more often in populations that relied on diets featuring a considerable maize content. In cribra orbitalia, numerous apertures penetrate the anterior portion of the orbital surface of the frontal bone, and the

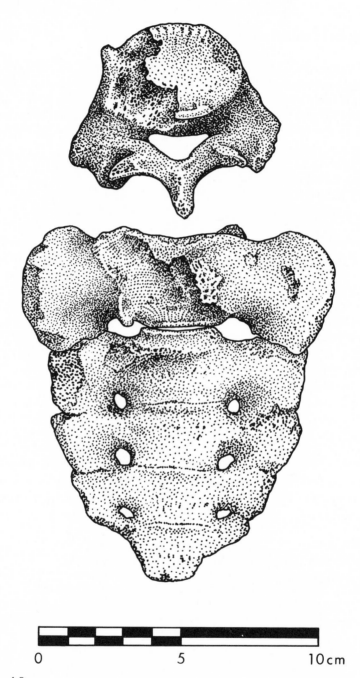

Figure 4-3
The Sacrum and Fifth Lumbar Vertebra from a Moorehead Phase Skeleton from
Kane Mounds

bone surface may be raised, extending into the orbit. In porotic hyperostosis, apertures penetrate the external table of the cranial vault, the external table can be thinned, and the diploe is often thickened. Abnormal diploic structure may be visible in radiographs as striations radiating from the inner to the outer tables, the so-called hair-on-end effect.

The percentage of crania displaying either cribra orbitalia or porotic hyperostosis in the Sand Prairie series is approximately three times greater than it was in the earlier sample (Table 4–2). The majority of the crania were not intact, although the most poorly preserved and highly fragmented specimens were excluded from the interpopulation comparison. Nevertheless, variation in bone preservation combined with any differential expression of the lesions in the two parts of the cranium where the conditions usually occur, the orbits and posterior vault, could obscure comparisons based on incomplete specimens. When only crania with at least one orbit and much, or all, of the posterior cranial vault are compared, the samples are reduced but the discrepancy in lesion frequency remains: Moorehead phase, $N = 68$, 7 percent affected; Sand Prairie phase, $N = 24$, 25 percent affected.

Three of the six Moorehead phase crania that exhibited the lesions belonged to children who died during their second or third years. These three individuals represented 38 percent of the children in this two-year interval with crania that could be examined for either condition. The affected Sand Prairie phase individuals were generally older at the time of death than their Moorehead phase counterparts. In addition, the lesions typically had a well-remodeled appearance, indicating that the period of nutritionally related stress that resulted in a pathological involvement of bone had occurred earlier in life. (See Martin, Goodman, and Armelagos 1985; Mensforth et al. 1978; Palkovich 1987; and Stuart-

Table 4-2
Skeletons with Cribra Orbitalia or Porotic Hyperostosis

Age	Kane Mounds	Affected		ESLSQ	Affected	
	N	N	%	N	N	%
0–2.9 years	13	3	23	3	1	33
3–14.9 years	11	0	0	7	2	29
+15 years	74	3	4	31	4	13
Total	98	6	6	41	7	17

ESLSQ: East St. Louis Stone Quarry

Macadam 1985 for discussions of the importance of differentiating active from inactive lesions.)

The greater number of remodeled lesions in the Sand Prairie phase population may reflect the fact that more young children lived through a period of chronic stress, which resulted in skeletal lesions that eventually healed, than survived in the earlier population. Differential survivorship is also suggested by the third-year mortality figures that dropped in the Sand Prairie phase population but continued at an elevated level in the Moorehead phase group.

American Bottom and Other Midcontinental Populations

Some evidence exists for variation in the mortality and morbidity patterns of populations drawn from different times during Cahokia's long slide to obscurity. It can be safely assumed, however, that the causes underlying any shifts in either mortality or morbidity were many. This uncertainty makes the interpretation of seemingly different patterns rather difficult, particularly when combined with the small size of archaeological skeletal samples and the problems inherent in making inferences about past conditions, human behavior, and the prevalence of pathological conditions in a living population from the frequency of lesions in a nonsurvivor sample. Nevertheless, alterations in the patterning of juvenile deaths and in the age distribution of nutritionally related skeletal lesions may reflect a change in the overall health of young children. Differences in mortality patterns, specifically during the second and third years, may be linked to variation in the age distributions of individuals exhibiting cribra orbitalia and porotic hyperostosis. Taken together, this information raises the possibility that many Sand Prairie phase children survived a period of initial stress, which resulted in bony manifestations of the disease process, only to succumb later to other causes of death. Other indexes of health, such as the combined periostitis and osteomyelitis figures for adults, remained essentially the same during the last two Mississippian phases. These findings underscore the importance of integrating complementary data sets in the assessment of prehistoric community health. In addition, future research should direct especially close attention toward the juvenile segment of American Bottom populations.

Lesions resembling those of classic skeletal tuberculosis are particularly significant given previous research conducted within western Illinois. Buikstra and Cook (1978, 1981; Cook 1984) have identified lesions closely approximating those of skeletal tuberculosis in specimens from the neighboring lower Illinois River Valley, and they suggest that the Cahokia area was a probable source for this infectious disease. When Cahokia was a major center, the numbers of people and the appreciable intraregional social interaction that occurred would have facilitated the maintenance of a communicable disease such as tuberculosis that is characteristically associated with crowded, unsanitary conditions. Tuberculosis can establish chronic infections in humans, particularly when it occurs as an endemic, as opposed to an epidemic, disease in the host population.

Apparently west-central Illinois groups maintained this disease well into the Sand Prairie phase, long after the floodplain in the vicinity of Cahokia had undergone a marked reduction in population. Persistence of the disease may be explained by intermittent interaction among distant groups that continued throughout the late prehistoric period. This contact is indicated by nonlocal raw materials at American Bottom farmsteads that the inhabitants of the region were able to obtain throughout the cultural and demographic transition from the Stirling to the Sand Prairie phase. In this context it is significant that lesions approximating those of classic skeletal tuberculosis also occur in a recently excavated skeletal series from the central Illinois River Valley (Milner and Smith 1990). This particular collection consists of skeletons from a contemporaneous, tribally organized Oneota society in a region of lower population density. For this group there is also abundant archaeological evidence of interpopulation contact, in this instance antagonistic as well as cooperative in nature.

Taking a much broader perspective—and one arguably altogether too global given the present state of knowledge and the degree of interobserver variation in recording methods—it appears that levels of community health varied among roughly contemporaneous late prehistoric populations (see discussions in Milner 1982; Powell 1988; and Rose et al. 1984). Overall, it seems as if the people of the American Bottom were more or less as healthy as the Mississippians of Moundville, Alabama (Powell 1988), and several late prehistoric populations from the Arkansas region (Rose et al. 1984). They were not as highly stressed as the Dickson Mounds "Middle Mississippian" (Goodman and Armelagos 1985; Goodman et al. 1984) and Norris Farms #36 Oneota (Milner and Smith 1990) populations of the central Illinois River Valley, some central Mississippi River Valley late Mississippian groups (Rose et al. 1984), and the Mississippian Averbuch population from central Tennessee (Eisenberg, 1986a, and Chapter 5, this volume). In light of this other information, it is tempting to suggest that archaeologists look to factors other than an increased disease load to account for the decline of the Cahokia-area cultural system.

Future Research

This study of American Bottom Mississippian period human remains clearly reflects several difficulties having to do with sample inadequacy, a problem that is all too familiar to archaeologists. First, additional large and adequately provenienced skeletal samples are needed to evaluate the results presented here for the Moorehead and Sand Prairie phase populations. Second, comparable skeletal collections for the Lohmann and Stirling phases do not exist. This is a serious omission inasmuch as the Stirling phase was the peak in Cahokia-area cultural development. Third, the populations represented by the Kane Mounds and East St. Louis Stone Quarry cemeteries were drawn from the residents of peripheral sites—the farmstead communities. Sizable, well-preserved, chronologically secure, and adequately documented skeletal series representing both the elite and the nonelite of the town-and-mound complexes are simply not available for study. Much remains to be learned from skeletal series that can only be obtained through additional excavations.

Furthermore, the estimates of relative population change provided here for the four Mississippian phases should be regarded as no more than the most reliable currently available figures based on excavation data. Additional research is needed to determine whether these demographic trends are representative of the American Bottom as a whole. Certainly the existing survey and excavation data from the floodplain and uplands underscore the importance of clearly delineating the geographical scale of research when addressing population-related issues. Such definition is particularly important when dealing with spatial and temporal variation in the distribution and density of people across a varied and unstable social landscape, such as that associated with the chiefdom level of sociopolitical organization.

Conclusion

Biological information on the adaptive success of human populations, especially that pertaining to morbidity and mortality, constitutes an integral element of archaeological interpretation. Taken together, alterations over time in human health and archaeological evidence of cultural change provide a means of identifying the processes underlying the evolution of human societies. The interrelated nature of archaeological and physical anthropological research cannot be overemphasized—one does not stand alone from the other in our study of past peoples and their cultures.

Archaeologists have only begun to identify the conditions that contributed to the cultural and demographic transformations associated with the florescence and later collapse of the American Bottom Mississippian cultural system. The observations on Mississippian period health that are presented here are best treated as an exploratory study. Additional fieldwork should be undertaken to excavate large skeletal series representing a broader temporal depth and different segments of the hierarchically organized Mississippian period society of the American Bottom.

Acknowledgments

The Kane Mounds skeletons were examined while on loan from Southern Illinois University at Carbondale. The East St. Louis Stone Quarry skeletons were excavated and analyzed as part of the FAI-270 Archaeological Mitigation Project, which was conducted by the University of Illinois and funded by the Illinois Department of Transportation. Rusty E. Smith drew Figure 4–3.

✳ 5

Mississippian Cultural Terminations in Middle Tennessee: What the Bioarchaeological Evidence Can Tell Us

Leslie E. Eisenberg

Cultural terminations have always been of great interest to anthropologists, demographers, economists, historians, and other researchers tracking the changing course of the great civilizations and their less complex counterparts. This phenomenon, also referred to as "collapse" or "cultural fatigue," is believed to have occurred throughout prehistory in diverse cultural periods and geographical locations (Hill-Clark 1981; Winters 1974a:xii; Winters n.d.:47–49).

Qualitative and quantitative changes in the material remains from the archaeological record have been employed as markers to identify changes in organizational complexity. In the New World, for example, the Middle Woodland cultures, the Maya, Mississippian cultures from the Midwest and Mid-South, and several late prehistoric southwestern groups appear to have experienced this transformation (Boesch 1984; Culbert 1973; Dean et al. 1985; Dragoo 1976; Minnis 1985; Upham 1984). The discipline of archaeology, whose ultimate goal is to understand the processes by which cultures change over time, seems especially well suited to describe and explain the phenomenon of cultural termination.

Explanations based on single variables have in recent years yielded to more complex, multicausal models to account for the disappearance of the often spectacular material evidence of a culture's existence (Dragoo 1976:19; Sheldon 1974:9; Styles 1981; Willey and Shimkin 1973). The factors most often causally implicated in the disappearance of various cultures have included climatic change, warfare, natural catastrophe, environmental degradation, demographic collapse, pestilence, invasion, migration, resource imbalance, nutritional stress, and disease (Griffin 1960; King and Roper 1976:149; Vickery 1970).

This chapter focuses on the late prehistoric period in the southeastern United States known as the Mississippian and in particular on those inhabitants of the central portion of what is today the state of Tennessee. This region experienced a widespread demographic decline prior to Euroamerican contact. It is hoped that the analysis of the human skeletal populations recovered from sites in this area will provide some meaningful insights into the specific factors that led to their decline.

The Mississippian was the latest and most complex aboriginal cultural tradition in the southeastern United States. It developed in situ from preceding Woodland cultures as early as A.D 900 and continued as late as the sixteenth century in some locations. The Mississippian tradition represents a quantitative and qualitative elaboration of many of the social, religious, political, and cultural practices known to have been important during preceding times. The cultural features characterizing this tradition include a subsistence base that relied heavily on intensive floodplain agriculture and a social organization that was hierarchically ranked (Griffin 1967; Peebles and Kus 1977; Smith 1978). This restricted conception of the subsistence base has recently been challenged by a number of studies that suggest that domesticates did not totally dominate Mississippian subsistence but constituted only one portion of the diverse plant food resources utilized at some sites (Blakeman 1974; Hudson 1976:80; Kline and Crites 1979:98; Lewis and Kneberg 1946:43, 46; Phillips et al. 1980:256). Settlements were for the most part permanent and sedentary, but shorter term occupations are also known. Cultural stability characterized these late prehistoric groups from their initial appearance until their decline.

The late prehistoric inhabitants of Middle Tennessee represent a local variant of Mississippian known as the Middle Cumberland culture, which developed around A.D. 1200 and lasted in some areas until the late 1600s (Ferguson 1972:3). Locally, they are referred to as the "stone grave peoples," because they were responsible for constructing the form-fitting limestone box graves described by many early Euramerican hunters and explorers who traveled in the area (Clark 1878; Fiske 1820; Haywood 1959; Jones 1876; Thruston 1897). According to these reports, the graves were particularly abundant in and around Nashville, Tennessee. The remains of small hunting camps are also mentioned in their chronicles (Clayton 1880:16). These accounts are of particular interest in view of complementary demographic information obtained from nineteenth-century burial excavations and more recent archaeological data that suggest that population density around Nashville was quite high during the late prehistoric period (Eisenberg 1986a; Thruston 1897:2, 28).

A number of explanations have been proposed to account for Middle Cumberland depopulation prior to Euramerican arrival and settlement in the region around A.D. 1650. Among the factors most often cited as possible causes are the introduction of French and Spanish epidemics into the area from the south, raiding from the north by the Iroquois, and wholesale population movement from central to eastern Tennessee (Berryman 1980; Ferguson 1972:45; Lewis and Kneberg 1955). It appears probable that the arrival of French and Spanish epidemics into the area would have come "after the fact"; substantive data in support of the proposed Iroquois raiding hypothesis are lacking, and the results of a biometric study by Boyd (1984) serve to discredit completely the east-ward migration theory.

This chapter presents both biological and archaeological evidence to examine the phenomenon of cultural terminations in Middle Tennessee: the bioarchaeological analysis of a large skeletal series ($N = 888$) re-covered from the upland village site of Averbuch (40DV60). All materials excavated from the site, including burials, are curated by the Depart-ment of Anthropology at the University of Tennessee, Knoxville.

Averbuch included three distinct cemeteries within a village area of approximately 11 acres (Figure 5-1). It has been dated between A.D. 1275 and 1400, falling squarely within the time frame outlined by Ferguson (1972) for a Middle Cumberland culture presence in the region. The site lies not on a floodplain or lower terrace (T–1) of the Cumberland River, as do the majority of other local sites in the vicinity of Nashville, but in a

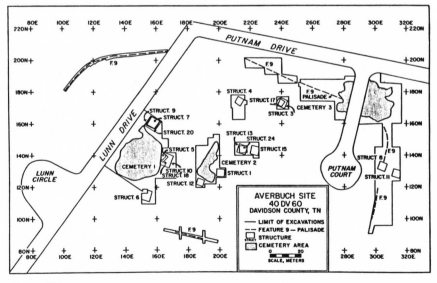

Figure 5-1
Map of the Averbuch Site (Berryman 1981:9)

different ecological/environmental zone, an upland slope some 9 km north of the river, at an elevation of over 500 feet above mean sea level. Its location in the uplands has been regarded as a response to high population density in the area. According to the current site interpretation, Averbuch represents a nonmound village occupation that "played a subordinate role in the as yet poorly understood late Mississippian settlement hierarchy in the Nashville Basin" (Klippel and Bass 1984:iii). The Mississippian site hierarchy classification scheme created by Fowler, applied most often to archaeological sites in the Midwest, would include Averbuch with other "fourth-line communities" (Droessler 1981:23).

Recent site survey data that offer a more accurate picture of Middle Cumberland settlement patterns suggest that the location of the Averbuch site may simply represent one chosen alternative within the possible range of settlement options open to late prehistoric period inhabitants of the Nashville Basin (P. Coats, personal communication 1984; Jolley 1980:64, 90). Given the rich carrying capacity of the region, the site may have been strategically located to take specific advantage of the resource diversity in two different neighboring ecological zones—the Nashville Basin and the Highland Rim. Alternately, its upland location may also reflect a logistical response to elevated levels of population density and may allude to an atmosphere where social predation may have been a circumscribing factor in the use of naturally abundant resources (Milner et al. 1988).

Analysis of the artifacts recovered from mortuary contexts indicates that, with a few exceptions, individuals buried at Averbuch were "ordinary householders and artisans" and not, in general, distinguished by high ranks and statuses (H. Winters, personal communication 1985). An analysis of lithic, bone, and shell artifacts recovered as grave associations indicates that existing social distinctions were clearly delimited by sex and age criteria (Kline 1984a; 1984b; Reed 1984a; 1984b; Romanoski 1984b).

Infectious and Nutritional Pathology in the Averbuch Skeletal Population

While not all disease lingers in the human body long enough to affect bone, certain diseases, especially those of a slow, chronic nature, may leave their mark (Ortner and Hunter 1981:236). Because disease levels reflect dynamic, ever-changing internal biological and external cultural responses, it is most informative from an epidemiological perspective to

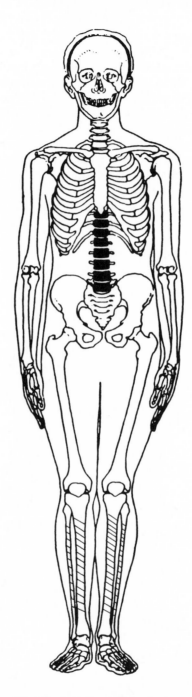

Figure 5-2
Skeletal Distribution of Vertebral and Long Bone Lesions (Solid black areas indicate resorption; diagonal lines mark proliferative periosteal and/or osteomyelitic
responses.)

view biological, cultural, and environmental variables as interacting elements in a complex human adaptive system. Acute and chronic biological stresses that affect the skeleton have the potential to provide information regarding related changes occurring within the other two systems. In effect, population levels of prehistoric disease can act as a cultural and environmental barometer of sorts, by tracking, measuring, and recording the effects of both internal and external systemic changes on the human skeleton.

Mounting evidence from the Averbuch skeletal research, as well as data from complementary studies of prehistoric health and disease among other Middle Cumberland groups, suggest that these sedentary late prehistoric populations were subject to health problems from both infection and iron-deficiency anemia (Boyd et al. 1983; Eisenberg 1985a, 1986a; Kelley and Eisenberg 1987; Wright et al. 1973). Results of an examination of these two conditions in the Averbuch skeletal series are discussed below.

Two distinct types of osseous lesions predominate in the burials from

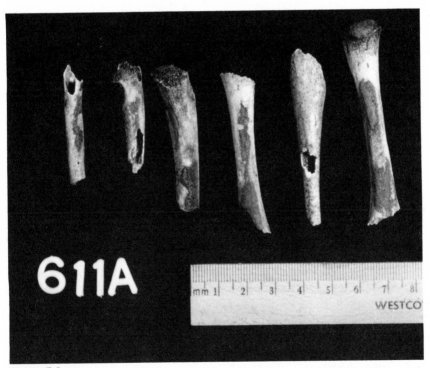

Figure 5-3
Active Periosteal Apposition on Subadult Long Bones (6 months to 1.5 years)

Averbuch (Figure 5-2). Proliferative lesions reflecting disturbances of the outer periosteal sheath of bone are most common in the appendicular skeleton. These lesions develop as an inflammatory response to one or more stimuli, one of which may be infection. Conversely, resorptive lesions are primarily distributed among the bones of the axial skeleton, with a particular predilection for the vertebral column. Such a well-defined, clearly patterned distribution suggests that at least two separate infectious processes may be responsible. An equally plausible scenario to explain this distribution may involve some type of systemic infectious condition(s) in the population that differentially affects the skeleton.

The tibia was chosen for intensive analysis not only because it was most frequently affected by subperiosteal apposition but also because the prevalence, degree of severity, and state of healing of tibial periosteal reactions (Figure 5-3) have been employed as generalized measures of infection in other populations (Lallo 1973; Mensforth et al. 1978). More than half of the tibiae examined exhibited some type of proliferative change—periostitis, osteomyelitis (a response to infection that involves the inner, medullary cavity of bone), or a combination of the two conditions. It has been suggested that circulation patterns in the metaphyseal area of the tibia, particularly during the growth period but also later in life, may trap and accumulate bacteria (Folkow and Neil 1971; Goodman and Armelagos 1985:15). This situation may serve, in part, to explain why the tibia is one of the most frequently affected bones in many population samples. The anterior shaft of the tibia is a very common site of traumatic injuries resulting from everyday activities that may play a part in the expression of infection. The prevalence, severity, generalized distribution, and often unhealed state of the tibial periosteal responses at Averbuch suggest that infection, rather than trauma, is the most likely explanation for the presence of this pathological condition.

When the distribution pattern of these lesions throughout the population was analyzed by state of healing (either active [unhealed] or healed at death), an interesting demographic pattern began to emerge (Figure 5-4). Those individuals in the youngest age cohort (fetal–2.5 years) exhibit the greatest frequency of active proliferative tibial lesions. A relative frequency of approximately 13 percent for active lesions is observed in those older than 2.5 years, which is suggestive of an endemic or chronic level of infection. Active lesion frequency exhibits a marked decrease in individuals between the ages of 35 and 50. Differences in the frequency rates of active and healed tibial lesions in the Averbuch skeletal series are statistically significant only in those individuals over the age of 15.

Proliferative Tibial Lesions

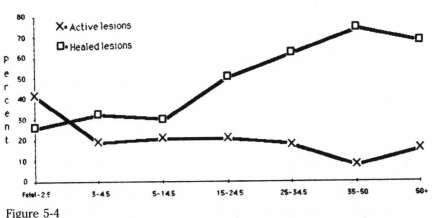

Figure 5-4
Relative Frequencies of Active and Healed Tibial Lesions by Age Group

Unhealed proliferative responses on the tibiae of subadults less than 2.5 years of age implies that active infection, perhaps tuberculosis, just prior to death may have compromised not only normal growth but overall life expectancy (Buikstra and Cook 1981). Additional work is needed to determine whether the periosteal reaction observed here can be attributed to a specific infectious disease syndrome, such as one of the treponemal infections (Cook 1976; Ortner and Putschar 1981:129–33; Powell 1985b, 1988; Steinbock 1976:137).

While not as generalized or widespread as the tibial periostitis, another type of skeletal pathology observed in the Averbuch series is the lytic lesion occurring in the spine, pelvis, lower long bones, and feet of many individuals. These destructive foci, usually observed as smooth-walled lesions surrounded by sclerotic margins, appear most commonly in the mid-to-lower thoracic and lumbar regions of the spine, where contiguous segments are frequently involved (Figure 5-5). The vertebral body alone is most often affected, although the posterior arch and the spinous process may be infrequently involved. The anterior aspect of the body seems to be the primary focus of many of the lesions, judging from the path of destruction of the lesion itself. Osteophytic (bony) bridging between spinal segments occurs with some frequency, apparently to reinforce and stabilize the resorbed and compromised vertebral area. The apposition of periosteal bone as a secondary response is not a common feature.

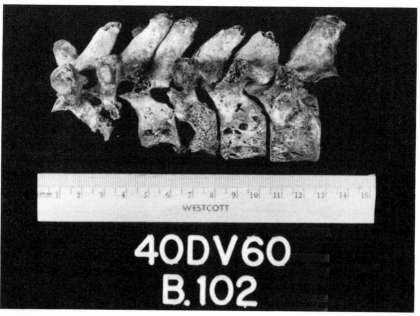

Figure 5-5
Resorptive Lesions in the Thoracic Vertebrae of a Female (30 to 34 years)

A detailed comparison of the demographic and anatomical patterning of these lytic lesions with diagnostic criteria of both modern tuberculosis (caused by *Mycobacterium tuberculosis* and related strains) and the mycotic disease blastomycosis (caused by the fungal organism *Blastomyces dermatitidis,* endemic in the southeastern United States) indicates that both diseases were endemic at Averbuch (Kelley and Eisenberg 1987). The predominance of adult male cases in this series points to mycotic rather than mycobacterial infection as the more common disease, although some individuals may have been afflicted by both. Given the opportunistic nature of mycotic disease, its frequent expression at Averbuch suggests indirectly a poor level of general health, as also indicated by widespread skeletal evidence of chronic anemia.

Cribra orbitalia (Figure 5-6) and porotic hyperostosis (Figure 5-7) are relatively abundant in the Averbuch skeletal series. These lesions have been interpreted in other New World prehistoric contexts as signaling the presence of iron-deficiency anemia. The appearance and distribution of these lesions have been associated, either directly or indirectly, with population aggregation and sedentism, where an increase in viral, bacterial, and parasitic infection possibly coupled with nutritional stress would be expected to lead to anemia (Kent 1986; cf. Reinhard 1988: 362–63). The presence of these lesions also appears to be related to diets low in iron and, possibly, those high in marine resources (Cybulski 1977; El-Najjar et al. 1976; Kent 1986; Mensforth 1985; Mensforth et al. 1978; Steinbock 1976; Stuart-Macadam 1985; Walker 1986). In Old World contexts, the hereditary hemolytic anemias produce similar cranial and orbital changes (Angel 1966b, 1967, 1971).

Interestingly, these types of skeletal pathology are present in the Averbuch sample despite the quantity and quality of food resources known to have been available prehistorically in the area, such as elk, white-tailed deer, turkey, migratory waterfowl, and hickory nuts (Crites 1984; Martin 1977; Romanoski 1984a; cf. Martin, Goodman, and Armelagos 1985:268). However, simple resource availability does not necessarily imply accessibility, for it is conceivable that in this late prehistoric context the social environment may have precluded the exploitation of the full range of plant and animal resources in the region. In other words, local conditions of social predation may well have restricted access to essential nutritional resources (Milner et al. 1988).

Another line of evidence that can be used to interpret these lesions is derived from stable carbon isotope analysis of a sample of burials from the Nashville Basin. The relatively low C13 values obtained for Averbuch (− 8.0 percent) and other Middle Cumberland sites located in that area implicate a subsistence base that included a high maize component (Buikstra et al. 1988). It is possible that the consumption of maize in ritual contexts may also have contributed to the values obtained. Clearly, the reasons for the appearance of these cranial lesions in the Averbuch sample are varied and complex and are most likely due to a combination of factors including population aggregation, infection, and diet.

The orbital (cribrotic) lesions found in almost 20 percent of the Averbuch population are almost equally distributed between males and females. Parallel frequencies of orbital and cranial lesions (Figure 5-8) in subadults between 3 and 4.5 years of age in the sample suggest that both of these conditions may reflect similar stresses, probably including the effects of weaning and weaning diets; bacterial, viral, and diarrheal diseases; and parasitic infections that are known in modern Third World contexts to be particularly devastating in children under 5 years of age (Kent 1986). Relative frequencies of these bony lesions diverge between the ages of 5 and 25 in the Averbuch sample, implying either that porotic hyperostosis alone may be a more sensitive nutritional stress indicator that is preserved in later life or that it may be measuring some additional health stress that does not promote a cribrotic response.

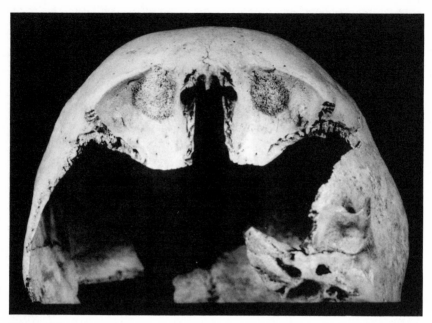

Figure 5-6
Bilateral Cribra Orbitalia in a Subadult (3.5 to 4.5 years)

Porotic lesions of the cranial vault were found in 39.07 percent (286/732) of all observable individuals at Averbuch (Table 5-1). Of those, 131 cases (45.8 percent) were active at death and 155 cases (54.2 percent) were healed. Adult individuals (those 15 years and older) manifested slightly higher frequencies (18.74 percent) of active porotic cranial lesions than subadults (16.48 percent). This finding is significant because it has been argued that these lesions in adults simply reflect anemia experienced in childhood, and they are regarded by some researchers as an inappropriate means of identifying an existing anemic condition in adults (Huss-Ashmore et al. 1982; Stuart-Macadam 1985; Wing and Brown 1979). However, in this series, the unhealed lesions are clearly indicative of anemia occurring in adulthood. These individuals may have been so chronically stressed that the remodeling of lesions was delayed beyond the normal period of recovery (M. L. Powell, personal communication 1986).

For individuals younger than 2.5 years of age, the percentages of healed (10.81 percent) and active (11.71 percent) lesions are nearly equal, suggesting that the stress(es) responsible for their occurrence might have been present prior to, and just after, birth. Porotic orbital

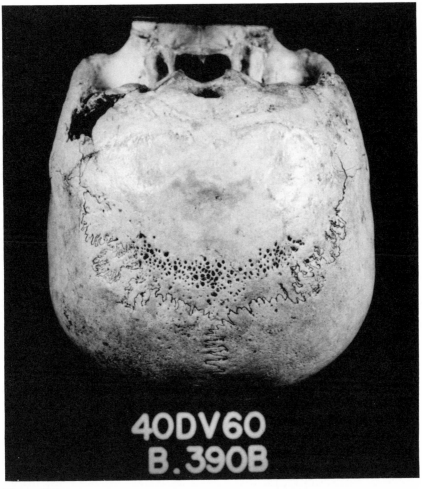

Figure 5-7
Porotic Hyperostosis in an Averbuch Female (18.5 to 19.5 years)

and cranial lesions appeared in from 4 to 10 percent of males and 19 to 27 percent of females at Averbuch. This pattern suggests that both sexes suffered from comparable levels of iron-deficiency anemia. The skeletal lesions noted at Averbuch have also been reported in burials from the Mayan site of Altar de Sacrificios in Belize. Frank P. Saul, who analyzed these burials, suggests that similar categories of lesions at Altar "strongly indicate the presence of disorders that would depress population energy levels" (1972:72). Such was probably the case at Averbuch as well.

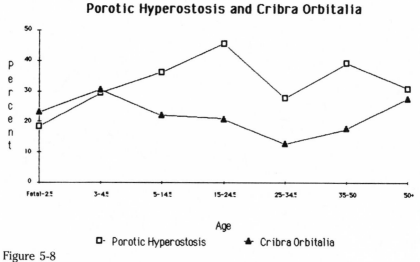

Figure 5-8
Relative Frequencies of Orbital and Cranial Lesions by Age Group

Discussion

More important than discussing the specific prevalence of particular diseases in archaeological populations is an understanding of the impact they may have had on long-term human adaptive success. The presence of anemia as inferred from this analysis may reflect not only the simple availability but also the absorption of certain critical nutrients. The dynamic effect of chronic infections, during which the body withholds iron from invading bacteria, fungi, and protozoa as an adaptive response (Weinberg 1974, 1977), in the production of severe anemia may have had disastrous implications for the biological and cultural success of the majority of Averbuch inhabitants.

The paleopathological data presented here and in more detail elsewhere (Eisenberg 1986a) indicate that infectious pathology (represented by periosteal tibial and lytic vertebral lesions) as well as iron-deficiency anemia (represented by orbital and cranial lesions) existed throughout the Averbuch population. Results of statistical analyses reveal that age, but not sex, is significantly associated with the presence of both infection and anemia in the population.

Specifically, the overall pattern and distribution of the infectious lesions point to differential diagnosis of tuberculosis and/or blastomycosis as well as of treponemal infection (Buikstra and Cook 1981;

Table 5-1
Percentages of Active and Healed Porotic Hyperostosis Cases by Age and Sex in the Averbuch Skeletal Series

Active Porotic Hyperostosis

Age	Sex			Row Total
	Indet.	Male	Female	
Fetal–2.5	11.71 (13/111)			11.71 (13/111)
3–4.5	16.67 (13/78)			16.67 (13/78)
5–14.5	21.95 (18/82)		50.0 (1/2)	22.62 (19/84)
15–24.5	30.77 (4/13)	20.48 (17/83)	20.99 (17/81)	21.47 (38/177)
25–34.5	0 (0/20)	20.27 (15/74)	28.57 (18/63)	21.02 (33/157)
35–50	25.0 (1/4)	20.83 (10/48)	4.55 (2/44)	13.54 (13/96)
+50	0 (0/1)	11.76 (2/17)	0 (0/11)	6.90 (2/29)
Column total	15.86 (49/309)	19.82 (44/222)	18.91 (38/201)	17.90 (131/732)

Healed Porotic Hyperostosis

Age	Sex			Row Total
	Indet.	Male	Female	
Fetal–2.5	10.81 (12/111)			10.81 (12/111)
3–4.5	15.38 (12/78)			15.38 (12/78)
5–14.5	23.17 (19/82)		50.0 (1/2)	23.81 (20/84)
15–24.5	0 (0/13)	34.94 (29/83)	25.93 (21/81)	28.25 (50/177)
25–34.5	5.0 (1/20)	16.22 (12/74)	22.22 (14/63)	17.20 (27/157)
35–50	25.0 (1/4)	31.25 (15/48)	25.0 (11/44)	28.13 (27/96)
+50	0 (0/1)	23.53 (4/17)	27.27 (3/11)	24.14 (7/29)
Column total	14.56 (45/309)	27.03 (60/222)	24.88 (50/201)	21.17 (155/732)

Ratio of Active to Healed Cases = 0.85 : 1

Subadults:
Active = 16.48% (45/273)
Healed = 16.21% (44/273)

Adults:
Active = 18.74% (86/459)
Healed = 24.18% (111/459)

Eisenberg 1985b, 1986a; Kelley and Eisenberg 1987; M. L. Powell, personal communication 1986). Tuberculosis is frequently characterized by high population mortality, particularly among children and young adults, either through primary infections or reactivation of dormant ones. Comparative studies suggest that blastomycosis or tuberculosis had become endemic in Mississippian populations in the Illinois valley and elsewhere (Buikstra 1976b). Mycotic infection is known to be highly opportunistic; that is, it is most often observed in individuals with low resistance and/or concurrent infection. Endemic treponemal infections, when not influenced by other illnesses, are not typically lethal (Hudson 1958). However, in this context, the synergistic impact of these three conditions may have had very significant effects on population health and survivorship at Averbuch.

Elevated mortality levels, particularly during the young adult years at Averbuch, are not an unexpected response to the presence and interaction of these diseases. Thus, evidence for chronic disease stress in the Averbuch series is consistent with what would be expected in a biocultural setting that included high areal population density and aggregation in permanent, sedentary villages where minimal levels of hygiene and sanitation existed (Kent 1986; Larsen 1982; Magennis et al. 1985; Mensforth 1985).

The peak prevalence of both iron-deficiency anemia and infection at approximately twenty-five years of age seen in this study corresponds graphically to a concomitant decrease in population survivorship during that period, evident in the mortality profile (Figure 5-9) constructed for the skeletal series by Berryman (1981:60). While the possibility exists that this parallel association may prove to be coincidental, it is highly suggestive of a period during the Averbuch lifespan when the synergistic effects of such morbid conditions may have overwhelmed the population by lowering the overall level of community health (Scrimshaw 1975).

From a cultural and economic perspective, the observation that the mortality in the adult population peaks at between twenty and thirty years suggests that a number of subsistence, cultural, and defense-related activities may have been affected. The loss of an important sector of economically active adults within the Averbuch population may have had a significant impact on the timely completion of all aspects of their subsistence round, which involved horticultural as well as hunting and gathering activities. Responsibility for the care and teaching of young children would also fall to this age group, and a decline in their numbers may have, over time, negatively affected the social reproduction of this late prehistoric polity (Bourdieu 1976) by dismantling the family structure and disrupting the cultural transmission of knowledge (A.-M. Cantwell, personal communication 1986).

An increased need for settlement defenses during the late Mississippian period is supported by evidence of palisade construction at Averbuch and at other Middle Tennessee occupations. Nonstructural evidence for an atmosphere of conflict and warfare is also confirmed by studies of the skeletal remains from these sites where traumatic injuries such as scalping, parry fractures, cut marks, and entrance wounds have been recognized. These conditions attest to the fact that this was a time in prehistory when social stress, accompanied by physical trauma, was occurring with increasing frequency, even in marginal locations (Eisenberg 1986b; Milner et al. 1988). These social stresses, which appear to have targeted adults between the ages of twenty and thirty-five at Averbuch, were an additional burden on an already anemic, biologically stressed, and energy-poor population.

From a biological standpoint, reproductive potential for females aged twenty to thirty-five must have declined simply because of the drop in their numbers (Clarke 1977:181). This situation compounded the problem even further by decreasing fertility levels during a period when the population required new members just to maintain its size and organizational structure. It has been estimated by Berryman (1981:71–73) on the basis of the crude mortality rate that the Averbuch population experienced a decrease of between 1 and 2 percent per year. The skeletal data document the presence of anemia among women in this age group and this iron deficiency would have come at a time when adequate iron intake would have been most critical during times of pregnancy and lactation and when maternal mortality would be most significant to continued levels of fertility, population growth, and stability.

Interpretations and Conclusions

An examination of the mortality profile generated by Berryman (1981), in combination with the disease load reported here for the Averbuch series, suggests that individuals who survived the initial childhood disease and stress period had a high probability of dying in young adulthood. If in fact Averbuch represents a natural population (which it may not), life expectancy at birth for Averbuch males and females was 17.4 and 14.6 years, respectively (Table 5-2), among the lowest documented for many historic or prehistoric populations examined (Berryman 1981:68). If recurrent disease episodes or one or more catastrophic events can be postulated to explain the rather unusual bi-

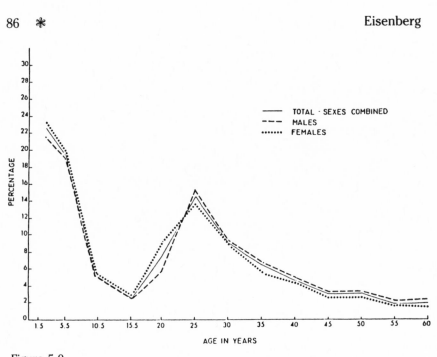

Figure 5-9
Male and Female Mortality at Averbuch (Berryman 1981:60)

modal mortality profile obtained (Buikstra and Konigsberg 1985; Buikstra et al. 1988), it appears that Middle Cumberland populations at sites such as Averbuch were severely debilitated by both heavy and chronic disease stress *and* by social predation that limited their access to abundant natural resources. This situation would have affected not only subsistence but political strength and demographic stability as well.

While this chapter underscores the significance of disease as one factor contributing to the disappearance of Middle Cumberland cultures, using Averbuch as a model, it should also be emphasized that no single explanation can adequately interpret processual change, especially at this level of sociocultural complexity. These data may offer one clue to understanding the complex set of events that culminated in the disappearance of Middle Cumberland cultures long before the Euramerican explorers reached Middle Tennessee. Additional factors may have included high population density, possible overreliance on selected subsistence resources, and participation in a tribute system, all of which may have overtaxed their production capabilities.

It is equally possible that what we currently regard as cultural terminations (evidenced in the Middle Cumberland by depopulation and areal abandonment) may involve the restructuring of social systems at a different level of organizational complexity. If such a process occurred in Middle Tennessee in Late Mississippian times, the material remains of such "reorganized" social systems might logically be expected to differ substantially from those of the preceding societies. The archaeological "invisibility" of the earlier social systems might then prompt an interpretation of cultural termination (Anderson and Schuldenrein 1985; Morse and Morse 1983:280–83; Palerm and Wolf 1960; Upham 1984). Consequently, when approaching the question of cultural terminations from the archaeological record, it may be necessary to modify both our site survey strategies and our material culture expectations accordingly.

Table 5-2
Comparative Life Expectancies

Life Expectancy at Birth in Several World Populations		
Populations	Dates	Life Expectancy
		(Years)
Larson, South Dakota	A.D. 1750–1781	13.7
Averbuch (F), Tennessee	**A.D. 1350**	**14.6**
Arroyo Hondo, New Mexico	A.D. 1300–1420	16.0
Averbuch (M), Tennessee	**A.D. 1350**	**17.4**
Indian Knoll, Kentucky	3000 B.C.	18.6
Nubia, Egypt	A.D. 1050–1600	19.2
Nanjemoy, Ossuary I	A.D. 1500–1600	20.9
Nanjemoy, Ossuary II	A.D. 1500–1600	22.9
Ancient Greeks	670 B.C.–A.D. 600	23.0
Kane Mounds	A.D. 1250	24.1
Moundville, Alabama	A.D. 1050–1550	28.0
Texas Indians	A.D. 850–1700	30.5
European ruling families	A.D. 1480–1579	33.7
U.S. Caucasian	A.D. 1800	30.0–35.0
U.S. Negro	A.D. 1900	33.8
English	A.D. 1000–1100	35.3
India (F)	A.D. 1951–1960	40.6
India (M)	A.D. 1951–1960	41.9
Pecos Pueblo	A.D. 800–1700	42.9
England and Wales (M)	A.D. 1965–1967	68.7
England and Wales (F)	A.D. 1965–1967	74.9

Modified from Berryman 1961:68 and Owsley 1975:84 with additions from Milner 1982:295; Palkovich 1980:30; and Powell 1985b:368.

Acknowledgments

Suggestions made by Mary Lucas Powell, Dennis Appleton, Eugene Boesch, and two anonymous reviewers on earlier drafts of this chapter have significantly improved both its content and its clarity. Any errors, misinterpretations, or omissions, however, remain my own.

The paleopathological analysis of the Averbuch skeletal series was funded in large part by a New York University Dean's Dissertation Fellowship. It was greatly facilitated by the faculty and staff of the University of Tennessee, Knoxville, Department of Anthropology.

✻ 6

Skeletal Evidence of Changes in Subsistence Activities Between the Archaic and Mississippian Time Periods in Northwestern Alabama

Patricia S. Bridges

One of the goals of physical anthropology is the reconstruction of past lifeways. One aspect of this reconstruction is the determination of the activities of prehistoric peoples. Admittedly, this determination is extremely difficult to do from skeletal remains alone. However, one can estimate the levels and kinds of forces that are placed upon the bones, because during life bones respond to changes in forces by adding or redistributing osseous material. An examination of the amount and distribution of bone in the shafts of long bones, then, can suggest what forces were placed upon them. This information, along with archaeological and historical data, can help to reconstruct the activities that might have produced those forces.

This chapter examines the evidence for changes in both the level and the types of subsistence activities between the Archaic and Mississippian time periods in the Pickwick Basin area of northwestern Alabama. To do so, it compares dimensions and strengths of the long bones in the two groups. Two major hypotheses about changes in long bone size and strength were tested. (1) Overall, the Mississippian agriculturalists should have long bones with larger external dimensions that were stronger under bending and torsional forces. Ethnographic peoples engaging in hoe agriculture have a more physically demanding life-style than modern hunter-gatherers (Lee and DeVore 1968; Sahlins 1972). If this pattern prevailed in the Pickwick Basin, the Mississippian Indians should have long bones reinforced against higher levels of mechanical loading. (2) There should be more increases in long bone size and strength for the Mississippian females than for the males. Historically, southeastern Indian women did the majority of the agricultural work (Adair 1930; Bartram 1853, 1928; Bossu 1962; Hudson 1976; Le Page du

Pratz 1947; Romans 1962; Swanton 1911, 1946; Tuggle 1973), as do women in most contemporary societies engaging in hoe agriculture (Boserup 1970; Brown 1970; Burton and White 1984; Ember 1983; Murdock and Provost 1973). It is likely that Mississippian women took over most of the duties related to subsistence, while retaining many or all of the household chores that Archaic women had carried out. If so, Mississippian women should show larger increases in dimensions and strength compared to the men. In addition, because of the wide variety of new activities associated with agriculture, it is likely that new forces would have been imposed over much of the postcranial skeleton. The changes in the females, then, should be widespread and generalized, reflecting the broad spectrum of new mechanical loading patterns. Mississippian men, on the other hand, were probably less affected physically by the change in subsistence duties. Males were therefore expected to show relatively fewer changes occurring over less of the skeleton.

Besides these general ideas about changes in overall activity levels, several related hypotheses concerning specific behaviors were tested. In historic times, pounding corn was "women's work" and southeastern Indian women spent a great deal of time in this task (Adair 1930; Le Page du Pratz 1947; Tuggle 1973). Because of the addition of such chores as pounding corn, Mississippian women were expected to show greater changes in the arms rather than in the legs.

Although it was predicted that males would not show such widespread changes as females, they were expected to show some minor differences. For example, the introduction of the bow and arrow should have changed forces operating on the arms. Throwing an atlatl would require a good deal of strength in one arm only, usually the right. Use of the bow would place forces on both arms. Therefore, it was predicted that Archaic males would have larger and stronger right arms. Mississippian males should have arms more nearly equal in size and strength.

Materials and Methods

The sample used in this study derives from a large burial collection excavated in the Pickwick Basin region of northwestern Alabama (Newman and Snow 1942; Webb and DeJarnette 1942, 1948a, 1948b). Of the 266 individuals chosen for analysis, 126 represented the Mississippian period and 140 represented the Archaic period.

A series of standard measurements was taken on all major long bones (femur, tibia, humerus, ulna, and radius). In addition, a subset of the group was chosen for biomechanical analysis (forty-nine left humeri and forty-two left femora). The bones were scanned using a computed tomographic scanner. From this process, accurate pictures were obtained of their cross sections at five levels along the diaphysis of each bone. Data on cross-sectional structure were recorded directly onto a magnetic tape in the form of an integer array of CT numbers, representing the relative density of bone (Bridges 1985). This information was used to determine cortical area of each cross section and area and polar moments of inertia, which estimate the resistance of the bone to bending and torsional forces (Dickie et al. 1984).

Findings

Findings from the metrical analysis showed that the Mississippian Indians had long bone shafts with larger external dimensions than did the Archaic Indians. In no case were the bones of the Archaic group larger than those of the Mississippian Indians. This result holds true even when the overall size of the bone is taken into account, which was done by calculating indexes by dividing each measure by the length of the bone. In general, Mississippian Indians had larger long bone indexes than did the Archaic Indians (Table 6-1). Their diaphyses, then, were not just absolutely but were relatively larger than those of the Archaic Indians.

To a large degree, these findings are borne out by the results of the biomechanical analysis. Obviously, bones that are thicker and have greater cortical area should also be stronger. The strength of a bone under compression is directly related to the amount of cortical bone in the cross section. For a variety of reasons, though, bones are frequently subjected to bending and torsional (or twisting) forces as well as simple compression. The resistance of a bone to these forces is determined not only by cortical area but also by how bone is distributed in the cross section. Clearly, a bone that is thickest in the mediolateral direction will be better able to resist forces operating along that direction. Therefore, it is necessary to examine both area and distribution of cortical bone in biomechanical studies of long bones. By using engineering beam analysis, it is possible to derive accurate estimates of the resistance of a bone to different forces.

This study compares several estimates of long bone strength derived from beam analysis: minimum and maximum bending strengths and torsional strength. Minimum bending strength is the resistance of the bone along the axis where it is weakest under bending forces. Maximum bend-

Table 6-1
Changes in Diaphyseal Indexes

Measure	Males		Females	
FEMUR	Left	Right	Left	Right
Midshaft				
Anteroposterior diameter		+		+
Mediolateral diameter	+	+	+	
Circumference	+	+		
Subtrochanteric				
Anteroposterior diameter	+	+	+	
Mediolateral diameter	+	+		
HUMERUS				
Midshaft				
Maximum diameter			+	
Minimum diameter	+	+	+	+
Circumference			+	+
Minimum				
Circumference			+	

Key: The "+" signs indicate a significant increase (p < .05) in the
Mississippian time period. If no significant change has occurred, the column
remains blank. Each dimension was converted to an index by dividing the
measurement by the length of the bone.

ing strength is the resistance of the bone along the axis where the bone
is strongest under bending. For these estimates, differences in overall
size of the bones examined have been taken into account by dividing
each variable by the maximum fiber length of the cross section multiplied by the length of the bone squared. (The maximum fiber length is
the distance between the centroid or "balance point" of the cross section and the most distant point on the outside of the section—see
Bridges 1985).

In this study, the Mississippian Indians have generally stronger bones
under bending and torsional forces (Table 6-2). Their bones remain
stronger even when the length of the bone is taken into account as described above. Therefore, the Mississippian group has long bones that
are both larger in external dimensions and stronger in terms of biomechanical variables than those of the Archaic sample.

In addition, as expected, major differences occurred in the patterning
of changes between the sexes. For the males, most of the changes in size
and strength occurred in the legs. Mississippian males had femora and

Table 6-2
Changes in Biomechanical Variables

Measure	Males					Females				
	Scan Number									
	1	2	3	4	5	1	2	3	4	5
FEMUR										
Area/length²	+	+	+	+						
Minimum bending strength	+	+	+	+	+		+			
Maximum bending strength	+	+	+	+	+		+	+	+	
Torsional strength	+	+	+	+	+		+	+		+
HUMERUS										
Area/length²	−					−				
Minimum bending strength	−							+	+	
Maximum bending strength	−							+	+	+
Torsional strength	−							+	+	+

Key: The "+" signs denote a significant increase in the variable in the Mississippian period. If no significant change has occurred, the column remains blank. A "−" sign indicates that the variable decreased significantly in the Mississippian period. Scan 1 is the most proximal scan and Scan 5 the most distal. Scan 3 is set at midshaft. Area/length² = cortical area divided by the length of the bone squared. Minimum bending strength = minimum area moment of inertia divided by maximum fiber length multiplied by length of the bone squared. Maximum bending strength = maximum area moment of inertia divided by maximum fiber length multiplied by length of the bone squared. Torsional strength = polar moment of inertia divided by maximum fiber length multiplied by length of the bone squared. (p < .05) tibiae that were thicker—absolutely and relatively—than were those of the Archaic males (Table 6-1). The same relationship is seen when looking at changes in biomechanical variables of the legs. Mississippian males had femora that contained significantly greater amounts of cortical bone and that were stronger under bending and torsional forces than were those of the Archaic males (Table 6-2). For maximum bending strength (Figure 6-1), Mississippian males are significantly stronger than Archaic males for the proximal and central femur (those levels nearest the hip and in the middle of the bone).

However, the same pattern does not hold true for the arms. Very few differences exist between Mississippian and Archaic males in external dimensions of the humerus, and no differences occur at all in biome-

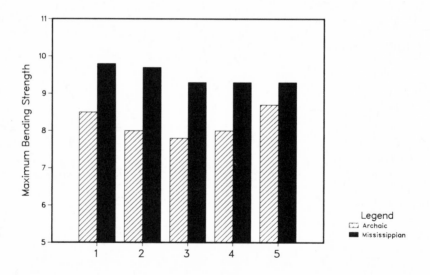

Figure 6-1
Maximum Bending Strength of Male Femora. Archaic males are shown by the slashed columns and Mississippian males by the solid columns. All five scans are included. Scan 3 is set at midshaft, with Scan 1 being the most proximal (nearest the hip) and Scan 5 the most distal (nearest the knee). Maximum bending strength = maximum area moment of inertia divided by maximum fiber length multiplied by the length of the bone squared. See Table 6-2 for significance values.

chanical variables. Therefore, the two male groups are essentially identical in terms of humeral strength (Table 6-2).

The females show a very different pattern of change. Mississippian females had femora that were somewhat thicker than are those of the Archaic females (Table 6-1). Fewer differences in femoral dimensions occur between the two groups, however, than existed for the males. The same is true for the biomechanical data. Mississippian females had femora that were absolutely and relatively stronger than Archaic females under bending and torsional forces for several levels of the femoral diaphysis. However, no significant changes exist in the amount of cortical bone (Table 6-2). Instead, Mississippian females achieved greater strength not by addition of bone (as did the males) but by a more efficient distribution of the same amount of bone.

The females show much greater changes in the arms than did the males. As opposed to the males, who showed few significant differences in the humerus, Mississippian females had humeri that were relatively much thicker than were those of the Archaic females (Table 6-1). The

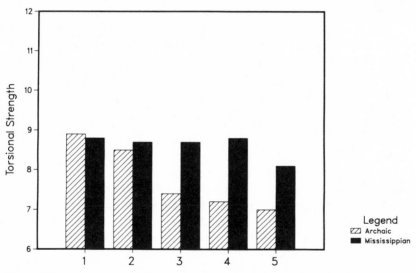

Figure 6-2
Torsional Strength of Female Humeri. Archaic females are shown by the slashed columns and Mississippian females by the solid columns. Scan 3 is set at midshaft, with scan 1 being the most proximal (nearest the shoulder) and Scan 5 the most distal (nearest the elbow). Torsional strength = polar area moment of inertia divided by maximum fiber length multiplied by length of the bone squared. See Table 6-2 for significance values. (Reproduced from Bridges 1989 with permission from *Current Anthropology*)

Mississippian females' humeri were also significantly stronger under bending and torsional forces than were the Archaic females', especially in the midshaft area and near the elbow (Figure 6-2). Again, the greater strength is not due to an increase in the amount of cortical bone (which stays the same or decreases near the shoulder) but to changes in the distribution of that bone.

In summary, both of the major hypotheses were supported. The Mississippian group in general had larger and stronger long bones than did the Archaic group, presumably as a result of a more physically demanding life-style. As expected, females showed more widespread changes occurring over both the arms and the legs. Males showed significant increases in the Mississippian time period only in their legs. These differences in male and female strength are likely to be related to changes in the division of labor and to the females' assuming most of the chores associated with agriculture.

The next goal of this research was to try to associate some of the differences in long bone structure with changes in specific behaviors. Mississippian women, as noted above, show a great number of increases in size and strength in their arms. However, these changes do not occur along the entire length of the humeral diaphysis but are concentrated in the distal part, near the elbow (Table 6-2; Figure 6-2). The Mississippian group is larger than the Archaic one for maximum bending strength at all scans, but this difference is significant only at the more distal levels (Scans 4 and 5, and Scan 3 at p = .10). In addition, for minimum bending strength and torsional strength, no significant differences occur at the two scans nearest the shoulder, while the Mississippian females are larger than the Archaic ones at midshaft and more distally. These data demonstrate clearly that it is the three most distal levels that are significantly larger (p < .05) in the Mississippian females, while no changes occur in the scans closest to the shoulder.

An examination of the changes in the external dimensions of the arm bones may help to explain these findings. The dimensions of the humerus at midshaft and at the point of minimum circumference near the elbow are most relevant to this comparison (Table 6-1). It is clear that Mississippian females, while generally larger than the Archaic ones, show more differences on the left side. In fact, their left sides are identical to their rights for this measure.

These changes in the degree of bilateral asymmetry may best be expressed by an index (left/right multiplied by 100). If the left and right sides are approximately equal, the index will be close to 100. In all cases, the Mississippian females have indexes of bilateral asymmetry closer to 100, indicating that their lefts are more nearly the size of their

Table 6-3
Index of Bilateral Asymmetry: Females

HUMERUS	Archaic	Mississippian	p
Midshaft maximum diameter	95	98	***
Midshaft minimum diameter	98	100	
Midshaft circumference	96	98	**
Minimum circumference	98	99	.08
ULNA			
Proximal maximum diameter	98	99	
Proximal minimum diameter	96	100	*
Proximal circumference	97	99	*

Key: This index is calculated by dividing the left side by the right and multiplying by 100. The closer the measure is to 100, the more symmetric are the two sides. One asterisk denotes that the difference is significant at $p < .05$, two that $p < .01$, and three that $p < .001$.

right humeral shafts (Table 6-3). This index differs significantly between Archaic and Mississippian females for maximum diameter and for circumference at midshaft.

These findings are generally supported by data on external dimensions of the forearms. In general, both the radius and the ulna have thicker diaphyses in the Mississippian group. However, fewer changes occur in the amount of bilateral asymmetry in the forearms than occur in the humerus. For the radius, no significant differences occur in this index. For both groups, females tend to have slightly larger right sides.

The pattern of change is somewhat different for the ulna. As noted above, the Mississippian females are significantly larger than are the Archaic females for both the left and the right sides. Moreover, the left ulna has increased relatively more than the right. However, one area shows the greatest amount of change: the proximal ulna (that area of the bone closest to the elbow) on the left side. The index of bilateral asymmetry for the ulnar shaft at the highest development of the interosseous crest (which is proximal to midshaft) clearly shows that, while both sides are larger in the Mississippian group, the left has increased relatively more than the right side (Table 6-3). For this level of the ulnar diaphysis (the area closest to the elbow) Mississippian females have more symmetric shafts than do the Archaic females.

In summary, Mississippian females show the following differences from Archaic females in their arms: (1) relatively greater external dimensions of all arm bones, (2) relatively stronger humeral diaphyses at midshaft and close to the elbow, (3) relatively greater increases in the humerus on the left side than on the right, and (4) relatively greater increases on the left side in the proximal ulna alone.

These changes are most likely to be due to an activity that required the use of both arms rather than the right arm alone. As a result, the left arm increased greatly in size and strength, until it became nearly identical to the right arm. Finally, the distinctive patterning of changes suggests that they are related to a change in the amount of extension and flexion at the elbow. The flexors and extensors of the elbow attach at the distal humerus (where the greatest changes occur) and at the proximal ulna (again, where the major changes occur in the forearm). It is most likely, then, that this complex of changes is related to a great increase in an activity requiring flexion and extension of the elbows on both the left and the right sides. These are precisely the motions that are used in pounding corn in the traditional manner of southeastern Indian women.

It was not possible to delineate such specific changes corresponding to different activities for the males. For the forearms, however, Mississippian males showed a striking decrease in the amount of bilateral asymmetry, primarily for the ulna (Table 6-4). Archaic males had relatively larger right than left forearms, while Mississippian males had left ulnae that were similar to or even slightly larger than their rights. The decrease in bilateral asymmetry suggests that the forces placed on the two sides were more similar in the Mississippian time period. It is possible that this difference is related to the use of the bow rather than the atlatl.

An unexpected result was the large increase in size and strength of the legs in the Mississippian males. This change included a significant in-

Table 6-4
Index of Bilateral Asymmetry: Males

RADIUS	Archaic	Mississippian	p
Midshaft maximum diameter	96	97	
Midshaft minimum diameter	97	101	*
Midshaft circumference	98	98	
ULNA			
Midshaft maximum diameter	95	101	**
Midshaft minimum diameter	94	101	***
Midshaft circumference	95	99	*

Key: See Table 6-3 for explanation.

crease in cortical area and was somewhat more pronounced near the hip. There was also an especially large increase in the mediolateral (or transverse) bending strength of the male femora.

It is unclear how to interpret these findings. Obviously, Mississippian males were imposing high levels of forces on their legs alone. It is unlikely that the overall increase in strength is due to an activity such as long-distance running, which imposes more anteroposterior forces closer to the knee (Ruff and Hayes 1983a). It is more likely that a variety of activities, which may have included long-distance raiding and hunting, agricultural or building chores, and possibly increasing involvement in the ball game, a vigorous sport regarded as preparation for warfare, may together be responsible for these increases in leg strength.

Discussion

In summary, an examination of long bone dimensions and strengths suggests major changes in activity levels between the Archaic and Mississippian time periods. Mississippian agriculturalists were generally stronger than Archaic hunter-gatherers. The changes in bone strength suggest that, for this region, the adoption of maize agriculture involved a major increase in the workload.

Although cortical area may be affected by a variety of other factors (including genetics, diet, and age), activity differences seem to be the most plausible explanation for the changes seen here. Nutritional differences, for example, would lead to systemic differences in cortical area. For example, obese individuals have generally thicker bones overall, including the finger bones, which do not function in weight-bearing (Garn and Solomon 1981). Given the *patterning* of changes seen here, it is unlikely that they result from a major change in diet, which should affect all bones equally.

Second, this study demonstrates changes in the division of labor between the two time periods. Mississippian females showed increased long bone size and strength over Archaic females for all body segments examined, including both the arms and the legs. The widespread nature of the increases in Mississippian females is probably related to the broad spectrum of new tasks related to subsistence. As detailed by historic observers, female duties covered an immense range of activities: from the majority of the field work and subsequent processing of agricultural products to preparation and cooking of other food, making pottery and baskets, gathering wild food, chopping and bringing home firewood, carrying water, and curing animal skins and making clothing from them, as well as weaving cloth (Adair 1930; Bartram 1928; Bossu 1962; Hudson 1976; Swanton 1946; Tuggle 1973). These tasks represent not only most of the household chores for which Archaic women would have been responsible but in addition an overlay of demanding tasks associated with agriculture. It is not surprising, then, to find an overall increase in strength in the Mississippian females.

Mississippian males, on the other hand, showed changes occurring over less of the postcranial skeleton than did the females. It is likely that the restricted nature of these differences was associated with fewer changes in subsistence activities. Apart from clearing the fields, helping in the planting and harvesting, and, of course, hunting, male input into subsistence may have been relatively small compared to the female contribution.

Besides these general changes in activity level and the sexual division of labor, some suggestions may be made concerning specific activities. The large increases in the arms of the Mississippian females are probably related to the pounding of corn. Historic southeastern Indian women used a wooden mortar and pestle for this task. The mortar was made from a log into which a hole had been burned (Adair 1930). The pestle was also wooden and usually 5 or 6 feet in length. For most of its length, it was about 2 inches in diameter, but a thick end of about 6 inches was retained as a weight at the top of the pestle (Hudson 1976). The woman stood before the mortar, grasping the pestle with both hands. In this position, the most efficient way to grind the corn is to flex both elbows, raising the pestle, and then to sharply extend (or straighten) the forearms, which drives the pestle into the corn at the bottom of the mortar.

Pounding grain using this level of technology is not by any means an easy task. One historic observer, William Tuggle, in detailing the arduous life of Indian women, points to grinding corn as an especially onerous task. He notes that "Beating sofkey [which is grinding corn to make hominy grits] with 10 lb pestles is like blacksmithing" (Tuggle 1973:96).

Other workers have linked corn grinding with increases in long bone robusticity and arthritis in the prehistoric southwestern United States (Hooton 1930; Merbs 1980; Miller 1982). It is also interesting to note that today, in groups that grow a staple crop requiring extensive processing, women often spend several hours each day in the preparation of food (Bleiberg et al. 1980; Dufour 1984). In fact, pounding seed crops by African women expends a great deal of energy—more than either hoeing or carrying water (Bleiberg et al. 1980). Given that grinding corn is such a strenuous activity, which is carried out frequently for long periods of time, it is not surprising that it should lead to recognizable changes in the arms.

Compared to the dramatic changes in the arms of the females, the differences in the forearms of the males seem almost trivial. In retrospect, the smaller level of change may not be surprising. Several workers have tried to link changes in body build or arthritis with spear throwing or archery, the best known being Alice Brues in "The Spearman and the Archer" (1960). Generally, these attempts have not been successful (Frayer 1981; Pickering 1984). It seems likely that routine chores, performed daily and for relatively long periods of time, would impose more consistent forces on long bones than the infrequent use of weapons.

In short, this study has demonstrated clear increases in the level of activities in the Mississippian time period in northwestern Alabama. More importantly, it linked these differences with changes in the division of labor and specific activities. As is suggested by historic accounts and modern ethnographic research, the majority of the new subsistence chores associated with agriculture probably fell to the lot of the women. One of these, the pounding of corn, was a regular and arduous task, reflected in the dramatic changes in female arms. Changes like these suggest that many significant differences in physique between prehistoric groups may be due not to relatively spectacular innovations in weapon type but to changes in routine activities or the "daily grind" of prehistoric peoples.

✳ 7

Biomechanical Adaptation and Behavior on the Prehistoric Georgia Coast

Clark Spencer Larsen and Christopher B. Ruff

The study of human skeletal morphology offers an important means by which both level and type of physical activity in past populations can be analyzed. Because the skeleton is influenced by a wide variety of environmental circumstances—especially physical activity and nutrition—during growth and development and adulthood, it provides us with a cumulative record of behavior and reflects how the body responds to particular functional demands in the face of these circumstances.

For example, study of degenerative joint disease (osteoarthritis) can provide information on degree of mechanical demand on various joints of the skeleton (e.g., Ortner 1968; Merbs 1983). The study of non-pathological articular modifications at specific joints can reveal habitual body postures that presumably reflect postures maintained during work activities (e.g., Ubelaker 1979). A number of workers have also noted the tendency for a relatively greater degree of robusticity, as determined by external bone dimensions, in skeletal elements from populations with mechanically stressful lifeways (e.g., Trinkaus 1984).

Although degree of robusticity represents an approximation of mechanical demand, actual shape differences offer, perhaps, a more precise measure of musculoskeletal stress. Various investigators have reported an increasing circularity in diaphyseal cross sections of the femur or tibia or both with the shift to sedentary lifeways that is associated with the adoption or intensification of agriculture in the American Southeast (Hoyme and Bass 1962; Larsen 1982), Southwest (Bennett 1973a), and Midwest (Perzigian et al. 1984), which is apparently part of a general worldwide trend since the Late Pleistocene (Buxton 1938; Brothwell 1981). For the femur, flatness is expressed by two indexes—platymeric for the area below the lesser trochanter and robusticity (midshaft). For the tibia, flatness is likewise expressed by two indexes—platycnemic for the area at the nutrient foramen and robusticity (midshaft). Some have suggested that degree of flatness of these skeletal elements in archaeological remains reflects nutritional quality (cf. Angel 1979). Based on a number of studies, however, it is more likely that long bone shaft flatness, at least for the lower limb, reflects general level of mechanical stress on the leg (Lovejoy et al. 1976; Larsen 1982; Ruff and Hayes 1983a).

It has become increasingly apparent that externally defined long bone shaft shapes based on linear measurements provide only a partial picture of behavioral adaptation as it is reflected in skeletal morphology. More precise information available from the mechanical properties of bones has added important knowledge of past function and behavior.

Like any other material, bone has mechanical properties, the most important of which are strength and stiffness. In addition to material properties of bone (e.g., density)—not to be considered in this discus-

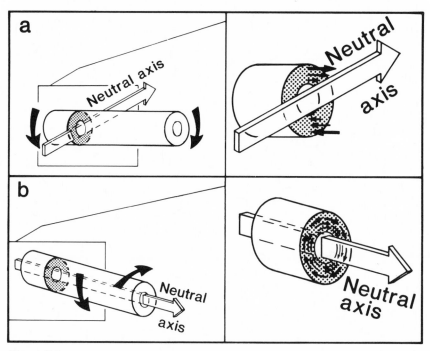

Figure 7-1
Bones subjected to Bending (a) and Torsion (b) Around a Neutral Axis. Note that bending actually involves a combination of tension and compression. The heavier arrows in each of the loading modes indicate a greater magnitude of stress at the periphery of the bones. (Reproduced from Larsen 1987 with permission from Academic Press, Inc.).

sion—the shape, size, and geometric configuration of bones contribute to mechanical integrity under different loading situations.

The long bones (e.g., femur, tibia, and humerus) are subject primarily to loading modes that are associated with bending and torsion (twisting). In both bending and torsion (Figure 7-1), the cross-sectional area (size) as well as the distribution of bone are important determinants of mechanical behavior in general and strength and stiffness in particular. Because the long bones are tubular, they are able to withstand stresses associated with bending from all directions. In engineering terminology, a long bone can be modeled as a hollow beam, and beam theory can be used to analyze structural strength and rigidity. In a beam undergoing bending, stress represents a function of distance from a neutral axis, which runs through the center of the section. Therefore, the greater stresses are located in the most distant fibers of the bone from this axis. In essence, then, to withstand these stresses, the bone cross section that is strongest and stiffest is that in which the material is distributed furthest from the neutral axis (Nordin and Frankel 1980; Lanyon and Rubin 1985).

In order to measure mechanical properties as an indicator of mechanical demand, a series of cross-sectional geometric properties are examined. Because of the cumbersome techniques involved in deriving some of the properties, until quite recently it has only been possible to examine very few individual remains. However, with the development of automated techniques involving noninvasive (e.g., Martin, Burr, and Schaffler 1985; Ruff and Leo 1986) and invasive approaches (e.g., Ruff and Hayes 1983a), it has become possible to examine and analyze geometric data from large numbers of skeletal elements. In this chapter, we report on one such study in which we examined cross-sectional geometric properties of the femur in relation to the transition from a subsistence regime based primarily on hunting, gathering, and fishing to one that incorporated maize as a significant component of diet on the prehistoric Georgia coast. We were especially interested in determining possible mechanical changes that occurred in the skeleton with this transition. The femur was chosen for study because this skeletal element is likely to reflect changes in locomotion and general patterns of activity as well as particular changes in the use of the lower limb.

The Georgia Coast

The Georgia coast has been the focus of a great deal of archaeological work since the nineteenth century. In the last decade, in particular, an impressive body of data focusing on prehistoric settlement patterns, subsistence reconstruction, human biological adaptation, and European/Indian interaction during the mission period have provided for a better understanding of adaptation, in both prehistoric and historic contexts. This body of data provides for important background work in our study of skeletal adaptation.

The dominant feature of the Georgia coast is a chain of barrier islands—the Sea Islands—that extends from North Carolina southward to northern Florida. The region is characterized by relative uniformity in rainfall, temperature, topographic features, vegetation, and fauna. It is part of a zone that represents a transitional area between the temperate northern Atlantic and the tropical southern Atlantic. The transitional nature of this region is reflected by a combination of tropical and nontropical resources (cf. Reitz 1982a, 1982b, 1988; Reitz and Scarry 1985).

Reflecting this diversity of resources, analysis of food remains from archaeological sites on the Georgia coast shows an exploitation by native populations of primarily estuarine/marine and terrestrial resources. In this regard, estuarine/marine resources, including fishes and invertebrates (especially shellfish), were the predominant faunal resources (Reitz 1982a, 1982b, 1988; Feitz and Scarry 1985), providing the major sources of protein. Reptiles, birds, and small and large mammals—including but not limited to raccoon, deer, opossum, and rabbit—and a number of plants (e.g., hickory nuts, acorns, persimmons, grapes) were also utilized during the entire prehistoric period and into the contact period. During the twelfth century A.D., maize began to play an important role in the subsistence economy. The use of maize by native populations during the contact period appears to have been emphasized even more than in the prehistoric period. (See Marrinan 1975; Jones 1978; Thomas and Larsen 1979; DePratter 1979; Larson 1980; Larsen 1982; Reitz 1978, 1982a, 1982b; Reitz and Scarry 1985; Steinen 1984; Crook 1980, 1984; Quitmyer et al. 1985; May 1983; Adams 1985; and DesJean et al. 1985 for discussions of Georgia coastal native subsistence.)

Subsistence-related activities undertaken by native populations occupying this region would, therefore, be associated with hunting, collecting, and fishing during the prehistoric period with the addition of field preparation and raising of crops, especially maize, during the later centuries prior to European contact. This study addresses specifically the impact of subsistence and activity changes associated with this major shift in adaptation.

Materials and Methods

Femora were obtained from a number of mortuary localities on the Georgia coast (cf. Larsen 1982). Twenty femora from a preagricultural group (pre–A.D. 1150) and twenty femora from an agricultural group (A.D. 1150–1550) were selected. All but three of the preagricultural femora postdate A.D. 500; most of the remainder of the sample dates between A.D. 1000 and A.D. 1150. All femora from the agricultural group are prehistoric and are primarily restricted to the period A.D. 1200 to 1450. Therefore, most of the femora used in this study are from a relatively restricted period of time. Given the well-established record of cultural continuity in prehistoric Georgia coastal populations, especially during later prehistory (see discussion in Larsen 1982), it is appropriate to suggest that biological change in this region did not likely result from population replacement.

These materials represent approximately equal numbers of females and males, thereby circumventing problems of size differences between sexes. In order to avoid potential problems of side asymmetry that is characteristic of limb bones, approximately equal numbers from left and right sides were used in the study. For this sample, the average age at death was twenty-five years for the preagricultural group and twenty-eight years for the agricultural group. Neither of these ages is significantly different from the average age at death for the entire population reported in an earlier study of demographic characteristics of these skeletal series (Larsen 1982, 1984).

Two locations were examined on each femur: the subtrochanteric region (inferior to the lesser trochanter) and the midshaft. Once properly oriented, the bones were cut transversely, the exposed sections photographed, and the photographs projected onto a digitizer screen. Both the subperiosteal and endosteal sections were then traced manually on the digitizer screen and geometric properties automatically calculated with a computer program (SLICE) developed for this specific purpose in another investigation (cf. Ruff and Hayes 1983a). This invasive approach was chosen over a noninvasive approach—that is, CT (computerized tomography) scans—because of a variety of problems associated with the technique and the nature of archaeological bone (cf. Ruff and Leo 1986). For our purposes, we determined that our results would be more reliable by using a direct measurement approach.

Specific femoral cross-sectional geometric properties that we examined include cortical area (CA), medullary area (MA), total subperiosteal area (TA), maximum second moment of area (I_{max}), minimum second moment of area (I_{min}), and polar second moment of area (J).

Cortical area, medullary area, and total subperiosteal area provide measures of amount and general distribution of bone; second moments of area depend on bone area and distribution of bone area with respect to the neutral axis of a cross section. Relatively large values of I or J reflect more outwardly distributed bone area. Simply put, large values of I reflect greater bending strength and large values of J reflect greater torsional strength.

Results

To standardize for differences in general body size, cross-sectional dimensions were first divided by bone length squared for areas and bone length to the fourth power for second moments of area before carrying out comparisons (Ruff et al. 1984). In the comparison of the preagricultural and agricultural femora, little difference in cortical area is revealed for either the subtrochanteric or midshaft regions (Figure 7-2). Medullary area and total subperiosteal area, however, show significant declines in the agricultural group relative to the preagricultural group. These results indicate that although bone area remains about the same, the distribution of bone becomes more tightly clustered about the centroid or neutral axis in the agricultural group. This distribution is reflected in markedly reduced subperiosteal and medullary areas of bone.

Examination of second moments of area (Figure 7-2) also reveals a decline in the agricultural group. It is apparent from both the summary data and the cross-section outlines shown in Figure 7-2 that bone is furthest distributed from the neutral axis in the preagricultural group. These differences directly reflect greater bone strength in the preagricultural femoral sample.

Discussion

In other studies of Georgia coastal skeletal variation, it was shown that a general reduction in body size and skeletal robusticity occurred after A.D. 1150 (Larsen 1981, 1982, 1984). Additionally, the frequency of degenerative joint disease declined (Table 7-1). Because degenerative joint disease is an age-related pathological process, the reduction in frequency of degenerative joint disease by itself does not mean a decline in mechanically related stress on bone joints, however. If a skeletal series contains a relatively greater number of older adults, it should have a higher frequency of joints exhibiting degenerative changes. In fact, the preagricultural sample has a greater number of older adults than the agricultural sample (Larsen 1982). However, statistical treatment (Kolmogorov-Smirnov and chi-square) revealed that the age distributions of individuals affected by the disease are not significantly different

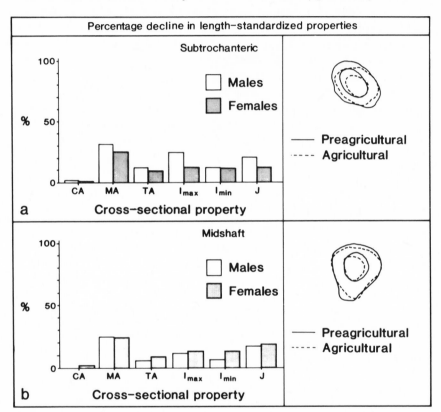

Figure 7-2
Percentage Decline in Femoral Subtrochanteric (a) and Midshaft (b) Cross-sectional Properties in Comparison of Georgia Coastal Preagricultural and Agricultural Groups (CA = cortical area; MA = medullary area; TA = total subperiosteal area; I_{max} = maximum second moment of area; I_{min} = minimum second moment of area; J = polar second moment of area). CA, MA, and TA provide measures of relative amount of bone tissue; the other variables—I (bending) and J (torsion)—indicate distribution of bone about the neutral axis. The differences between the preagricultural and agricultural groups are summarized in the cross sections figured at the right of the bar graphs (after Ruff et al. 1984; reproduced from Larsen 1987 with permission from Academic Press, Inc.)

(p = .05). Therefore, we suggest that the changes in degenerative joint disease are consistent with the findings reported here in cross-sectional geometric properties.

The present discussion is a further investigation of this hypothesis through direct examination of specific cross-sectional geometric properties that reflect strength of bone. Although reduction in body size and skeletal robusticity can result from both decline in nutritional quality and decline in mechanical demand, the findings in this investigation would seem to indicate that it is possible to differentiate more clearly between dietary and mechanical factors.

Two important changes stand out in comparison of the two subsistence groups. First, there is a reduction in the amount of bone, but when standardized for length the difference in bone areas within cross sections becomes negligible. Second, there are significant reductions in

Table 7-1
Frequency of Preagricultural and Agricultural Adult Articular Joints Affected by Degenerative Joint Disease (Females, Males, Indeterminate Sex Combined)

Joint	Preagricultural		Agricultural		% Change[2]	p[3]
	%	N[1]	%	N[1]		
Cervical	26.4	53	5.3	132	−21.1	ns[4]
Thoracic	8.0	50	5.3	131	−2.7	ns
Lumbar	44.4	45	17.8	118	−26.6	.001
Sacrum	2.7	40	3.4	87	+0.7	ns
Shoulder	4.0	149	1.0	289	−3.0	ns
Elbow	9.1	176	2.3	307	−6.8	.001
Wrist	4.9	142	0.4	266	−4.5	.05
Hand	0.0	82	1.2	245	+1.2	ns
Hip	4.1	169	0.3	290	−3.8	.005
Knee	13.7	183	6.5	291	−7.2	.01
Ankle	4.4	158	0.4	285	−4.0	.005
Foot	0.0	81	0.4	232	+0.4	ns

Data from Larsen 1982.
[1]Number of articular joints observed for presence or absence of degenerative joint disease.
[2]Computed by the formula: % agricultural − % preagricultural.
[3]Chi-square significance levels.
[4]Not significant (ns).

medullary area and subperiosteal area. These reductions lead to a tighter distribution of bone, thus decreasing second moments of area. Therefore, although the relative area of bone material is equivalent, the bending and torsional strengths of the preagricultural femur are greater than in the agricultural femur.

These alterations can lead to but one conclusion: that there are distinct reductions in mechanical strength in the agricultural group relative to the preagricultural group. Although these changes might reflect differences both in nutrition and in mechanical loadings, the type of geometric remodeling observed—redistribution of bone with no change in bone area per se—is most likely to reflect mechanically related demands. It would seem, therefore, that the change in lifeway during the Mississippian occupation of the Georgia coast was toward a less demanding pattern—mechanically speaking—than in earlier periods.

Comparisons of these data by sex indicates that both males and females showed approximately equal declines in measures of bone strength. However, earlier studies of skeletal size based on external bone dimensions showed that females exhibited relatively greater overall body size reduction than males. This trend suggests that the greater body size reductions in females may have been due primarily to nutritional factors (see also discussion in Larsen 1982, 1984).

It is interesting to note as well that with respect to shaft shape, males in the agricultural group show a greater increase in circularity than females, particularly at the midshaft. Therefore, an actual decline occurs in level of sexual dimorphism in bone shape in this section of the femur. This pattern would strongly suggest that sexual differences in type of activity that affect femoral shaft shape may actually have been reduced in the later subsistence group (cf. Ruff and Hayes 1983b; see also Ruff 1987). Thus, measures of sexual dimorphism in bone strength reveal a somewhat different pattern of temporal change than what is exhibited in measures of general body size.

In sum, the results of this investigation indicate that reduction in musculoskeletal stress was experienced by both sexes in the transition to subsistence economy. The greater changes in general body size of females may reflect a greater component of maize in their diets relative to males. This conjecture is supported by a greater frequency of dental caries in females compared with males, a factor that Larsen has interpreted as reflecting a greater proportion of carbohydrates in the female diet than in the male diet (cf. Larsen 1983a).

A limited number of studies have examined bone strength and differences between archaeological populations that practiced different subsistence economies. Brock (1986; Brock and Ruff 1988) has examined a

series of skeletal remains representative of hunter-gatherer and agricultural populations from the southwestern United States. Like the results presented here, this investigator noted greater bone strength in the
hunter-gatherer samples. These results were interpreted as reflecting an
adaptation to greater mobility and generally greater mechanical demands in hunter-gatherers than agriculturalists.

Bridges (1983, and Chapter 6, this volume) has found generally the
opposite trend in materials examined from Alabama in the shift from
hunting and gathering to agriculture. On the surface, the data presented
by Brock and by us would seem to contradict those presented by
Bridges. Rather than representing contradictory data, however, we be-
lieve that these studies point to the complexity of mechanical adaptations that are associated with the shift to agriculture. Indeed, the use of
the terms hunter-gatherer and agriculturalist probably grossly over-
simplifies the issue. That is, these regions in all probability represent
very different adaptational and behavioral circumstances in late prehistory. With regard to the Southeast in particular, the transition to agriculture is probably only one factor of many that are involved in the
economic shift as represented in Alabama on the one hand and the
Georgia coast on the other. The Alabama and Georgia coastal populations were exploiting a number of common terrestrial resources. However, the range of marine and estuarine resources depended upon by the
coastal populations in Georgia undoubtedly contributed to a very different mechanical adaptation relative to Alabama populations. It should
be stressed that the findings based on the two series from the Southeast
(Georgia coast and Alabama) and, for that matter, the single series from
the Southwest, should be considered not as general models but rather
as specific to the regions studied. More regional studies examining skeletal change in relation to mechanical properties are needed before general conclusions can be drawn.

These data are pertinent to broader issues in prehistory, in particular
the amount and kind of labor involved in the food quest in the transition
from hunting and gathering to agriculture. We are speaking not just with
reference to the Georgia coast or the southeastern United States but
rather with respect to changes that have been documented worldwide.
The amount of time and labor hunter-gatherers expend in the food quest
relative to agriculturalists has been hotly debated by a wide spectrum of
anthropologists (cf. Roosevelt 1984). A number of workers have provided
detailed data on amount of time devoted to specific labors in both subsistence economies and combinations, and generally there is little
agreement as to whether hunter-gatherers devote relatively more or less
time to acquisition of food than agriculturalists (summarized in Gross

1984). The data presented by Brock (1986; Brock and Ruff 1988) and in this study (see also Ruff et al. 1984) suggest that the food quest may have been more demanding among hunter-gatherers than among agriculturalists in at least two areas: the Southwest and the Georgia coast.

Conclusions

This study emphasizes the skeleton as an ever-changing mechanical tissue and organ. In particular, study of cross-sectional geometric properties of archaeological bone provides greater meaning for the statement (Wolff's Law) that in an area of bone subject to mechanical demand, bone is deposited, and in areas where there is a lack of mechanical demand, bone is resorbed.

We suggest that approaches such as the one outlined in this chapter go far in providing precise information regarding the degree to which a population is stressed mechanically. These data used in conjunction with more traditional approaches to skeletal analysis of activity and behavior will help to clarify a number of behavioral issues in the archaeological past. In a very real sense, then, the analysis of cross-sectional geometric properties is a link between archaeological and behavioral contexts. As such, it is an important example of application of midrange theory (cf. Brock 1986) leading to a more precise understanding of earlier human populations.

Presently, we are examining cross-sectional geometric properties of humeri from precontact Georgia coastal sites in order to ascertain possible mechanical changes in the upper limb. Additionally, as part of a broader study of the impact of European contact on Native American health and adaptation on St. Catherines Island, these geometric properties are under investigation in both the upper and lower limbs of postcontact populations. It will be especially interesting to observe the effects of the impact of increased focus on maize agriculture and increased settlement nucleation and, presumably, sedentism on skeletal morphology and adaptation in these populations.

Acknowledgments

This research was supported by the Edward John Noble Foundation, the St. Catherines Island Foundation, the Smithsonian Institution, the National Science Foundation (grant BNS–8406773) (to Larsen), and a National Institutes of Health (NIH) Traineeship (AM 07112) (to Ruff). We thank Dr. Douglas H. Ubelaker for permission to study femora housed in the collections of the National Museum of Natural History, Smithsonian Institution. We also thank Dr. Wilson C. Hayes for making available facilities in the Orthopaedic Biomechanics Laboratory, Beth Israel Hospital, Boston, used in the bone cross-sectional analysis. Dennis O'Brien prepared the artwork for the figures. The figures are reproduced with permission from Academic Press, Inc.

✳ 8

Sifting the Ashes: Reconstruction of a Complex Archaic Mortuary Program in Louisiana

Ann Marie Wagner Mires

> The mortuary customs of savage and barbaric people have a deep signifi-
> cance from the fact that in them are revealed much of the philosophy of
> the people by whom they were practiced. Early beliefs concerning the
> nature of human existence in life and after death, and the relations of the
> living to the dead, are recorded in these customs. The mystery con-
> cerning the future, love for the departed who were loved while here; rever-
> ence for the wise and good who may after death be wiser and better;
> hatred and fear of those who were enemies here and may have added
> powers of enmity in the hereafter—all these and like considerations have
> led in every tribe to a body of customs of exceeding interest as revealing
> the opinions, the philosophy of the people themselves. (Powell 1880:iii)

Death is a universal human "rite of passage" whose physical manifestations are often preserved in the archaeological record. Ethnologists
have collected a wealth of data on North American Indian mortuary
customs, representing a wide range of cultural groups (Bushnell 1920;
Swanton 1911, 1946; Yarrow 1880; among others). From these and from
worldwide studies, a body of theory has been developed aimed at reconstruction of the social systems that gave rise to these customs (Binford
1972; Brown 1971, 1981; Saxe 1970). A major assumption of this body of
theory is that the response of a social group to the death of one of its
members would bear a predictable relation to that individual's status in
life, that is, one's social persona (Binford 1972), and consequently to the
organization of that society, that is, egalitarian or stratified (O'Shea
1984). Archaeological analysis of Archaic North American Indian sites
would seem to suggest that their hunting-gathering way of life would
produce a simple burial program reflecting predominantly ascribed
status by sex and age, with a lesser dimension of achieved status obtained within individual lifetimes (Rothschild 1979). However, the limitations of this assumption are challenged by the complexity of some
Archaic mortuary series, including the one described in this chapter.

The "role" theory of mortuary practices has been recently criticized by Pearson (1983), who alternatively proposes a broader interpretive framework. Using data from Victorian and modern England, he argues that burial ritual is susceptible to ideological manipulation within the construction of social strategies, regardless of the deceased individual's status in life. The dead are "manipulated" by the living depending upon how the living perceive the dead within the context of competing social relationships.

Pearson's viewpoint harks back to the goal of the early ethnographers of mortuary studies, which was elucidation of the opinions, philosophy, and customs of the people themselves as reflected in their mortuary rituals. He believes that the burial ceremony must be seen as an encapsulation of the larger social system, which is dynamic and can vary with time. Minor variations that represent dynamic processes may appear in individual burials within the larger cemetery. Too often our view of the past is static, due in part to the stasis of the material remains. Death and its social correlate burial, like other rites of passage, were probably manipulated by the living in the past, as in the present, to suit changing perceptions in social relations. Pearson was fortunate to have historical data to reconstruct the changing ideological mind-set of the nineteenth- and twentieth-century British, but most archaeologists must make do with incomplete data sets—individual burials, cemeteries, and sites— when attempting to reconstruct past behavior and social systems within regional contexts.

These products of human behavior can be viewed as the end result of collective action. The traditional view suggests that burials and cemeteries are laid out according to a rigid set of specific rules. Alternatively, an informed cemetery analysis suggests that rules potentially are constructed and *re*constructed. Burials reflect in their forms the material application of those dynamic rules. Variability exhibited in the material record is the result of the application of those rules at specific instances. This awareness of sources of variability informs our analysis of the dynamic nature of collective action.

If we are to understand the ideological framework behind the physical manifestations of burial ceremonies, we must first understand the group responsible for the ceremonies. This dimension includes group size, subsistence regime, intra- and intergroup social relations, residential stability and mobility. Archaeologists and physical anthropologists working in tandem can synthesize biological and cultural data recovered from mortuary contexts in an attempt to understand social processes that influenced the creation of a site. An understanding of site formation processes and the plan of the mortuary area are essential to comprehension of the originating group's social objectives. The Archaic period in Louisiana was essentially unknown prior to the excavation of the Cowpen Slough site (Ramenofsky 1986). With its investigation, the Archaic period as a separate spatial, temporal, and cultural entity was established as distinct from the Poverty Point cultural phenomenon postdating the Archaic. The recognition of a distinct cultural entity displaying a considerable amount of complexity both in the mortuary features and in the site as a whole prior to the Poverty Point period is an important first step toward understanding this yet unexplored regional phenomenon. Additional systematic testing is necessary before this period will be well documented.

Site Description

The Cowpen Slough site, 16CT147, is located in Catahoula Parish, Louisiana, directly southwest of Larto Lake, a remnant oxbow of the Mississippi River (Figure 1-1). The site itself lies on a relict channel of an ancestral river, presently known as Cowpen Slough. The cultural deposit is a long linear strip that parallels the outside bend of the relict channel, representing an estimated use area of 1,500 m^2 (Figure 8-1). The buried deposit represents an undulating aboriginal surface quite different from the present land surface, with a 2 percent slope from north to south and as much as a 7 percent slope east to west. The depth of the midden varies from 30 to 100 cm (Ramenofsky and Mires 1985).

The site was discovered in 1975 during the cutting of a drainage ditch, and systematic test excavations were conducted by Louisiana State University in 1983. Radiocarbon dates were obtained predating the Poverty Point period, which prompted more extensive excavation by LSU the following year. Both cemetery and noncemetery areas were identified and are described in detail elsewhere (Ramenofsky and Mires 1985). An unknown portion of the cemetery had eroded into the drainage ditch; of the remaining 22 m^2, one-half (11 m^2) was excavated.

Grain size analysis of sediments both within and outside the archaeological deposit was performed to determine the sedimentological history of the intact deposits at Cowpen Slough. Prior to 4,500 B.P., this area was affected by fluvial processes from the Arkansas or Ouachita river systems (Ramenofsky and Mires 1985). The sterile sandy loams underlying the cultural matrix were deposited in a high-energy environment, probably during the formation of a levee and/or point bar. Occupation of the site began around 4500 B.P. after the levee and point bar system had stabilized. The soils from the first archaeological stratum are loams. The

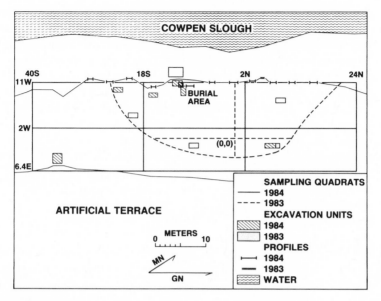

Figure 8-1
Cowpen Slough: Site Plan

earliest phase of occupation is Late Archaic and appears to be continuous up until around 3100 B.P. At this time there was a shift in fluvial systems and the Mississippi River flowed through the basin, spreading sediments through backwater flooding. Present-day Larto Lake may occupy part of its old channel. The soils from this stratum are characterized as clay loams. The second phase of occupation spans the period between 3100 and 2800 B.P. and represents the Poverty Point component at the site. Site use shifted from intensive to intermittent, with the later occupation probably coinciding with times of low water. The earlier alluviation had terminated prior to the Mississippi deposition, but by 2800 B.P. that river had abandoned its channel in the vicinity of Cowpen Slough. Aboriginal activity appears to have terminated around that time (Ramenofsky and Mires 1985).

Description of the Cemetery

All of the human remains were recovered from one area of the site, located along its western edge bordering the cut ditch (Figure 8-2). Site use as a whole spanned approximately 1,700 years, from 4500 to 2800 B.P., but the use-life of the cemetery itself was considerably shorter.

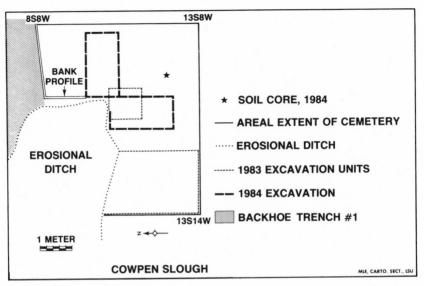

Figure 8-2
Plan View of Test Units Within the Delimited Cemetery Area

Three methods of analysis were utilized to establish the use-life of the cemetery portion of the site: (1) grain size analysis, (2) C^{14} analysis, and (3) stratification. Taken collectively, the data suggest that cemetery use was restricted to the earliest phase of occupation, if not specifically to the period between 4500 and 4000 B.P.

Sedimentological analysis of feature and nonfeature soil samples from the cemetery reveal a homogenous cluster of loams. These loams are indicative of the earliest archaeological stratum, and their presence places cemetery use solely within the initial period of occupation, 4500 to 3100 B.P. No clay loams were found within the cemetery, but the prior mechanical removal of the top level of this portion of the site made it impossible to determine exactly how much clay loam may have existed above it.

Numerous samples intended for radiocarbon analysis were obtained from the cemetery. A large chunk of wood recovered from the multiple cremation deposit lying at the very top of Feature 7, the only nonbone sample recovered, yielded a date of 4200 + 180 years B.P. All other samples taken were of cremated and unburned bone, but unfortunately the organic content of the bone was so reduced by diagenesis that radiocarbon dating was impossible. If this single date is accepted, then the multiple crematory deposit (Feature 30) and the flexed burials within Feature 7 all predate 4000 B.P.

Table 8-1
Human Burials at Cowpen Slough: Demographic and Mortuary Data

Feature	# of Ind.	Age	Sex	Burial Mode
Layer 1				
5	1	indeterminate	indeterminate	secondary, unburned
7b	4	subadult	indeterminate	primary, unburned
		subadult	indeterminate	primary, unburned
		adult	indeterminate	primary, unburned
		adult, 18+ years	female	primary, unburned
8	3	adult, senile	male	primary, unburned
		adult, 35+ years	male	primary, unburned
		adult, 18+ years	female	primary, unburned
24	1	adult	indeterminate	secondary, unburned
43	1	adult, 21–35 years	male	indeterminate, unburned
Layer 2				
23a/b	1	adult	indeterminate	secondary, unburned
26	3	subadult, 4–10 years	indeterminate	secondary, cremation
		adolescent, 11–17 years	indeterminate	secondary, cremation
		adult, 21–35 years	male	secondary, cremation
30	3	subadult, 0–6 months	indeterminate	secondary, cremation
		subadult, 9 months–3 years	indeterminate	secondary, cremation
		adult, 40–44 years	male	secondary, cremation
31	2	subadult, 0–6 months	indeterminate	primary, cremation
		adult	female	primary, cremation
38: 32, 33, 34	5	subadult, 0–6 months	indeterminate	primary, cremation
		subadult, 9 months–3 years	indeterminate	primary, cremation
		subadult, 4–10 years	indeterminate	primary, cremation
		adolescent, 11–17 years	indeterminate	primary, cremation
		adult, 21–35 years	female	primary, cremation
40	2	subadult, 4–10 years	indeterminate	primary, cremation
		adult, 35+ years	male	primary, cremation

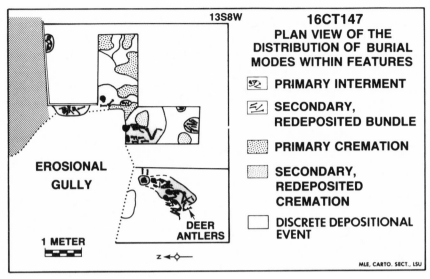

Figure 8-3
Plan View of the Distribution of Burial Modes Within Features

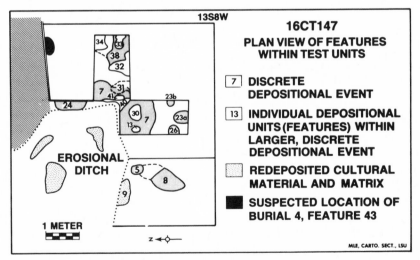

Figure 8-4
Plan View of Burial Features

Because the other burial deposits could not be dated absolutely, cemetery stratigraphy was examined to establish their relative temporal placement. The vertical stratification in the cemetery segregates the deposits into two layers (Table 8-1). The earlier, lower layer lies between

13.42 and 13.92 msl (meters above sea level) and contains both primary (articulated) unburned burials (Features 7b, 8, and 43) and secondary (disarticulated) unburned interments: Features 5 and 24. The later, overlying layer lies between 13.92 and 14.32 msl and consists of a variety of deposits: secondary disarticulated unburned remains (Feature 23a/b), primary cremations burned in situ (Features 31, 32, 33, 34, and 40), and secondary cremations burned elsewhere before deposition in this locus (Features 26 and 30). The upper layer of deposits are horizontally discrete. The cremated deposits in Feature 30 directly overlie the earlier Feature 7b, which contains four flexed primary burials. This overlapping but nonintrusive positioning suggests that placement of later deposits may have been made with foreknowledge of the earlier deposits. The two layers of burial deposits are thus distinguished from one another both by vertical location and by variation in body treatment.

Deposition in the cemetery took one of two distinct forms. The deposits in the lower layer are all contained within subsurface pits dug into the sandy loam below the top of the aboriginal surface. In the upper layer, all but one (Feature 26) were placed not in pits but directly on the extant surface and mounded with the adjacent midden. Four distinct modes of burial are evident, but not all appear in both layers (Figures 8-3 and 8-4). Primary articulated interments were located only at the base of subsurface pits (Features 7, 8 and 43) in the lower layer. Disarticulated unburned interments were placed either on the surface (Feature 23a/b)

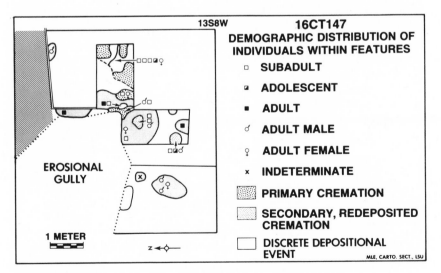

Figure 8-5
Demographic Distribution of Individuals Within Features

in the upper layer or in pits (Features 24 and 5) in the lower layer. The in situ cremations in the upper layer (Features 31, 32, 33, 34, and 40) were all surface deposits with evidence of burning underlying the bone clusters. Redeposited cremations (found only in the upper layer) assumed both forms: Feature 26 was deposited in a pit, and Feature 30 was placed on the ground over Feature 7.

The depositional events involved both single and multiple individuals (Figure 8-5, Table 8-2). The smaller deposits (e.g., Features 5, 23a/b, 24, and 26) were distinct spatial entities evidently placed each at a single event. The larger deposits (e.g., the constellation of Features 32, 33, and 34), on the other hand, represent sets of carefully placed remains apparently representing consecutive burial events.

Feature 7 is a massive pit, more than 65 cm in depth, 180 cm in length, and 142 cm wide. Two distinct layers of burial activity occur at this locus. The top layer contains a constellation of three surface deposits (collectively, Feature 30): two primary and one secondary cremation. The second layer, separated from the first by a sterile zone of approximately 8 cm containing no cultural materials, consists of four flexed primary burials in a pit (Feature 7).

Features 32 and 33 lie on top of and partly within an area of burned soil designated as Feature 38. The configuration of the burned area strongly suggests that bodies or skeletal elements were placed along the perimeter of a cone-shaped fire. The center of the fire had very little bone placed in it and remained elevated, but the weight of the bone around the edges compacted the coals and ash down into the underlying matrix. This crematory fire represents a single episode of use. A high percentage of charred or incompletely burned bone from Features 32 and 33 suggests that the fire was not sustained for a long period of time.

Table 8-2
Frequency of Features by Number of Individuals Across Burial Modes

Number of Individuals	Primary Interment	Secondary Interment	Primary Cremation	Secondary Cremation
1	1(43)	3(5,23a/b,24)		
2			2(31,40)	
3	1(8)			2(26,30)
4	1(7)			
5			1(38)	

(#) = Feature number

Table 8-3
Distribution of Age Categories Across Burial Modes

	Primary Interment	Secondary Interment	Primary Cremation	Secondary Cremation
Subadult	2	0	5	3
Adolescent	0	0	1	1
Adult	6	2	3	2
Indeterminate	0	1	0	0
Total	8	3	9	6

Feature 34, lying along the northern perimeter of Feature 38, was a pile of poorly preserved, disarticulated, unburned bone overlain by a thin layer of charred bone. These unburned bones were apparently piled up near the crematory fire but were never placed in the flames. A few charred bones either rolled or were pulled from the fire and were deposited on top of this unburned material. Skeletal elements from five separate individuals were randomly distributed among these three bone piles (Ramenofsky and Mires 1985).

The number of individuals contained within each burial deposit varies across burial modes (Table 8-2). The majority of the deposits contain more than one individual. The disarticulated noncremated interments each appear to contain only one individual, but this conclusion is biased by the poor condition of the unburned material and the difficulty in distinguishing more than one individual among the bone fragments present. Traditional techniques for determining the minimum number of individuals represented (Ubelaker 1978) were applied to the cremated skeletal remains. Aging and sexing criteria were applied to 1,000 burned bone fragments that displayed diagnostic characteristics (Bass 1971; Moorrees et al. 1963a, 1963b; Murphy 1959; Ubelaker 1978). The total number of individuals from the cremations represents a conservative estimate.

The sample from the cemetery yielded 26 individuals: 10 subadults, 2 adolescents, 13 adults, and 1 indeterminate (Table 8-3). Both sexes were represented among the adults (Table 8-4). Seventeen of these individuals displayed more specific age indicators and created the subset used in the mortality profile (Figure 8-6). This subsample, though small, approximates a normal demographic profile, with the probability of dying being the greatest for infants and older adults (Weiss 1973). Despite the very poor bone preservation and sampling bias, this profile suggests that there were no cultural proscriptions on the part of this cultural

Table 8-4
Sex Distribution of Adults Across Burial Modes

Age in Years	Primary Interment	Secondary Interment	Primary Cremation	Secondary Cremation
Adult (18+)	2 F, 1 ?	2 ?	1 F	0
Young Adult (21–35)	1 ?	0	1 F	1 M
Old Adult (+35)	2 M	0	1 M	1 M

M = Male, F = Female, ? = Indeterminate

16CT147

MORTALITY GRAPH REPRESENTING THE NUMBER OF INDIVIDUALS DYING WITHIN EACH AGE CATEGORY, SEXES COMBINED (N = 17)

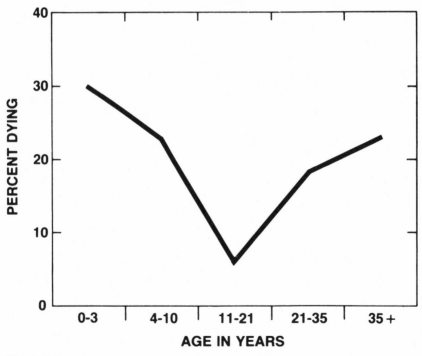

Figure 8-6
Mortality Graph Representing the Number of Individuals Dying Within Each Age Category. Sexes Combined (*N* = 17)

group against the inclusion of individuals of both sexes and all ages in this mortuary precinct.

Interpretations

In the Late Archaic period, the aboriginal inhabitants of this site selected a locale at the western edge of their habitation area on a mature levee in which to bury their dead. The concentrated constellation of burials suggests that the cemetery was reused by the same group of people (perhaps including both site and adjacent nonsite residents) within a restricted period of time. The archaeological record at Cowpen Slough suggests year-round occupation of the site by a population practicing a diffuse-redundant subsistence strategy exploiting a wide niche breadth (Ramenofsky 1986). Although interlayer variability in burial modes can be attributed to possible temporal factors, a great deal of intralayer variability must be explained.

As stated earlier, the majority of the deposits contain multiple individuals (Table 8-2). Laboratory analysis of the cremated deposits has suggested that the preincineration condition of the individuals within features was highly variable. Some of the individuals were burned in the flesh, while others were burned in a dry bone condition (for a discussion of the techniques used to distinguish these conditions see Baby 1954 and Buikstra and Swegle 1980). These data suggest that certain individuals were processed and curated for final deposition at a later date (Figure 8-7). The different burial modes entailed different levels of processing

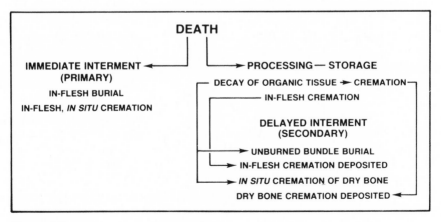

Figure 8-7
Processing of Individuals Following Death

and curation of human remains. The primary articulated burials exhibit no processing of the elements, only simple laying out of the body, whereas the dry bone cremations that were redeposited had gone through numerous levels of mortuary processing. The intralayer variability results from these differing levels of processing and curation.

The features in the upper layer containing multiple extensively processed individuals may represent both sequential and contemporaneous deposits. The particular burial mode chosen for any particular individual (burial mode does not segregate by age or sex variables) may have been a function of time elapsed before final deposition and/or of spatial distance from the cemetery, particularly if the area was used by nonsite (but culturally associated) residents. Individuals within a single deposit may, despite different levels of processing, represent specific kin groups, or, alternatively, they may represent simply individuals who died within a particular period of time. Whatever the case, each nonprimary interment represents the termination of a particular sequence of processing and curation activities.

Many ethnographic and archaeological studies of hunter-gatherers have focused strongly upon human-land relationships in their search for critical factors governing population distribution and social interactions. Within this cultural-ecological paradigm, ecological constraints (including subsistence regimen) dictate the essential arrangement of people across the landscape and in part determine the context of social relations and organizational development. This theoretical framework assumes that hunter-gatherers adapt in a straightforward manner to their environments and that this process is constrained and directed sufficiently to produce an optimum solution under any given circumstance (Bettinger 1980). This viewpoint focuses on one very visible by-product of human activity; settlement and subsistence remains. As a consequence, it reduces multifaceted aboriginal peoples to mini-max strategizers carefully calculating spear size ratio to desired calories. Personal and group directives are considered to account only for unexplained idiosyncratic variability in the archaeological record, of minor interest to anthropological inquiry.

Few archaeologists have addressed the role of social relations and group directives as a viable influence upon the arrangement of people across the landscape. Wobst (1974, 1976) has introduced the mating network as a behavioral concept that integrated adjacent settlement populations and serves to shape the form and structure of cultural behavior at individual settlements. The mating network is synonymous with the maximum band and defines the largest social entity beyond the local group that has behavioral correlates (Wobst 1976). Wobst argues that, given low population density, mating networks would remain "open" and overlapping to ensure optimal access to potential mates across reasonable distances. This flexibility allows each local group (minimum band) equal options for mate exchange and works against the development of sharply defined social boundaries, signified by local stylistic elaboration. As population density increases, so does the local pool of potential mates, thus reducing the need for open and overlapping mating networks. Closure of the mating network is dependent upon a certain population density threshold and fertility rates high enough to ensure maintenance (Wobst 1976). Concurrent with closure is the need to symbolize ethnicity or band affiliation within and between distinct mating networks. In order to counteract the central place tendency of a closed mating network, social mechanisms may have been developed by the social unit to increase solidarity within the mating network:

> the number of occasions can be increased during which several local bands get together for ritual and other reasons, thus reducing the differential in communication efficiency between the participating groups; territorial symbolism and ritual can be intensified to increase the affiliation of local groups with the area they habitually exploit; stable patterns of intrasocietal mate exchange can be encouraged . . . to make an individual's mate choice more predictable; and since marginal local groups are closer to resources exotic to the area, they can improve their locational lot by intensifying inter-societal exchange. (Wobst 1976:55)

Wobst (1976) further contends that these processes can be monitored in archaeological remains, albeit ones rarely encountered, including portable art, burial rites, cave painting, dress, and items that measure intensity of inter- and intrasocietal exchange. Bender (1985) has applied this behavioral model to the prehistoric hunting and gathering populations of North America. As population density increased, the open mating networks operating during Paleo-Indian and Early Archaic times were reduced. Closure in these regional groups offered social and economic advantages. Stylistic elaboration ensued, probably within a context of social gatherings and exchanges (Bender 1985). The florescence of burial ritual in the Late Archaic period may reflect such an expression of intensified social cohesion.

Charles and Buikstra (1983) have examined one particular aspect of stylistic elaboration of burial ritual: spatial segregation of the mortuary domain. The degree of delimitation of the mortuary domain correlates positively with the importance of ritual affirmation of corporate groups within the larger society (see Saxe 1970 for an extensive discussion of this topic). The absence of a specified mortuary domain suggests little or no resource competition and consequently no need to affirm the corporate structure of the group responsible for control of critical but limited resources. The establishment of a cemetery area indicates a degree of sedentism, which may include seasonal mobility, as well as definition of corporate group boundaries within an ecological territory. Inclusion within the cemetery reflects inclusion within the corporate group.

A cemetery consisting of primary interments in a site in a major river valley may indicate a large, sedentary group within a densely populated area, whereas a cemetery of secondary burials along a peripheral drainage may indicate a small, highly autonomous group that returned occasionally to this locale to bury its dead. The degree of spatial structuring within the cemetery may indicate the degree of competition among groups for critical resources. In larger population aggregates, the corporate groups will be most distinct, leading possibly to inclusion in separate cemeteries or in spatially distinguished areas within a single cemetery. For instance, cemeteries with strongly defined internal differentiation spaced throughout a region may indicate competition at two levels: (1) among villages and (2) among lineages within each village.

Both Bender (1985) and Charles and Buikstra (1983) examined certain behavioral correlates that may have directly influenced the observable archaeological record. Using Pearson's model (1983) suggesting that burial ritual is susceptible to ideological manipulation within the construction of social strategies, we should be able to model predicted spatial configurations of mortuary areas that would result from various social strategies. The open and closed mating networks proposed by Wobst (1976) provide a valuable background for this exercise.

Burial ritual within the context of *an open system* would involve local band disposal of the dead with little or no stylistic symbolizing to differentiate that particular social unit from others within the mating network. Burial form would be dictated by residential mobility; that is, primary burial would represent people who died while resident at the site, while secondary burial would signify those who died while absent from the site. The internal structure of the cemetery would consist of discrete interments with little spatial variability. Grave goods, if present, could reflect the age, sex, and achievements of the individuals with whom they were placed.

In contrast, burial ritual within the context of *a closed mating system* would emphasize aggregated disposal by the corporate group as a means of symbolizing the internal cohesion of that social unit. The rite of burial would provide a vehicle for redistribution and exchange of information, mates, sumptuary goods, grief, and so forth, as well as a means of strengthening bonds of sodality between groups (Bender

1985). The common interment of the dead would serve the social function of reinforcing the social relations of the living. The internal structure of the cemetery might be quite complex, with considerable variety in burial mode, spatial relationships, and symbolic context. Grave goods within this context could be selected to symbolize individual status and to signify corporate group affinity.

The absence of comparative data from other Late Archaic cemeteries in Louisiana makes interpretation of the mortuary pattern observed at Cowpen Slough a very tentative exercise. Nonetheless, comparison of the available data with the theoretical propositions of Wobst, Bender, and Charles and Buikstra concerning archaeological manifestations of certain social strategies does reveal certain interesting points of agreement. The presence of a spatially delimited cemetery area within the site, rather than the burials being scattered through the living area, suggests (1) consistency of occupation, whether year-round or seasonal, (2) definition of corporate group boundaries within an ecological territory, and potentially (3) operation of a closed mating network. The inclusion of all ages and both sexes, with no grave goods, signals the precedence of corporate group identity over individual or subgroup status (e.g., adult males). The presence of primary interments only in the lower and not in the upper layer of burial deposits suggests that through time site occupation may have shifted from continuous to occasional, with the site retaining a strong ritual significance as the designated mortuary area for a particular group of people.

The "common" burial exemplifies the collective action of the corporate group to "manipulate" the dead by curating them until they could be interred with the rest of the group in order to reaffirm the relations of the living. At the same time, the diversity exhibited in the upper layer displays how the "rules for interment" were constructed and/or reconstructed at specific instances to suit the needs and directives of the living.

The Cowpen Slough site has provided a glimpse of life at a very early time in Louisiana's prehistory. It is hoped that this description and preliminary analysis of the mortuary complex uncovered there will stimulate further excavation at this site and the discovery of additional Late Archaic sites in the region.

Acknowledgments

Many people made this work possible. I would like to acknowledge Louisiana Delta Farms Plantation for financial and professional support of our research efforts. The continued support and encouragement of the late Mr. William Baker, avocational archaeologist and farm manager with Delta Farms, initially got us involved with the project. His love for archaeology and the "Delta" region provided inspiration and support for all aspects of the project. Ann F. Ramenofsky, project director, guided and advised through many aspects of the fieldwork and laboratory analysis. The friendship and collegiality exhibited at the field school, as well as the true grit of those participating in the rigorous excavation of such a complex burial locus, are greatly appreciated and highly commended. I would like to thank Mary Lucas Powell for her encouragement of this work. And I would like to acknowledge the aboriginal inhabitants of the Cowpen Slough site and the opportunity we as members of the present have had in glimpsing the past.

✳ 9

The Prehistoric People of Fort Center: Physical and Health Characteristics

Patricia Miller-Shaivitz and Mehmet Yaşar İşcan

Until recently, reported analyses of prehistoric human skeletal remains from Florida have been few in number. Over the past ten years, however, a number of descriptive studies (İşcan 1983; Carr et al. 1984; Miller-Shaivitz 1986; İşcan and Kennedy 1987; Kennedy and İşcan 1987; İşcan and Kessel 1988) and paleopathological and nutritional analyses (Dailey and Morse 1984; İşcan and Miller-Shaivitz 1985; İşcan et al. 1989) have appeared. In spite of these and earlier studies (Snow 1962; Bullen 1972; Saunders 1972), it is obvious that knowledge of the physical and health characteristics of the people of prehistoric Florida is still minimal.

Our analysis of the human skeletal remains recovered during the excavation of the Fort Center site by W. H. Sears (1982) is summarized here. (For a more extensive report, see Miller-Shaivitz 1986.) In addition to a description of physical and health characteristics of this population, we examine the hypothesis that this sample represents individuals of high socioeconomic status, including mortuary specialists and their families. The results are then compared with data from other prehistoric Florida population samples.

Archaeological Background

Fort Center is situated in the cultural area known as the Okeechobee Basin (Milanich and Fairbanks 1980; W. H. Sears 1982). The dominant topographical feature of the region is Lake Okeechobee, a freshwater lake occupying about 1,825 km^2 of the south-central peninsula. The surrounding land is flat and is often covered with water during the rainy season (May through September).

Elsie Sears (1982) noted that the botanical remains represent two main categories of plants, wetland and grassland, in addition to the

cultivar maize. Faunal remains from the site include aquatic and terrestrial mammals, turtles, snakes and other reptiles, amphibians, and
various birds (Hale 1984). An analysis of the fauna indicated that the
people living at the site preferred deer, bowfin, and gar as food items.

The Fort Center site, one of several representing the Belle Glade
culture within the Okeechobee Basin, was excavated over several field
seasons by W. H. Sears, beginning in 1966. In his monograph (W. H.
Sears 1982), he indicated that the region was occupied from 450 B.C. or
earlier until the time of Spanish contact. Four cultural periods were recognized archaeologically, largely from radiocarbon dates and the seria-
tion of ceramics. Sears hypothesized that the site became a specialized
mortuary center during the Period II occupation (A.D. 1–500/1000) with a
charnel house and platform constructed on a platform mound next to an
artificial pond for the purpose of processing and housing the remains of
the dead from the surrounding region (Figure 9-1).

The ceremonial nature of the site was inferred from the existence of
earthworks (mounds and embankments), the charnel structure, and numerous associated features including bundled burials, wooden carvings
of a variety of animals, plummets, polished stem points, celts, daggers,
carved bone pins, and ceramics (including Pasco Plain and Perico Plain
chalkware). Hopewellian items such as platform pipes and quartz crys-

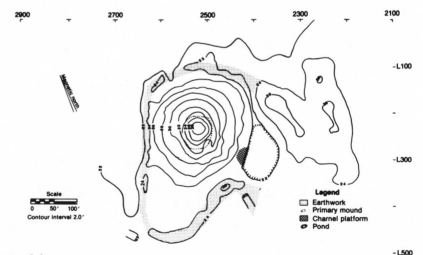

Figure 9-1
Mound and Pond Complex (W. H. Sears 1982. Used by permission of the Board of
Regents of the State of Florida).

tals were also found, as well as evidence of lime burning (Steinen 1982).

Sears reported that the site contained approximately 300 individuals associated with the mortuary facilities. According to his reconstruction of mortuary ritual, the dead were macerated in the charnel structure and their bundled remains placed on a wooden platform built out in the artificial pond (Figure 9-2). At some point, the platform burned for unknown reasons and collapsed into the pond, scattering the bundled burials and associated artifacts. A number of the burials were salvaged from the pond and redeposited on the platform mound after the charnel house was removed, and the mound subsequently was covered with sand (Milanich and Fairbanks 1980). Several of the recovered bone and wooden items were blackened from exposure to the fire, and the human remains were disarticulated and commingled, sustaining considerable damage. None of the crania retained intact facial regions, nor certain associations with their mandibles, and few postcranial bones remained complete. None of the bones could be definitely associated with one another and thus individuals could not be reconstructed, a situation very commonly reported from prehistoric sites in southern Florida (Snow 1962). The preservation of the remains ranged from good to poor because of damage from the fire, collapse of the platform, the nature of the soil, and the continual flooding of the pond.

W. H. Sears (1982) concluded that the Fort Center site represented a high-status community within a ranked society (see also Hale 1984). However, he did not specify whether all of the individuals whose remains were recovered actually resided there throughout their lifetimes or were brought there for mortuary curation because of high achieved status. In the present study, the Fort Center remains were compared with other skeletal samples in the region to test for patterned differences in stature, skeletal robusticity, or health status that might reflect superior nutrition or physical development among these supposedly elite individuals.

Figure 9-2
Reconstruction of the Charnel Platform with Burial Bundle (W. H. Sears 1982. Used by permission of the Board of Regents of the State of Florida).

Materials and Methods

In the present study, 121 crania (complete and fragmentary) of adults and subadults were examined. Postcranial elements analyzed included 23 humeri, 23 femora, 27 tibiae, and many fragmentary vertebrae and other bones. Age and sex were evaluated using criteria in Krogman and İşcan (1986). For crania, age estimates were based upon ectocranial suture closure (Todd and Lyon 1925) rather than upon the more reliable endocranial suture closure because of damage to endocranial surfaces. Osteometric techniques followed Bass (1987). Sex estimates for postcranial remains were obtained from midshaft circumferences of the femur (Black 1978; DiBennardo and Taylor 1979) and tibia (İşcan and Miller-Shaivitz 1984) as well as other bone dimensions (Krogman and İşcan 1986). Stature was calculated using Genovés's (1967) formulae for Mesoamericans. Only complete elements were utilized in estimates of stature and robusticity. In addition, complete femora ($N = 12$) and tibiae ($N = 16$) were radiographed for the presence of transverse growth arrest lines.

All skeletal elements were examined for evidence of disease and trauma. Diagnoses of pathological lesions were made with reference to standard paleopathological sources (Steinbock 1976; Ortner and Putschar 1981), clinical texts (Aegerter and Kirkpatrick 1975), and consultations with radiologists and orthopedists. Specimens suspected to display pseudopathological conditions were analyzed by gross inspection and compared with known cases in the literature (Wells 1967; Campillo 1977; Morse 1983).

This Belle Glade population sample was compared with other prehistoric samples from sites from the east and west coasts of Florida (unspecified occupation dates) (Hrdlička 1922), the Bayshore Homes site in St. Petersburg (Weeden Island period) (Snow 1962), and the Margate-Blount site in Margate (Glades II period) (İşcan 1983).

Results

Only six individuals (7.6 percent) younger than twelve years were represented by crania ($N = 79$) for which age and/or sex could be determined (Table 9-1). It is unclear whether this underrepresentation represents poor preservation or differential burial practices (Tainter 1978; Jacobsen and Cullen 1981). Adults aged twenty-one to thirty-five years make up the majority of the sample (61 percent), and no individuals were aged older than fifty-five years. Young female adults (eighteen

Table 9-1
Age and Sex Composition of Cranial Sample from Fort Center (N = 79)

Age	Male N	Male %	Female N	Female %	Sex Unknown N	Sex Unknown %	Total N	Total %
4–6 years	—	—	—	—	2	33	2	2.5
7–12 years	—	—	—	—	4	67	4	5.1
13–17 years	—	—	—	—	—	—	—	—
18–20 years	3	8	8	23	—	—	11	13.9
21–35 years	28	72	20	59	—	—	48	60.8
36–55 years	8	20	6	18	—	—	14	17.7
+56 years	—	—	—	—	—	—	—	—
Total	39	49	34	43	6	8	79	100

to twenty years) outnumber males, but this pattern is reversed in the older age categories. The male/female cranial ratio is 100:87 (39/34).

Table 9-2 summarizes craniometric data. Sexual dimorphism was evident but to a minor degree in such measurements as minimum frontal breadth and porion-mastoid height. The average cranial index approxi-

Table 9-2
Cranial Metrics of Fort Center Adults

Variables*	Sex	N	Range	Mean	SD
Cranial length	M	25	161–193	175.6	7.01
	F	29	145–185	170.9	7.41
Cranial breadth	M	27	132–153	142.6	5.11
	F	29	120–151	137.4	7.50
Minimum frontal breadth	M	15	88–101	94.3	4.56
	F	18	87–100	94.7	3.45
Maximum frontal breadth	M	23	107–131	118.2	5.41
	F	28	95–132	113.9	7.55
Horizontal circumference	M	20	495–544	510.8	11.39
	F	17	467–511	493.1	12.91
Parietal thickness	M	37	3–8	4.9	1.40
	F	38	2–9	4.3	1.39
Porion-mastoid height	M	15	19–31	24.5	3.66
	F	13	19–30	23.9	3.09
Cranial index	M	22	73.3–90.8	81.4	4.31
	F	26	73.2–91.5	81.2	4.51

*Dimensions are in mm.

Table 9-3
Cranial Metrics: Comparative Data from Florida Sites

Measurements and Indexes	Sex	Fort Center Mean	N	Margate-Blount Mean	N	Bayshore Homes Mean	N	East Coast Mean	N	West Coast Mean	N
Cranial length	M	176	25	182	2	178	11	181	11	180	78
	F	171	29	170	5	170	18	170	7	172	33
Cranial breadth	M	142	27	140	2	145	13	144	11	145	78
	F	137	29	136	5	140	19	136	7	140	33
Minimum frontal	M	94	15	98	2	97	14	—		—	
breadth	F	95	18	92	4	93	18	—		—	
Maximum frontal	M	118	23	—		121	12	—		—	
breadth	F	114	28	—		108	17	—		—	
Horizontal	M	511	20	511	2	508	8	—		—	
circumference	F	493	17	487	4	492	16	—		—	
Parietal thickness	M	5	37	7	2	10	16	—		—	
	F	4	38	5	4·	9	20	—		—	
Cranial index	M	81.4	22	77.0	2	82.1	11	79.8	11	81.0	55
	F	81.2	26	79.8	5	82.4	16	81.1	7	81.2	33

Modified from Miller-Shaivitz 1986: Table 7 incorporating data from Margate-Blount by İşcan 1983, Bayshore Homes by Snow 1962, and east and west coast Florida by Hrdlička 1922.

Table 9-4
Postcranial Metrics: Comparative Data from Florida Sites

Measurements and Indexes	Sex	Fort Center Mean	N	Margate-Blount Mean	N	Bayshore Homes Mean	N	All Areas in Florida Mean	N
Humerus									
Maximum Length	M	—		326	3	306	3	323	18
	F	287	2	309	3	307	7	294	8
Maximum head	M	48	3	47	3	45	10	—	
diameter	F	41	6	41	2	41	7	—	
Maximum midshaft	M	—		24	3	25	7	24	40
diameter	F	21	2	21	3	22	8	21	45
Minimum midshaft	M	—		18	3	18	7	18	40
diameter	F	16	2	14	3	16	8	15	45
Robusticity index	M	—		19.9	3	21.3	3	—	
	F	19.4	2	17.0	3	19.9	6	—	
Femur									
Maximum length	M	445	4	444	1	432	3	—	
	F	420	2	—		416	4	—	

(Table 9-4, continued)

Measurements and Indexes	Sex	Fort Center Mean	N	Margate-Blount Mean	N	Bayshore Homes Mean	N	All Areas in Florida Mean	N
Bicondylar length	M	439	3	—		424	3	442	20
	F	417	2	—		417	4	409	8
Maximum head	M	44	3	46	1	46	8	—	
diameter	F	43	7	—		42	11	—	
Anterior-posterior shaft	M	30	10	31	1	34	5	31	86
diameter	F	27	5	—		28	9	26	36
Mediolateral shaft	M	26	2	26	1	27	5	27	86
diameter	F	24	5	—		25	9	24	36
Midshaft circumference	M	89	10	91	1	92	6	—	
	F	80	5	—		81	9	—	
Robusticity index	M	13.2	3	12.9	1	14.4	4	13.1	20
	F	12.3		—		13.1	4	11.9	8
Tibia									
Maximum length	M	368	5	374	1	379	1	367	12
	F	—		—		355	3	335	10
Anterior-posterior shaft	M	36	9	37	1	35	4	34	56
diameter	F	33	6	—		32	3	28	55
Mediolateral shaft	M	25	9	26	1	24	4	23	56
diameter	F	21	6	—		22	3	19	55
Midshaft circumference	M	85	10	—		93	4	—	
	F	79	3	—		85	3	—	
Platycnemic index	M	71.1	9	70.3	1	—		—	
	F	65.3	6	—		—		—	
Stature*	M	164.3	4	164.2	1	168.9	33	165.0	
		(163.4)	5	(164.5)	1				
	F	155.9	2	—	0	164.0	28	150.0	

Modified from Miller-Shaivitz 1986: Table 12 incorporating data from Margate-Blount by İşcan 1983, Bayshore Homes by Snow 1962, and all areas of Florida by Hrdlička 1922.
*Estimated from complete femora and tibiae according to Genovés 1967 for Fort Center and Margate-Blount; from unspecified bones according to Trotter and Gleser 1958 for Bayshore Homes; from unspecified bones according to Hrdlička 1922 for all areas in Florida. Values in parentheses are from tibiae.

mated 81 for both sexes, classifying the population as predominately brachycranic. Table 9-3 presents comparative data from the Margate-Blount, Bayshore Homes, and east and west coast sites. In general, the Fort Center people did not differ markedly from these other populations in cranial dimensions. The Margate-Blount sample displayed the lowest cranial index and the Bayshore Homes sample the greatest parietal thickness.

Postcranial data for adults from Fort Center and the comparative sites are summarized in Table 9-4. Several differences are apparent, despite the small sample sizes. The Fort Center population displays shorter humerus and tibia lengths and longer femur lengths than the other populations but more gracile transverse shaft dimensions (with the exception of tibia anteroposterior and transverse diameters). The average male stature was estimated as 164.3 cm ($N=4$) and the average female stature as 155.9 cm ($N=2$), similar to those for the Margate-Blount population but somewhat shorter than the other populations sampled.

Table 9-5 lists frequencies of selected pathological conditions, several of which are illustrated in Figures 9-3 through 9-7. The most prominent cranial pathology was hematologic in etiology: 8 of the 121 crania examined (6.6 percent) display the diagnostic lesions of porotic hyperostosis in bones of the vault, with some degree of parietal thickening. The three

Table 9-5
Paleopathology at Fort Center

Pathological Conditions	N	Cranial	Post-Cranial	%
Infections of Bone	6	1	5	1.8
Osteitis and periostitis	1	0	1	0.3
Osteomyelitis	4	0	4	1.2
Treponematosis	1	1	0	0.3
Tumors of Bone	5	5	0	1.5
Osteoma	1	1	0	0.3
Meningioma	1	1	0	0.3
Perforation	3	3	0	0.9
Diseases of Joints				
Osteoarthritis	22	0	22	6.8
Deformities	0	0	0	0.0
Trauma				
Fractures	21	4	17	6.5
Hematological Disorders				
Porotic hyperostosis	8	8	0	2.5
Disturbances Unknown	1	1	0	0.3
Wormian Bones	1	1	0	0.3
Synostoses	3	3	0	0.9

Number of bones examined includes both cranial and postcranial bones.
Some specimens display multiple lesions. Total $N=325$ bones examined.

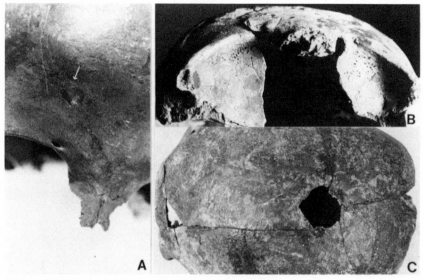

Figure 9-3
Cranial Pathology at Fort Center. (A) Specimen (#B69-81) with a button osteoma superior to the right brow ridge. (B) Subadult (#B68-66) with bilateral cribra orbitalia. (C) A specimen (#B68-11) with a single lytic lesion of both parietal bones.

subadults also display cribra orbitalia (Figure 9-3B), but this condition is absent in the five adults (three females, one male, and one of unknown sex).

Four skulls of adult males showed evidence of healed depressed fractures in the frontal, parietal, or lambdoid regions. One eighteen- to twenty-year-old female skull bore severe erosive lesions on frontal and parietals indicative of treponemal disease (Figure 9-4A and B): serpiginous cavitation without perforation on the ectocranial surface and slight pitting on the corresponding endocranial surface.

One adult cranium displays a button osteoma (Figure 9-3A), with a small erosive lesion immediately endocranial to the tumor. Another adult male aged thirty-six to fifty-five years displayed multiple cranial pathological lesions: a circular perforation near bregma, a depression inferior to lambda, medial bulging of the left supraorbital region, and a deformed and bulging nasion. The perforation is most likely the result of a neoplastic process, for example, meningioma (Figure 9-3C), and the depression may represent a healed fracture or premature fusion of the lambdoid suture.

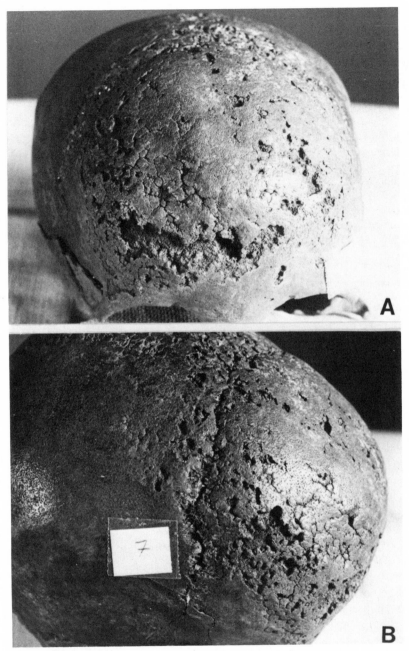

Figure 9-4
Cranium (#B69-45) with Possible Treponemiasis, Displaying Nodular and
Serpiginous Cavitation. (A) Frontal view. (B) Lateral view.

Table 9-6
Descriptive Statistics of Dental Conditions

VARIABLES	N	%
HYPOPLASIA ($N = 1,279$)		
None	1,204	94.14
Slight	30	2.35
Moderate	39	3.05
Heavy	6	0.47
CARIES ($N = 1,279$)		
Absent	1,244	97.26
Minor	20	1.56
Advanced	15	1.17
HYPERCEMENTOSIS ($N = 310$)		
Absent	285	91.94
Slight	9	2.90
Moderate	12	3.87
Heavy	4	1.29
CALCULUS ($N = 1,279$)		
Absent	902	70.52
Moderate	318	24.86
Heavy	59	4.61
DEGREE OF ATTRITION ($N = 1,279$)		
None	146	11.42
Enamel only	648	50.66
Dentine visible and enamel	409	31.98
Dentine visible only	71	5.55
Worn to neck	5	0.39
ALVEOLAR RESORPTION ($N = 630$)		
None	33	5.23
Up to 3 mm	337	53.49
3 mm to 6 mm	234	37.14
Over 6 mm	26	4.13
PERIAPICAL ABSCESS ($N = 381$)		
Absent	379	99.48
Present	2	0.52

Modified from Isler and İşcan 1986. N = teeth observed.

The dental features and pathology of the Fort Center population have previously been reported by Isler and İşcan (1986) and are summarized here in Table 9-6. Out of almost 1,300 teeth, only 3 percent displayed minor to advanced dental caries. Hypercementosis was observed on 8 percent of the observed roots. Fewer than 6 percent of the teeth displayed linear enamel hypoplasia, but some evidence of this developmental defect may have been obliterated by attrition: 38 percent of the teeth showed exposure of dentine. The most striking dental characteristics were the high percentage of alveolar resorption and the almost complete absence of periapical abscesses.

The most frequently observed postcranial pathological condition was osteoarthritis, followed by fractures and inflammation (osteomyelitis and periostitis). Radiographs revealed no trace of transverse growth arrest (Harris) lines in femora or tibiae. A total of twenty-two individual

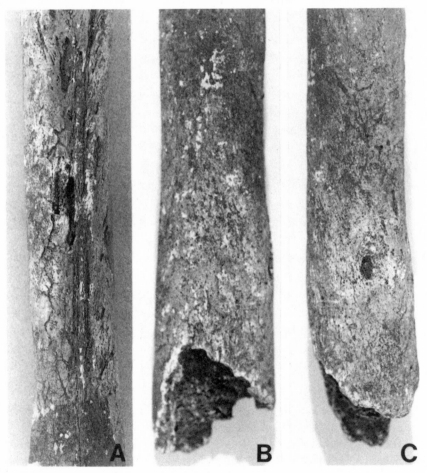

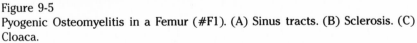

Figure 9-5
Pyogenic Osteomyelitis in a Femur (#F1). (A) Sinus tracts. (B) Sclerosis. (C) Cloaca.

bones displayed osteoarthritis: nineteen vertebrae (mostly lumbar), two radii, and one ulna.

Two tibiae and four femora exhibited gross evidence of inflammatory response. Periostitis was diagnosed in one tibia with two "frosted" lesions. A tibia with medial thickening and anterior bowing (boomerang shin) was diagnosed as another case of treponematosis (Figure 9-5A). One osteomyelitic femur displayed varying degrees of sclerotic reaction and a cloaca, involucrum, and sequestrum (Figure 9-5A-C). Fractures in the extremities were equally distributed between upper and lower limb bones. An example of a healed fracture of the distal humerus is illustrated in Figure 9-6B and C.

Pseudopathological conditions were also observed in eight long bones of the upper and lower extremities. Five bones (humerus, radius, femur, and two tibiae) displayed surface alterations evidently resulting from cultural manipulation (e.g., cutting) rather than from true pathology, animal gnawing, or environmental agents (e.g., weathering, root damage). The femur shaft (Figure 9-7A) shows several horizontal striated grooves. Another specimen, the proximal end of a left tibia (Figure 9-7B), bears eighteen notches or short horizontal grooves spaced 3 to 6 mm apart on the posterior surface. These grooves extend distally to about 49 mm inferior to the nutrient foramen, but their proximal limit is unknown because of damage to that region of the bone. The first groove trails off in a serpentine pattern. These marks may be the result of maceration (defleshing cuts).

Discussion and Conclusions

In spite of the difficulties involved in working with the fragmentary remains from Fort Center, it was possible to obtain selected information on health and physical characteristics. The sample consisted mainly of mature adults aged twenty-one to fifty-five years, with few subadults and no elderly (fifty-six years or older). As noted previously, this disproportionate representation may reflect differential preservation, burial, and/ or archaeological recovery. Females outnumbered males in the youngest adult age category, but this trend was reversed in the later years.

Osteometrically, the Fort Center population was generally similar to the other prehistoric Florida samples available for comparison. The femoral robusticity index is lower than the average for the Bayshore Homes sample but comparable to the averages for the samples reported by Hrdlička (1922). The Fort Center population was generally somewhat more gracile but approximately as tall as the other populations, with the

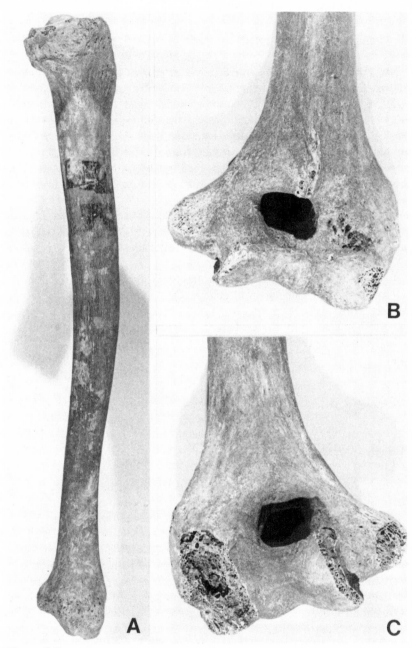

Figure 9-6
Postcranial Pathology. (A) "Boomerang shin" (medial thickening) in a left
tibia (#U27). (B) Anterior and (C) posterior surfaces of a left humerus
(#U71) showing a bony growth superior to the coronoid fossa and an en-
larged septum resulting from fracture.

Figure 9-7
Pseudopathology. (A) Right femur (#B98817) showing horizontal striated grooves. (B) Left tibia (#U-56) with eighteen small grooves on the posterior surface lateral to the nutrient foramen.

exception of the larger and more robust Bayshore Homes people.

In terms of skeletal pathology, both cranial and postcranial specimens displayed anomalies in growth and development, trauma, inflammatory response, and hematologic disorders. These conditions were not unique to this site but have been reported from other Florida sites as well (Hrdlička 1922; Snow 1962; Bullen 1972; Saunders 1972; Carr et al. 1984; İşcan and Miller-Shaivitz 1985).

Generalized bone inflammation (periostitis) was observed in several individuals, suggesting an infectious origin, and one individual displayed gummateous cranial lesions typical of treponemal disease. Similar lesions have been reported by Snow (1962) from the Bayshore Homes site, by Bullen (1972) for various sites, by İşcan (1983) for the Margate-Blount site, and by İşcan and Miller-Shaivitz (1985) from Highland Beach. Taken together, this evidence for treponemal disease in the Florida peninsula spans several centuries.

Some of the pseudopathological alterations on bones may reflect the mortuary maceration processes suggested by W. H. Sears (1982), for example, defleshing of skeletons prior to curation. These marks were observed only on one specimen, but the macerating tools commonly in use may not have regularly scored the surface of the bones if, for example, the fingernails of the morticians were employed in this task, as described elsewhere for the historic Choctaw (Swanton 1946; Kidwell and Roberts 1980).

The analysis of dental pathology suggested that the most outstanding problems were attrition and alveolar resorption (Isler et al. 1985; Isler and İşcan 1986). The prevalence of caries (3 percent of teeth) was low, suggesting that these people practiced a mixed subsistence economy. As indicated by Patterson's study of southern Ontario populations (1984), the caries rate approximates 1.5 percent for hunter-gatherer groups, 4.7 percent for those with mixed economies, and 11.8 percent for horticulturalists.

Hematologic disease is a good indicator of health status, as it reflects poor nutrition, other diseases, and parasite loads. Of the 121 Fort Center crania examined, 8 specimens (6.6 percent) display porotic hyperostosis, with the 3 subadults also displaying cribra orbitalia. It is assumed that they suffered from severe chronic iron-deficiency anemia resulting from bacterial and parasitic infections and/or iron-deficient diets.

Evidence of skeletal trauma may provide inferences about physical activities and stresses. Traumatic injuries at Fort Center include both skull and long-bone fractures. Several bones of the spine and appendicular skeleton display osteoarthritic changes. These lesions did not differ radically in frequency and anatomical location from those observed in the Bayshore Homes sample.

W. H. Sears (1982) saw the Fort Center site during the Period II phase as occupied by a group of mortuary specialists and their families, who may have been accorded superior social status by the inhabitants of the surrounding region whose bodies they ceremonially processed after death. The biological hypothesis drawn from this interpretation is that the Fort Center population might have enjoyed superior health, compared with their "constituents" in the region, because of a better diet and freedom from the typical round of arduous physical activities. The gracility of their long bones does suggest lower habitual levels of strenuous physical activity than, say, the inhabitants of the Margate-Blount site, and the low observed level of bone inflammation suggests a relatively healthy population. However, given the small sample size and the disarticulated and commingled nature of the skeletal remains available for study, these conclusions must be tentative at best. Further research at other major and minor sites in the Okeechobee Basin is essential for a better understanding of the lives of the prehistoric inhabitants of this rich and complex region.

Acknowledgments

The authors gratefully thank Stephen A. Shaivitz and Walda E. İşcan for their editorial comments. William Watkins, Denise R. DeFazio, and Ashley Abel at Florida Atlantic University provided photographic assistance. We appreciate the constructive criticisms of volume editors Mary Lucas Powell and Patricia S. Bridges.

❋ 10

Status and Health in Colonial South Carolina: Belleview Plantation, 1738–1756

Ted A. Rathbun and James D. Scurry

Variations in social rank within complex sociopolitical systems are often considered to influence differential access to valued goods and services. It is often assumed that factors that influence longevity, growth, and health in general are preferentially available to *particular* social classes. Our colleagues in social anthropology have documented such differential access in the economic and political realms, and archaeologists have attempted to reconstruct social systems through dwelling, mortuary, and artifact analysis (Chapman et al. 1981). But only recently have bioarchaeologists begun to examine the biological consequences of differential status, as expressed in the skeletal system. Several recent osteological studies discuss the various pitfalls in assuming that overall patterns of skeletal data necessarily indicate similar types of underlying social and biological phenomena. Palkovich (1983) rightly points out that some factors may be enhanced or disguised by superimposed patterns in social stratification. Cook (1983) makes a convincing argument for considering the importance of regional or historically specific factors for patterns of biological differences associated with status. Other examples of the consequences of cultural change upon the skeletal system have been presented (Milner 1983a; Goodman et al. 1983; Larsen 1983b; Bradtmiller 1983). The gender and age differences that affect the division of labor, participation in certain activities, and access to specific resources may also vary with types of stratified society.

The plantation system as developed in South Carolina during the Colonial period is a peculiar example of a highly stratified society. Social position was institutionally marked by biological ancestry with rigid boundaries for participation in the social, economic, and political spheres of society. The inhumanity of this system is well known, but only recently have the biological consequences and archaeological evidence come under examination. It is often assumed that the plantation slavery system over wide areas was essentially the same and that the systematized social inequities necessarily produced health differences between the status groups. Gibbs and co-workers (1980), in their study of nutrition in slave society from historical and archaeological sources, argue convincingly that such research should focus on specific eco-zones within a limited time frame. The ideal osteological research strategy, of course, would include large samples of ancestral, contemporary, and descendant groups. Inasmuch as ascribed status was a significant feature of this stratified system, those activities based on gender and age should also be examined and compared both diachronically and synchronically.

The data on slaves and masters presented here, however, had a more serendipitous origin. No large population samples are available, so the sample discussed here is compared with data from similar limited studies. Although the sample from the Belleview Plantation of the coastal ecozone in South Carolina is quite small, comparisons with other groups from similar times in other areas reveal some shared aspects. Empirical skeletal data on mortality, general health indicators, and nutritional factors do not support the contention of wide differences between high- and low-status groups with respect to health. This statement should in no way be construed as an apology for the slavery system, but as Gibbs suggested, the lack of significant differences "may be considered as evidence that the black slaves actively participated in changing their diet and thereby increased their chances for survival" (Gibbs et al. 1980:177). The majority of the skeletons from Belleview are probably from the Edward Croft family, who owned the plantation from 1738 to 1756. Detailed comparisons with other planters and slave groups during the Colonial period appear to reflect a commonality rather than marked differences between status groups.

Belleview Plantation: The Setting

Belleview Plantation is located west of U.S. Highway 17 near Charleston, South Carolina. It encompasses 561 acres that border on the Wando River to the north and west and on Hobcaw Creek to the south. Available historical documents indicate that the plantation originally consisted of four separate tracts that were consolidated into the present configuration in 1841 (CCRRMC/Y-10:377–78). The name Belleview was given to the plantation sometime prior to the Civil War, as it first appears on a record of conveyance in 1862 (CCRRMC/R-14:263).

The economic development of Belleview can be described generally as a combination of agricultural and industrial bases with shifting periods of emphasis. During the first two-thirds of the eighteenth century, the primary economic activity was plantation agriculture. This conclusion is suggested by the wills and inventories of several of the owners that list slaves, cattle, sheep, and a variety of agricultural products among their property (CCROPJIAS/R-2:531–32). Of particular interest is the will of Edward Croft that bequeathes the produce from his orange groves to his wife and sons (SCRSSW/1752–1756/7:501–03). While the production of oranges was not uncommon in South Carolina during the Colonial period, most were grown for home consumption (Gray 1958:826). Records indicate, however, that the groves at Belleview exceeded 4,000 trees (Jones 1958:194n).

By the end of the Colonial period, general agricultural productivity in Christ Church Parish had declined as the soils in the area had been overworked and exhausted (PSPG/B-17:174). During the 1760s, shipbuilding began to replace agriculture as the primary economic activity. This shift is suggested by the sudden influx of four known shipwrights into the Belleview area and by a series of plats that indicate the construction of a shipyard on the southern portion of the plantation (Bolling 1786:79). This rise of shipbuilding in the Belleview area is generally consistent with the growth of shipbuilding in other areas of the state, as a series of shipyards were built in South Carolina between 1740 and 1773 (Sellers 1934:62–63).

During the nineteenth century, Belleview Plantation appears to have been used as a residence with some small-scale commercial and subsistence agriculture. This pattern of land use continued into the late 1950s, when the property was sold to Gulf Oil Corporation. It was maintained as a recreational/hunting retreat until 1973, when the plantation was purchased by the South Carolina State Ports Authority and scheduled for marine port facilities development.

Recovery of the Skeletal Samples

In 1979, an archaeological survey of the plantation was conducted in anticipation of proposed construction of marine terminal and docking facilities. At the time of the survey, approximately 100 acres of the tract had been cleared. In the process, a large limestone vault marker and several smaller crypt fragments were recovered from a 70 by 90–m area. The marker displayed an epitaph to Edward Croft, but no date or mention of others in the vault was included. Shovel testing in the immediate area of the crypt materials failed to locate any burials, and recommendations were made for the machine removal of the upper 1 to 1.5 feet of disturbed overburden and inspection of the undisturbed and lighter strata below. This procedure also failed to locate any burials or associated features, as the original clearing activities had moved the crypt materials much further than indicated by the scatter of debris. During the construction of the docking facilities, however, several skull and long bone fragments were recovered from an equipment maintenance excavation. A 50 by 50–foot area was pedestaled and preserved while construction of the dock continued. Subsequent salvage excavations by volunteers produced thirteen clusters of human skeletal material in differing stages of preservation and articulation (Figure 10-1). Subsequent construction in the area revealed four additional individuals from an adjacent construction backfill deposit.

Five of the bone clusters represented relatively intact burials that contained some coffin and clothing items. Burials 2 and 3 produced several bone buttons, coffin nails and handles, and a fragment of cypress wood with an elaborate design of brass tacks. Noel-Hume (1969:157–58) notes that many coffins had their occupant's name and date of death embossed across the coffin lid. Unfortunately, however, the information originally contained on the wood could not be determined from the fragmentary section. Similarly, the iron coffin nails and handles were corroded beyond temporal identification. Several of the more intact individuals had a green stain on the skull or other bone, probably from shroud pins.

Historical and Demographic Profile of the Edward Croft Family

While positive identification of the individuals interred at Belleview is as yet unsubstantiated, both historical and demographic data indicate that the majority of the burials probably represent the remains of the family of Edward Croft. This conclusion is suggested by the vault marker with his name inscribed and by a plat of the plantation that places a vault in the general vicinity of the burial and vault marker locations (Payne 1843).

Although the exact date of Croft's acquisition of Belleview is unknown, available historical sources indicate that by 1738 Croft maintained the plantation with thirty-eight slaves. In addition to his planting activities, Croft also owned retail stores in Charleston and Georgetown and was active in the Indian trade (Edgar and Bailey 1977:175). Listed among his other property were lots in Beaufort and Georgetown, a 500-acre plantation on the Winyah River, a 55-ton ship, and a pew in St. Philip's Church in Charleston (SCRSSW/1752–1756/7:501–03).

Croft was also very active in local affairs and politics. In 1745 he was

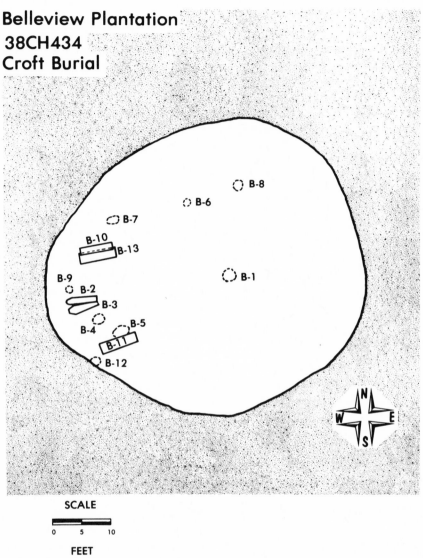

Belleview Plantation
38CH434
Croft Burial

SCALE

0   5   10

FEET

Figure 10-1
Burial Distribution at Belleview Plantation, South Carolina

elected to the fourteenth royal assembly from Prince George Winyah Parish. He also served as tax collector and inquirer for Christ Church Parish, tax inquirer for the city of Charleston, judge of the Admiralty Court, and captain in the militia (Edgar and Bailey 1977:175).

Because the records of Christ Church Parish were destroyed, little is known about the complete structure of the family. Available records indicate, however, that Edward married three times and had a total of sixteen children (nine, three, and four, respectively, with each wife). The deaths of at least three of the children before they reached maturity is suggested by the reuse of certain names with subsequent children.

Edward died in 1756 and willed his Belleview property to his wife and son Edward Peter (SCRSSW/1752–1756/501–03). The plantation was maintained by the younger Croft until the 1760s when it was sold to J. Mortimer Williams, a shipwright.

While complete reconstruction of the Belleview burial sample is impossible, several inferences may be made concerning its structure. It seems most probable that the plantation remained under Croft ownership until the death of Edward's third wife. This arrangement would have allowed for Croft and all three wives to be interred there. In addition, the three children that died before reaching maturity should also be included. Given the demographic patterns of Colonial populations, this distribution would indicate that a minimum group of one adult male aged fifty-five to sixty, three adult females, and three children would be in the family cemetery. The other skeletal remains in the immediate vicinity most probably represent other members of the extended family. Enough cranial material was preserved to allow morphological evaluation for racial diagnosis of several individuals as white. Fragmentary skeletal remains were circumstantially identified as representing members of the white population segment by the grave materials and general morphological characters. At least two of the skeletons from the adjacent backfill deposit appear to be of black individuals, based upon morphological aspects of the pelvis and complete femora (Stewart 1979; Gilbert 1976).

Osteological Analysis and Comparative Samples

After the initial finds, the skeletal material was removed by volunteers under less than ideal archaeological conditions in a race with the construction schedule. The local archaeological community was, unfortunately, less than enthusiastic about the potential importance of such material, despite efforts made to emphasize the importance of human remains as a historical and archaeological resource (Rathbun 1981).

The basic osteological analysis was complicated by the fragmentary and poorly preserved nature of some of the bone. However, a variety of data sets was obtained for comparisons with other samples. At this time, only the dental data from the site have been thoroughly analyzed. The Newton Plantation on Barbados (Corruccini et al. 1982) can serve as a base for some comparisons for the blacks of Belleview Plantation, because slaves entering Charleston were often transshipped from there. Specific African origins for South Carolina slaves have been suggested by Pollitzer (1958). Angel (1976) also provides data on Colonial blacks and whites as well as seventeenth-century English and modern black and white samples. Skeletal information on the Colonial planters and slaves at Clifts Plantation in Virginia is provided by Aufderheide et al. (1981). Other data for blacks were gleaned from unpublished reports from College Landing in Virginia and Catoctin Furnace in Maryland (Angel 1977, 1980; Angel and Kelley 1983).

The lead content analysis of the Belleview skeletal series, as well as that from Clifts, College Landing, and Catoctin Furnace, was conducted by Aufderheide et al. (1982) using a well-established methodology (Wittmers et al. 1981).

Results

Mortality is often considered a sensitive measure of health status and of the successful adaptation of a population. During the Colonial period, historical sources indicate a higher mortality rate, especially of children, than is reflected in the various skeletal series available today. Corruccini et al. (1982) reported a twenty-year life expectancy from historical records of the Barbados plantation, but his skeletal sample indicated a twenty-nine-year life expectancy and much lower infant and child mortality than the records reflected. At the Belleview Plantation, age at death after fifteen years for the white population sample (Table 10-1) is generally comparable to that at Clifts and slightly lower for males than the Colonial U.S. average. The black individuals at Belleview were over forty years of age at death.

Gibbs and co-workers (1980:205) suggest that slave female mortality from childbirth complications was significantly lower than for whites; however, census data from Charleston from 1822 to 1848 reflect a mortality rate of 19/100 for black and 9/100 for white infants. Mortality rates from all causes were 178/10,000 for blacks and 111/10,000 for whites, with the major cause of childhood death for both groups being diarrhea and for adults, tuberculosis. Respiratory and nervous system disorders accounted for many other deaths in both groups and age categories. Discrepancies between historical and skeletal data must be evaluated

Table 10-1
Age at Death: Belleview Plantation and Comparative Data

I. Belleview Plantation: Age at Death

	B–2	3–6	7–12	13–20	21–30	31–40	+40	Adult
Whites	1	2	2	2 M?	1-F	2-F	1-M	2
							1-F	
Blacks							1-M	
							1-F	

II. Mean Adult Age at Death

	Belleview	Clifts[1]	College Landing[1]	Catoctin Furnace[1]	Colonial U.S.[2]	Modern U.S.[2]
White male	30.3	31.8			39.6	43.8
White female	32.0	37.0			31.9	38.6
Black male	+ 40	30.5	36.3	35.7	35.7	42.0
Black female	+ 45	34.0	36.3	35.4	38.6	31.3

[1]Comparative data from Aufderheide et al. 1981.
[2]Comparative data from Angel 1976.

before final conclusions can be drawn, but generally speaking, the average lifespan was short for both whites and slaves.

Infection

A major contributing factor to early mortality for both groups, according to historical sources, appears to be acute infection (Table 10-2). Chronic infection at Belleview was not reflected in the skeletal material. Although all the white males had slight evidence of localized periosteal infections, sample size precludes conclusive statements. Episodic interruption of normal growth reflected in the dentition and postcranial skeleton may be related to a variety of infections. Malaria was endemic to this ecozone, and periodic epidemics occurred. Yellow fever, scarlet fever, typhoid, and typhus epidemics are well documented in the area during the Colonial period. Differential mortality due to prior population adaptation and exposure to childhood diseases such as mumps, measles, chicken pox, and whooping cough has been reported (Gibbs et al. 1980:202). Whooping cough was a major cause of death for infants in both groups. Treatment through purging and bloodletting

Table 10-2
Nonspecific Infections

	Belleview Plantation	Clifts[1]	College Landing[1]	Catoctin Furnace[1]
White male	3/3	0/3	—	—
White female	1/3	0/1	—	—
White subadult	0/5	—	—	—
Total	4/11 (36%)	0/4		
Black male	1/1	1/6	2/6	2/9
Black female	0/1	0/3	1/8	2/8
Black subadult	—	0/3	0/3	0/4
Total	1/2 (50%)	1/12 (8%)	3/17 (18%)	4/31 (13%)

[1]Comparative data from Angel 1976, 1977, 1980; Aufderheide et al. 1981.

probably exacerbated the effects of the diseases. Other local health factors include intestinal parasites, which were especially common from April through October. Hookworm was particularly harmful, and other intestinal worms such as threadworm, various tapeworms, and roundworm were common. Bacilliary and amoebic infections also contributed to the death rate through diarrhea and dysentery for both the white and the slave groups.

Stature

Analysis of stature as a generally accepted indicator of health is complicated by the varying origins of both the black and the white immigrants of the seventeenth century. Although a secular increase in adult body size of American populations in the recent century is well known, the effects of diet and living conditions in early eighteenth-century South Carolina was less well documented. Angel (1976) has cautioned us about accepting a rapid or a steady rate of increase from this period to present times.

The average stature of the white males at Belleview is comparable to the 169.3 cm average for seventeenth-century London, but the Belleview females, white with an average of 162.0 cm, are considerably taller than the 155.2 average white female Londoner from that time (Table 10-3). The black males also show a strong similarity to the average heights of West African males (165.3 cm), but no base data for females of these probable ancestral groups are available. The one black female at Belleview was 5 cm taller than the 155.9 cm average of other Colonial blacks

Table 10-3
Mean Stature Estimates

	White Male	White Female	Black Male	Black Female
Belleview	170.3	162.0	166.0	161.0
Clifts Plantation	168.9	163.7	171.6	157.0
College Landing	—	—	—	162.0
Catoctin Furnace	—	—	—	156.4
1600s London	169.3	155.5	171.6	—
Colonial U.S.	173.4	159.8	172.0	155.9
Modern U.S.	174.1	163.6	169.0	161.2

Stature in cm from formulae developed by Trotter 1970.

Comparative data from Aufderheide et al. 1981; Angel 1976, 1977, 1980.

and was similar to modern averages. The different biological background of the blacks and whites at Belleview complicate any assessment of status difference related to stature.

Harris Lines

Radiographic examination of selected adult long bones revealed a range in frequency of interruptions of normal growth and recovery. The average number of growth disruption episodes for white males at Belleview was 3.0, with a range of 0, 3, and 6 lines. White females showed an average of 1.7, with a range of 0, 1, and 4 lines. The black male had 7 lines, and the female had only 1. Statistical differences could not be evaluated due to sample size and lack of data from comparable groups. It should be noted that the males in both groups at Belleview appear to be more susceptible than females in the expression of this trait. The multiple occurrences of the Harris lines generally coincided with linear enamel hypoplasia of the dentition among the whites. No teeth were recovered from the slave sample.

Trauma and Fractures

Trauma and fractures in a skeletal population reflect the level of violence or work-related accidents. Angel (1976) attributed the significant rise of fractures, particularly to the head, from the Colonial period to modern times to violence. Fractures were relatively rare at the Belleview plantation: only one child and one adult male exhibited healed fractures to the radius.

Indicators of possible work-related stress were noted in both black and white groups at Belleview. Because the sample is relatively young, degenerative changes in the vertebral column were minimal, but stress herniations of vertebral disks were noted in the young males, and lower back stress was evident in the female skeletons, both young and old, white and black. Some hip stress around the acetabula was also present for both racial groups. The primary contrast between the two groups was the more marked stress at the shoulder joint for the black individuals. This response has been noted for the Clifts Plantation workers, and Angel and Kelley (1983) attribute this response to heavy lifting by the ironworkers at Catoctin Furnace, Maryland.

Dentition

A decline in dental health has been documented from the Colonial to the modern period (Angel 1976). Antemortem tooth loss is associated with advancing age as well as poor dental hygiene. At Belleview, both blacks and whites had lost most of their molars before death. In comparison with contemporary groups, the whites appear to have a slightly higher rate of tooth loss. Table 10-4 indicates the number of teeth lost per dentition. Tooth loss was also frequent in the slave populations on Barbados, with 51 percent of the sample exhibiting at least one lost tooth (Corruccini et al. 1982). The high rate of hypercementosis noted for these slaves was not evident for either slaves or planters at Belleview.

Carious lesions were frequent among the whites at Belleview Plantation, and all adults showed at least one lesion. Both crown and interproximal caries were present. Table 10-4 indicates the number of teeth per mouth affected. No clear differences were evident between black and white dentitions. Among slaves in the Caribbean, 20 percent of the sample had crown caries and 57 percent had interproximal caries (Corruccini et al. 1982). At Belleview, all adults exhibited at least one carious lesion. The mean number of lesions per dentition was 2.7 for males and 1.8 for females.

Linear enamel hypoplasia is often considered an indicator of developmental or metabolic insult. The enamel defects occurred universally among the whites at Belleview, with the lines being palpable and in many instances multiple. Females were less affected than were males, both in severity and in frequency.

Table 10-4
Antemortem Tooth Loss, Linear Enamel Hypoplasia, and Dental Caries: Comparative Data

I. Mean Number of Teeth Lost Antemortem				
	Belleview	Clifts	Catoctin Furnace	Colonial U.S.	Modern U.S.
White male	8.0	1.7	—	6.9	12.2
White female	6.3	32.0	—	8.5	9.6
Total	7.2	16.8	—	7.7	9.6
Black male	5.0	6.2	8.0	6.7	9.4
Black female	—	3.0	8.0	6.8	8.8
Total	5.0	4.6	8.0	6.8	9.1
II. Mean Number Linear Enamel Hypoplasias Per Individual				
White male	4.3	—	—	1.8	1.6
White female	1.8	—	—	2.0	1.6
White subadult	2.5	—	—	—	—
Black male	—	—	—	1.6	2.0
Black female	—	—	—	1.5	—
III. Mean Number Carious Lesions Per Individual				
White male	2.7	3.7	—	2.4	3.8
White female	1.8	—	—	4.2	5.5
Total	2.2	3.7	—	3.3	4.7
Black male	—	5.3	—	2.3	4.9
Black female	—	5.7	—	4.1	1.9
Black subadult	—	6.7	—	—	1.9
Total	—	5.9	—	3.2	3.4

Comparative data from Angel 1976, 1980.

The ubiquitous nature of hypoplasia was noted among slaves in Barbados, with 97 percent of the anterior and 99 percent of the posterior teeth showing at least one lesion. American slave frequencies could not be determined, but six of fifteen individuals at Clifts Plantation are reported as exhibiting the dental defect (Angel, personal communication, 1976), but it is unclear whether they occurred among the planters or the workers. One black female at College Landing had "striking" lesions that had formed between 2 and 4.5 years of age (Angel 1977).

The frequency and age of occurrence of the defects suggest both cultural and biological features. Among the Belleview whites, multiple relatively severe episodes are noted. Females were less frequently affected than males and the lesions were less severe. The age of occur-

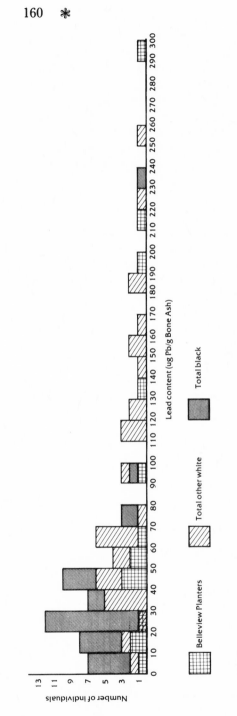

Figure 10-2
Frequency Distribution of Lead Content in Skeletal Populations from Virginia, Georgia, Maryland, and Belleview Plantation, South Carolina

rence, as determined by the methodology of Goodman et al. (1983), varies throughout childhood but peaks between ages three and four. Although the peak at approximately age four among the Barbados slaves was attributed to nutritional inadequacy (Corruccini et al. 1982), especially at weaning, it is unlikely that this explanation is the only cause among the whites at Belleview. The synergistic effects of parasites and fevers with metabolic disturbance, rather than simple nutritional inadequacy, is a more likely explanation for the defects occurrence in this group. It is unfortunate that no teeth from the slave sample at Belleview were available for examination.

Skeletal Lead Content

Differences in the skeletal lead burden of landowners and workers in the Colonial plantation system have been documented (Aufderheide et al. 1981). Samples from the Belleview skeletons, when analyzed by the same methodology (Wittmers et al. 1981), revealed a similar pattern (Table 10-5). The white sample at both plantations revealed a high level

Table 10-5
Skeletal Lead Content: Belleview Plantation Whites

Burial No.	Lead Content (mg/g ash)	Bone	Age (years)	Sex
B-1	1.88	Tibia	50–60	M
B-2	29.21	Tibia	35–39	F
B-3	51.36	Tibia	18–22	F
B-4	45.23	Rib	?	?
B-5	16.21	Fibula	7–8	?
B-6	41.93	Tibia	?	?
B-7	67.47	Femur?	3–5	?
B-9	220.50	Rib	?	?
B-11	138.00	Tibia	16–18	M
B-12	15.80	Rib	7–8	?
B-13	56.16	Tibia	35–40	F
Male $\bar{X}$	76.8			
Female $\bar{X}$	89.3			
Subadult $\bar{X}$	43.0			
Total $\bar{X}$	69.7			

of skeletal lead that is probably attributable to food preparation and storage methods. Comparisons with other seventeenth- and eighteenth-century groups reveal a consistent difference between whites and blacks, the latter both of slave and freed status (Figure 10-2). Skeletal inclusion of lead is, of course, age progressive, but the total differences as well as the individual variation revealed through analysis of variance (Table 10-6) showed some interesting significant differences by sex, location, and social status.

The skeletal lead content of the whites at Belleview had a mean value of 69.7 mg/g, which fell between the planters (mean 111.3) and workers (mean 31.4) at Clifts Plantation in Virginia. Analysis of variance comparing Belleview whites to all blacks indicated a significantly elevated level among the whites. Aufderheide et al. (1985) report a mean range for whites of 52.8–111.3 and for blacks of 29.2–41.9 during the Colonial period. When Belleview whites were compared to other white samples, no significant differences were noted. Within regional white samples, the Middle Atlantic groups had a slightly higher lead burden than those of the Southeast. These southern whites, however, carried a significantly higher lead burden than did the Middle Atlantic blacks. Aufderheide et al. (1982) indicate an average lead burden of 67.7 mg/g bone ash for white skeletons associated with Irene Mound in Georgia.

Regional comparisons through variance analysis indicated that both sexes in the white groups had significantly higher lead burdens than their black counterparts. No significant difference by gender was evident within the white samples, but black females had significantly higher levels than the black males. Differential access by females to food prepared for the white masters and their families is the most likely explanation for this difference. Aufderheide et al. (1981) provide a plausible example at Clifts Plantation in Virginia.

The deleterious effects of significant lead exposure among the Roman and eighteenth-century English aristocracy have received considerable recent attention (Nriagu 1983). Hodge (1981) discounts the popular notion of lead poisoning from water pipes in ancient Rome. No evidence of saturnine gout could be documented from the Belleview or other Colonial skeletal samples, but it is interesting to conjecture about the contribution of a high lead burden to the second- and third-leading causes of death for children and adults in the 1850 Charleston census: nervous system disorders. Prasad (1978:366) summarized a number of clinical features of lead toxicity that involve the nervous system.

Osteological analysis of skeletal lead content has the potential for an important contribution to the study of biological correlates of social class. Contamination of skeletal samples by groundwater must always

Table 10-6
Comparison of Bone Lead Levels in Blacks and Whites: Analysis of Variance

Sample groups	F-Statistics	Critical Value @ 0.05
Belleview and total blacks:	14.51	3.99**
Belleview and total whites:	0.10	4.02
Whites and blacks (non-Belleview)	20.03	3.94**
Total black female and total white female	15.39	3.22**
Total black female and total black male	9.20	3.18**
Total black male and total white male	16.91	3.15**
Total white female and total white male	0.19	3.18
Middle Atlantic blacks and Southern whites*	8.09	3.11**
Middle Atlantic whites and Southern whites*	3.55	3.15**

*Comparative data from Aufderheide et al. 1981; Aufderheide et al. 1982; and Aufderheide et al. 1985.
**The null hypothesis for all tests is that the two sample groups are equal so conclude significant differences in the sample.

be considered (Waldron 1983), but at Belleview none of the grave materials had significant lead content, and the soil had a lead level of 21 mg/g soil and a pH of 6. The water from shallow aquifers in the area is less than .05 mg of lead per liter of water.

Conclusions

Although the sample sizes of master and slave groups at the Belleview Plantation in South Carolina are inadequate for conclusive statements, it appears that health similarities were more pronounced than were differences between these two groups of clearly unequal social status. The skeletal lead burden was more severe in the white sample than in the black. Comparisons with other Colonial samples seem to complement these findings. The workloads of the black and white groups differed, with the black slaves generally performing more physically demanding tasks. Even with the very marked difference in living conditions, the general level of health, dietary adequacy, and exposure to infections as inferred by skeletal pathology showed no major differences on the basis of social position. Instead, both groups were subject to similar burdens posed by their environment. Gender and age differences within and between the social groups are another aspect that must be considered in evaluating the effects of status upon skeletal system in subsequent studies.

The analysis of the Belleview samples and comparisons with other Colonial groups support the contention that empirical analysis of specific populations in their unique ecological and cultural settings yields a more specifically accurate picture of health conditions than modeling from historical and deductive perspectives alone.

Acknowledgments

A number of individuals have contributed to the completion of this research. Thanks are extended to the construction company at the Charleston, South Carolina, Ports Authority for accommodating the salvage activities; the students in the 1979 University of South Carolina Human Osteology class who helped excavate, reconstruct, and preserve skeletal materials; Kate Singley and John and Carolyn Winberry for their volunteer efforts; Kathryn Propst for her contributions in data collection and final manuscript preparation; and Cheryl M. Fowler, Dorothy Tart, and Willa Stevens for table and manuscript production. Special thanks are extended to Joann Walgren and A. C. Aufderheide for the lead analysis. The late Dr. J. Lawrence Angel of the Smithsonian Institution kindly provided unpublished data from other Colonial sites for comparative analysis.

✳ 11

Bioarchaeology in a Broader Context

Bruce D. Smith

Over the past two decades the Midwest and Southeast have witnessed a dramatic expansion of the archaeological data base, due primarily to changes in federal law and the resultant healthy increase in funding for archaeology. Paralleling this expansion has been a less widely recognized but equally dramatic upsurge in innovative problem-oriented research. This upsurge, due in most part to the recent abundance of young scholars doing research in these regions, has placed midwestern/ southeastern archaeology at the forefront of the discipline in terms of the complexity of research questions asked and the quality of the answers obtained. Rather than being based on the shrill promises of some newly proposed ideological proto-paradigm, the recent innovative development of archaeology in America's heartland represents a reorientation of research design within the context of a long-standing atmosphere of "normal science." Thus while the broad research goals pursued in midwestern/southeastern archaeology today are not all that different from those identified twenty years ago, the paths for approaching those goals are far more numerous and often go in rather unexpected directions. The establishment of these new pathways to knowledge also reflects a significant maturing of the discipline of archaeology in terms of both the perceived and the realized informative value of different categories of archaeological information.

How these changes in both the anticipated and the realized contributions of different data categories represent a maturation of the discipline can be briefly outlined. A long-standing, and in many situations still operative, template for doing archaeology features a principal investigator archaeologist as organizer and primary intellectual force. This individual oversees data collection and performs the analysis of the "real" archaeological materials recovered, that is, the lithics and ceramics. While recognized as important under the banner of interdisciplinary studies, materials representing "peripheral" data categories (e.g., plant remains, human and animal bones, and so forth) are handed over to specialists for analysis, and their reports are included as separate chapters or, all too commonly, as appendixes in the final publication. While these specialists provide narrowly focused analyses within their areas of expertise, it is the archaeologist/organizer who addresses, in the concluding interpretive chapters, any broader issues of importance for which such peripheral data sets might have relevance.

Why would other data categories be considered peripheral to rocks and potsherds? Lithic and ceramic assemblages (along with *modified* items of bone and shell) were of premiere importance within the Midwest Taxonomic System because they played such a major role in establishing the degree of cultural similarity between archaeological assemblages recovered from different sites. In addition, formal attributes of ceramic and lithic artifacts continue to be of great value as sensitive temporal markers. It should also be mentioned that a wide range of new and quite innovative research questions are now being addressed through analysis of lithic and ceramic assemblages. But the same can also be said of the "peripheral" data categories, particularly as increasing numbers of researchers trained in anthropology have become interested in the information potential of archaeological materials other than lithics and ceramics. They have begun to seek answers to both new and long-standing research questions through analysis of these once marginal data sets, and they have begun to develop innovative methodologies and techniques to obtain them. As a result, the distinction between "core" and "peripheral" data sets (and researchers) has broken down to a substantial extent, with the value of each category of archaeological material determined by its relevance to the specific research questions under scrutiny.

As these once peripheral data categories gain parity with lithics and ceramics in terms of acknowledged research potential, the roles assumed by researchers working with the data categories have also changed. Narrowly focused specialized treatments, addressing research questions devised either by the project organizer or by the discipline most closely related to the particular data category (e.g., botany, zoology, physical anthropology, and so forth), are being replaced with increasing frequency by research oriented directly at answering the broader anthropological questions usually addressed only by the "real archaeologist" project organizers.

This trend toward data category equality understandably has caused some uncertainty and unease, particularly within the ranks of the "real archaeologists"—those having analytical expertise limited to lithics and ceramics—who have reservations about "peripheral data category specialists" not only approaching the "big house" but actually stepping up on the front porch to speak about major questions of prehistory. An atmosphere of ambivalence still sometimes settles over the front porch in such situations, with the challenge, "What you doing up by the big house?" left unspoken only because of the overriding urge to hear what the intruders have to say.

At the same time, the speakers may often be somewhat difficult to categorize, adding another aspect of ambiguity. This difficulty in categorization in turn constitutes another healthy symptom of maturation of the discipline, in that it reflects an accelerating tendency for archaeologists to develop greater expertise in any and all data categories that appear to hold the promise of shedding light on research questions that interest them. As a result, archaeologists are now often characterized according to a particular research focus—for example, the development of complex societies—rather than by specialization in a particular data category or time period.

The emergence of bioarchaeology, as illustrated by the chapters in this edited volume, provides an excellent example of the three general trends in midwestern/southeastern archaeology briefly outlined above: (1) data set parity; (2) innovative pursuit of ways in which once peripheral data sets can yield new information relevant to major research questions; and (3) an accelerating tendency for researchers to gain first-hand expertise in the analysis of a variety of different data sets, all of which relate to research questions of interest.

Human skeletal material constitutes the primary data category analyzed in each chapter, and Larsen's and Ruff's statement (Chapter 7) aptly describes the orientation of the authors: "These data are pertinent to broader issues in prehistory." Each of the chapters addresses such issues within a regional framework of analysis and a long-term developmental perspective. The inclusion of burial populations from Florida, South Carolina, Georgia, Alabama, Tennessee, Illinois, Arkansas, Louisiana, and Mississippi gives the volume a well-balanced geographical coverage (Figure 1-1).

With the exception of the study by Ann Marie Wagner Mires (Chapter 8) of the Late Archaic burial population from the Cowpen Slough site in Louisiana, the chapters all share a general concern with the adaptational success of agricultural populations. Miller-Shaivitz and İşcan (Chapter 9) find no evidence to support Sears's contentions that the ca. A.D. 200–600 Fort Center burial population from south Florida was both agricultural and elite. The examination of health at Belleview Plantation by Rathbun and Scurry (Chapter 10) impressively demonstrates the invaluable contribution that analysis of historic period burial populations can make to a fuller and more accurate understanding of eighteenth-century plantation lifeways; it also illustrates the need to master and combine historical, bioarchaeological, and archaeological data sets to gain such an improved understanding.

The remaining six chapters (2–7) all address either the initial emergence, subsequent development, or eventual decline of the late prehistoric ranked agricultural societies of the Midwest/Southeast that are commonly lumped together under the general descriptive label of "Mississippian." The authors of these six chapters make a point of emphasizing (as do Rathbun and Scurry) that a far-ranging cultural phenomenon such as the Mississippian tradition must be approached not as a monolithic and homogeneous processual problem with a single universally applicable set of explanations but rather as a mosaic of regionally distinct and sometimes quite different developmental trajectories: "Empirical analysis of specific populations in their unique ecological and cultural settings yields a more specifically accurate picture of health conditions than modeling from historical and deductive perspectives alone" (Rathbun and Scurry, Chapter 10).

The necessity of regional analysis is underscored by the biomechanical studies of pre-Mississippian and Mississippian populations in northwestern Alabama (Bridges, Chapter 6) and coastal Georgia (Larsen and Ruff, Chapter 7). Bridges documents an increase in upper arm strength (specifically the distal humerus and proximal ulna regions for flexor and extensor attachment) for females in the agricultural (Mississippian) burial population of the Pickwick Reservoir relative to earlier Archaic populations, and she links this increase to the long arduous hours spent by late prehistoric women pounding maize in wooden mortars. This skeletal indicator of the processing of maize (or other indigenous cultigens?) has obvious important applications as another biological marker of the initial shift to, and intensity of, a population's dependence on foods processed by that technique.

The chapters by Milner, Powell, and Eisenberg further illustrate the diverse results of regionally specific analyses and interpretation. Eisenberg (Chapter 5) describes the poor health status of the Averbuch burial population (central Tennessee, A.D. 1275–1400) and suggests that the skeletal evidence for poor nutrition and chronic infection can be linked to competition and conflict over agricultural land, with resulting population nucleation. High population density in turn led to higher infection rates and chronic nutritional problems, which had an adverse impact on social and biological reproduction and general level of adaptive success. While the precontact decline of Middle Cumberland polities, including the one represented by the Averbuch cemeteries, may well have followed a course similar to the one outlined by Eisenberg, the Moundville (Alabama), and American Bottom (Illinois) populations described by Powell (Chapter 3) and Milner (Chapter 4), respectively, exhibit relatively few indications of inadequate nutrition or poor response to high disease loads, "it is tempting to suggest that archaeologists look to factors other than an increased disease load to account for the decline of the Cahokia-area cultural system" (Milner, Chapter 4). Powell also provides convincing evidence of the relatively good level of adaptation of all segments of the Moundville chiefdom, calling into question the recent sweeping generalizations regarding the adverse impact of agriculture on the health of human populations and its inevitable nutritional separation of the elite- and lower-status individuals within ranked societies.

The chapters by Milner and Powell also reflect a broadly based yet detailed grasp of scattered and disparate fragments of archaeological information relevant to the research questions they are pursuing, which is a clear indication of anthropological archaeologists at work rather than narrowly focused "peripheral data set" specialists. The provocative chapter by Rose, Marks, and Tieszen (Chapter 2) provides another convincing example of this ability to master and coherently interpret a variety of different kinds of data relevant to a particular research problem. Working with archaeological, archaeobotanical, and bioarchaeological data sets from the central and lower Mississippi Valley (including δ values, caries rates, and SEM analysis of molar surface wear patterns), Rose et al. look at the nature and timing of the transition to maize-based agriculture in the Eastern Woodlands and its relationship to the initial emergence of ranked Mississippian polities. This complex and still poorly understood processual puzzle has been the focus of archaeological attention for over a half century, and the chapter by Rose et al. provides both an important advance toward clarification of the Mississippian emergence and a convincing demonstration of the central role played by bioarchaeology in understanding such trajectories of cultural development. While Rose et al. concluded that "changes in subsistence patterns in both the lower and central portions of the Mississippi River Valley are extremely complex and not well understood," they do present an interesting hypothesis relating to Late Woodland period plant husbandry systems that deserves further discussion as a concluding example of the substantial contributions to be made by bioarchaeologists to midwestern/southeastern archaeology.

At least three native North American seed-bearing plants were domesticated in the Eastern Woodlands by 1500 B.C. (sumpweed, sunflower, and goosefoot). The seeds of these three cultigens, along with a number of others (including maygrass, knotweed, and little barley), began to show up in abundance in cultural contexts after 500 B.C., reflecting the establishment of regionally variable "premaize" garden systems over a broad area of the interior midlatitude eastern United States. Not introduced into the East until after A.D. 200, maize appears to have been adopted as just another starchy seed crop into already existing garden or field cropping systems and, according to Rose et al., did not become the dominant agricultural crop for another 1,000 years (post–A.D. 1200).

Rose, however, noticed a dramatic increase in grit load and caries rates in several Coles Creek (A.D. 800–1000) populations, *prior* to the ascendancy of maize as a dominant field crop. He proposed that a shift to heavy reliance upon indigenous starchy seeds preceded the transition to maize-based agriculture in the East, at least in the lower Mississippi Valley. This provocative hypothesis gains additional support from archaeobotanical assemblages recently recovered along the Mississippi Valley corridor. Dating to approximately A.D. 400, a large pit at the Newbridge site in west-central Illinois was found to contain a large volume of carbonized seeds of goosefoot *(Chenopodium berlandieri)* and knotweed *(Polygonum)*. Recent reanalysis of this mixed two-species seed assemblage has shown the *Chenopodium* to be a thin-testa domesticated variety. Similarly, the knotweed specimens at Newbridge exhibited extremely thin achenes and may also represent a domesticated seed crop (Asch and Asch 1985).

Recent restudy of the *Chenopodium* and *Polygonum* seeds recovered from two adjacent pit features at the Middle Mississippian (A.D. 1300) Gypsy Joint site in Missouri has shown them to be quite similar to the Newbridge specimens.

Geographically and temporally bracketed by Newbridge and Gypsy Joint, several late Woodland period sites in the American Bottom have also recently yielded large samples of mixed *Chenopodium* and *Polygonum* seeds from pit features that on preliminary examination also appear to be domesticated varieties.

The co-occurrence of these two possible domesticates in cultural contexts separated by three hundred miles and almost a thousand years suggests the initial early Late Woodland development of a true crop complex that endured, at least along the Mississippi Valley corridor, well into the Mississippian period. Apparently grown, harvested, and processed together, the two plant species *Chenopodium* and *Polygonum* making up this "C-P Complex" would fit fairly well into Rose et al.'s hypothesis concerning the development of greater reliance on indigenous starchy seed crops prior to the transition to maize-based agriculture in the eastern United States. There would be an interesting developmental dualism, certainly, if it turned out that after being initially added to existing plant husbandry systems centered on indigenous starchy seed crops, the shift to maize as a primary food crop only duplicated the earlier shift to greater dependency on cultivated crops that had centered on the indigenous "C-P Complex."

While the foregoing discussion is highly speculative, such guessing in advance of definitive data is well within the tradition of midwestern archaeobotany and also serves to suggest possible paths of bio-archaeological investigation of the "C-P Complex" hypothesis. Inasmuch as both *Chenopodium* and *Polygonum* are C-3 pathway plants, stable carbon isotope analysis would be of value only in establishing the limited dietary role of maize. Strontium analysis, however, might be employed to monitor a shift to greater reliance on plant foods, although it would not identify an increase in consumption where cultivated plants simply replaced wild plant foods. While neither the thin-testa chenopod nor the "paper-thin achene" knotweed could directly produce the tooth-wear abrasion patterns observed by Rose et al., grinding these seeds with stone implements could increase a population's dietary grit load, producing the molar damage described. In reference to processing requirements, it would be interesting to see if biomechanical signatures of plant processing similar to those described by Bridges (Chapter 6) might shed light on the "C-P Complex" hypothesis. Finally, while changes in caries rates represent another marker of increased consumption of starchy foods, the information contained in Rose et al. (Table 2-1) suggests that this indicator will not be of much help in this particular situation.

The nature, relative importance, and geographical and temporal boundaries of the "C-P Complex" remain to be established, and bio-archaeology has an important role to play in unraveling this and many other questions of prehistoric cultural development in the Midwest and Southeast.

✳ 12

Out of the Appendix and Into the Dirt: Comments on Thirteen Years of Bioarchaeological Research

Jane E. Buikstra

> A human burial contains more anthropological information per cubic meter of deposit than any other type of archaeological feature. (Peebles 1977:124)

> Many paleoanthropologists may have in the past deceived themselves into thinking that they were part of conjunctive, bioarcheological investigations by providing descriptive addenda to site reports. This deception was, of course, but one symptom of a common malaise revealed also in the traditional monograph, through which most anthropologists appeared as technicians, or data bearers. (Blakely 1977a:1–2)

> A new form of regionally based, interdisciplinary research in mortuary site archaeology and human osteology has been developed in the course of the present study. With the active participation of both archeologists and physical anthropologists in all phases of research design, members of our "bio-archeological" research group made the initial decision to focus upon the investigation of biocultural change within the Woodland period. (Buikstra 1977:69)

Fourteen years ago, in 1977, the University of Georgia Press published *Biocultural Adaptation in Prehistoric America,* designed to promote communication and cooperation between physical anthropologists and archaeologists (Blakely, ed. 1977). Based on a symposium held as part of the Southern Anthropological Society meetings during the previous year, this volume urged conjunctive "bio-archeological" research directed toward the biocultural understanding of humankind's past.

Many of the 1977 papers focused upon the same archaeologically rich southeastern region that serves as the organizing element for this volume. More than a decade has passed, and the Blakely symposium thus becomes a useful touchstone against which to measure how much we have learned, how new techniques have added to our appreciation of the past, and how we should renew our efforts if we are to mine the remarkable archaeological record of the Southeast most effectively.

The participants in the 1977 symposium frequently underscored their sense that the objectives of bioanthropology were changing. The impact of the "new" physical anthropology (Washburn 1952), which to a great extent developed as a reaction to the domination of the field by descriptive osteological study, was being felt in skeletal biological research as population biology and problem orientation replaced typological thinking (Blakely 1977a; Robbins 1977). Also influential was the "new" archaeological emphasis upon subsistence and settlement systems, as well as the Saxe-Binford theories that related social behaviors to archaeologically recoverable mortuary site patterning (Willey and Sabloff 1980; Saxe 1970; Binford 1971). In the face of common anthropological research goals, an integrative or holistic "biocultural" approach was urged by Blakely, who also called for closer cooperation between skeletal biologists and archaeologists. The last point was underscored by several of the participants, notably Robbins and Buikstra who emphasized the need for cooperation in pre-field planning, excavations that included persons skilled in osteological recognition and recovery, and intensive integration of skeletal biologists in all stages of research design and execution. Buikstra coined the term "bio-archaeological" for this type of integrative, problem-oriented research. In closing, Peebles, as an archaeologist, argued strongly and compellingly for the value of mortuary site and skeletal biological research in the total fabric of archaeological study of the past.

In his introductory essay, Blakely (1977a) placed the responsibility for refining and executing a conjunctive bioarchaeological approach upon the shoulders of scholars from both relevant anthropological subdisciplines: archaeology and biological anthropology. Bioanthropologists were urged to escape from descriptive appendexes and to communicate the potential of the human biological dimension for enhancing biocultural studies of the past. In a complementary mode Peebles (1977:115) urged archaeologists to listen and act: "The variety of successful methods and procedures described in these papers demands that archaeologists extend their excavation techniques to recover adequate samples of data from such analyses. . . . It is evident from these papers that such extra effort will be repaid many times over, and both biological and cultural anthropology will be the richer." Thirteen years after these clarion calls, as emphasized by Powell et al. in the introduction to this volume, bioanthropologists have indeed stepped far beyond the descriptive appendixes that dominated earlier research. An ever-expanding literature in anthropology and archaeology amply illustrates this fact.

Less certain, however, is the archaeological response to the conceptual, technical, and methodological advances illustrated in recent bioarchaeological studies. Archaeologists such as Smith (Chapter 11, this volume), as with Peebles a decade ago, clearly are listening, yet the degree to which specialists are being invited "up to the big house" when excavation strategies are designed remains a crucial issue. As illustrated in several of the chapters in this volume, the major factors limiting advancement in bioarchaeological research center on the quality and quantity of skeletal remains and contextual data. The need for representative samples of sufficiently large size continues to be crucial. In recent years, bioanthropologists have expended a great deal of energy in an effort to convince archaeologists that skeletal biological study can address numerous significant research questions of mutual interest. Mutually designed research strategies, however, remain an elusive goal.

As correctly noted by the symposium organizers in their introduction to this volume, the research reported here can be regarded as state-of-the-art bioarchaeological study. Paralleling trends in the field at large, there is a focus here upon the study of diet, health, and adaptation, with certain traditional issues such as genetic relationships now receiving minor emphasis. The impact of agricultural intensification upon the human condition, addressed as one of several topics in 1977, now serves to focus much contemporary research in bioarchaeology (e.g., Cohen and Armelagos 1984). Not surprisingly, this subject correspondingly dominates the present symposium volume.

In 1977, the diversity of Mississippian adaptations was just beginning to be appreciated. Bioanthropologists who contributed to Blakely's volume tended to view agricultural intensification and Mississippian as monolithic constructs, frequently generalizing from single sites or regions to the full cultural or adaptational systems. In his closing remarks, Peebles perceptively contrasted the apparent differences in health status between the Fort Ancient and Middle Mississippian groups reported by Robbins and Blakely, respectively. This diversity, recognized (epi)genetically by Wolf (1977) for inherited features, is more fully defined by the participants in the current symposium. Were the Blakely title to be borrowed for the present volume, it would undoubtedly be modified to read "Biocultural Adaptations in Prehistoric America."

At the time of Blakely's symposium, studies in paleopathology were newly expanding from an emphasis upon the study of specific diseases and disease diagnosis to include the use of "nonspecific" skeletal markers to characterize population health. The most obvious example of this is Robbins's (1977) discussion of periosteal remodeling as part of a disease syndrome characteristic of at least two Fort Ancient communities. Perzigian's (1977) discussion of dental defects and asymmetry also moves in this direction, as does Buikstra (1977) in her discussion of acute and chronic nonspecific stresses. Even so, the issue of treponematosis, long speculated about in skeletons from the Southeast (Jones 1876), remains a subject of discussion today, as it did in 1977 (Buikstra 1977:78, citing Cook 1976). As emphasized below, it is important to strike a balance between disease diagnosis and the evaluation of nonspecific indicators, just as it must be realized that the relationship between community health and patterns noted in a mortality sample is only infrequently isomorphic (Cook 1981; Bumsted 1984).

The appreciation of both diachronic and synchronic differences in Mississippian adaptations has also focused interest upon bioarchaeological investigations in explaining the various Mississippian "depopulations." In 1977, depopulation and Old World epidemic disease introduced by Spanish explorers were commonly linked (e.g., Blakely 1977b:53). Research in Middle and Upper Mississippian populations reported here makes it clear that major changes in population structure and distribution predated Colonial contact by many decades or even centuries. Clearly, the complex relationships between biological, cultural, and social variables oft cited by today's researchers must focus on the American context; Spanish diseases will not often afford a convenient caveat.

In 1977, Blakely argued that the methods of osteological observation had changed less than the objectives of physical anthropology. This statement would clearly be disputed today as electron microscopy and computerized axial tomography are used to investigate the impact of ancient lifeways on skeletal and dental structures. Gilbert (1977) and Robbins (1977) described the application of an experimental new method—trace element analysis—in the reconstruction of ancient dietary patterns. The first paper describing another important biochemical technique—stable carbon isotope analysis—also appeared in 1977 (Vogel and van der Merwe). The frequent application of these sophisticated methods in the studies reported here signals the fact that scholars working in the Southeast continue to be on the innovative edge of bioarchaeological research.

The chapters in this symposium volume thus cover a wide range of issues, with several significant themes emerging. Among these are the facts that we must now consider Mississippian adaptations in the plural and that the impact of these upon the human condition varied considerably, given other social and environmental variables. The importance of maize in the Mississippian diet may have been overemphasized; the ill health commonly associated with Mississippian adaptations may appear prior to maize dependence in (at least) some areas; and there remains the important question of Mississippian terminations.

The rich archaeological record and a productive tradition of bioarchaeological research make the Southeast a unique place to investigate the Mississippian development and demise, serving as a model for similar investigations elsewhere. The chapters in this volume well illustrate an initial step in this effort. Given that this form of conjunctive study is relatively new, it is not unexpected that more significant problems are isolated than are resolved. But then, asking the right questions is a very important first step in effecting significant research.

Several chapters in this collection describe other exciting new directions for bioarchaeological research. The investigation of the impact of activity patterns on skeletal morphology obviously has great potential, both in defining diachronic changes associated with subsistence tasks and in investigating intrapopulation division of labor. In addition, little-known periods, such as the Late Archaic of Louisiana and the Middle Woodland of Florida, are examined, thus providing baseline, landmark bioarchaeological studies. The use of historical series, such as the plantation sample reported by Rathbun and Scurry, also holds excellent promise, both for illuminating incomplete textual documentation and for providing models useful in understanding the prehistoric condition.

The chapters presented here fall into three topical groups: (1) those that focus upon exploring the range of Mississippian adaptations (Rose, Marks, and Tiezen; Powell; Milner; and Eisenberg); (2) those that develop methodology for describing activity patterns from the study of skeletal remains (Larsen and Ruff; Bridges); and (3) case studies of previously unreported sites (Miller-Shaivitz and İşcan; Mires; Rathbun and Scurry). The following discussion is similarly structured.

Mississippian Adaptations

The third moon is that of the Small Corn. This moon is often impatiently looked for, their crop of large corn never sufficing to nourish from one harvest to another. (Du Pratz 1972:320)

. . . at their meals, when their food is distributed, none is presented to the women, till all the males have received their share, so that a boy of two years old is served before his mother. (Du Pratz 1972:325)

One topic of some antiquity in archaeological circles is that of cultural terminations. This is a complex issue, as emphasized by Eisenberg, who notes that there is evidence of severe epidemic disease and nutritional stress in many late prehistoric series and that protohistoric epidemics would have been too late to affect these groups. She illustrates this point, using the Middle Cumberland Averbuch series from central Tennessee (A.D. 1275–1400). Her measures of health status are periosteal reaction on the tibia and porotic changes of the skull. The former is interpreted as an indication of infectious pathology and the latter as the synergistic effect of a relatively high population density, abundant endemic disease, and nutritional stress. Although the rates of periostitis are higher than 50 percent in some age groups, the fact that the majority of cases are healed suggests that, as is the case at Moundville, the lesions represent a chronic disorder that may have depressed overall health levels but was not necessarily the ultimate cause of death. Further, it should be noted that there is considerable time depth for prevalence of periostitis of slightly more than 50 percent in Woodland Indians from Illinois (Cook 1976), in the face of significant population increase. A regional central Tennessee diachronic perspective would serve to clarify the situation remarkably, allowing researchers to identify new age-specific patterns, perhaps indicative of previously unknown diseases, and to establish long-term trends in skeletal markers of disease and nutritional stress. Until this diachronic patterning is known, it is difficult to assess the full impact of the seemingly severe pathology at Averbuch.

In this study, as in others from the volume, proper attention is paid to the multiple potential causes of cribra orbitalia and porotic hyperostosis, only one of which is iron-deficiency anemia associated with overreliance upon maize. Although interpretative arguments tend to focus on maize-related, nutritional explanations, these authors clearly recognize that anemia can develop in association with parasitic and other infections, and the synergism between diet and disease is emphasized, as are the cultural determinants of diet.

Eisenberg carefully describes the lesion patterning for her periostitic/osteomyelitic and resorptive disease syndromes before attempting to apply labels drawn from modern medical experience: treponematosis, tuberculosis, and blastomycotic infections are all potential plagues of the Averbuch population. Elsewhere (Kelley and Eisenberg 1987) she draws a detailed comparison with other prehistoric populations for the observed patterning of lytic lesions and explores extensively the expected ontogenetic patterning of the modern diseases blastomycosis and tuberculosis.

Eisenberg's observed elevated young adult mortality would be expected in the context of a tuberculosis-like pathology, and symptoms of stress in young juveniles, including periostitis, would similarly be anticipated (Martischig 1952; Edeiken and Hodes 1973; Buikstra and Cook 1981). Buikstra and Cook (1981) report that cribra orbitalia and periostitis only occur in neonates and young infants in Illinois Mississippian populations where resorptive vertebral lesions suggestive of tuberculosis appear. Thus, the pattern reported here by Eisenberg for both tibial lesions and cribra orbitalia in juveniles must be interpreted along *with* her information about infectious disease. Clearly, the use of periostitis and cribra orbitalia frequencies as indicators of nonspecific disease and nutritional stress in comparison with, for example, earlier populations where the tuberculosis-like disease did not exist could produce misleading results.

The Averbuch series also presents a remarkable demographic pattern, as noted by Eisenberg. The large number of young adult deaths is exactly what one would expect to see in the face of a tuberculosis-like epidemic, not unexpected here and accompanied by the appropriate array of lesions (Buikstra 1976a; Buikstra and Cook 1981). That a catastrophic explanation may be appropriate is also suggested by the results of a recent paleodemographic study conducted by Konigsberg and myself (Buikstra and Konigsberg 1985). When we had removed what we felt to be the effect of distinctive traditions of age estimation among our colleagues through principal components analysis, we found that the Averbuch probability of dying pattern (q_x) for adults closely resembled that of Crow Creek, a known massacre site. Thus, full explanation of the Averbuch patterning awaits further analysis of mortuary and habitation sites from the Cumberland Basin.

Milner also addresses the issue of cultural terminations, working with data from the American Bottom region. His study, strengthened by a diachronic perspective, well illustrates the importance of combining the study of age at death with disease profiles. He reports, for instance, that the relatively recent Mississippian peoples from the East St. Louis Stone Quarry site have twice as many cases of cranial porosity as the earlier Moorehead phase Kane Mounds sample. Milner might have inappropriately concluded that he had identified evidence for health status deteriorating through time. Instead, noting that many lesions were apparently healed and that childhood mortality was relatively low and peaked later in the East St. Louis Stone Quarry samples, he argues that the most recent groups provide evidence for individuals *living* with a chronic condition. His conclusion contrasts with the pattern common to earlier populations, where juveniles apparently succumbed to initial dietary or disease stresses—a less healthful circumstance. As Milner's study illustrates, we must remember that we are dealing with mortality samples and that survival in the face of ill health may produce more extreme evidence of skeletal pathology than immediate death in the face of dietary or disease insult. Estimates of declining population numbers, derived from counts of farmstead structures, support a gradualist model of population decline and dispersal in the American Bottom, after the Stirling phase maximum during the A.D. 1050–1150 period. Infectious diseases, treponemal and tuberculosis-like, persist through the period, with—as noted above—an argument to be made for better juvenile health during the more recent Sand Prairie times. On this basis Milner argues compellingly that factors other than infectious disease load must be sought to explain Cahokia's long "slide to obscurity."

Milner's closing comments should be underscored. The health of Mississippian peoples apparently varied greatly across space and through time. It is perhaps unfortunate that the pioneer studies of Mississippian pathology focused upon Dickson Mounds and Fort Ancient sites, which may turn out to be special, extreme cases when the broad spectrum of Mississippian adaptations is viewed.

The Moundville series, reported here by Powell, serves as an instructive example of a Mississippian population presenting little evidence for ill health. This sample from the second largest Mississippian population center is roughly contemporary with Milner's Sand Prairie phase, postdating the population maximum at Cahokia by two centuries, and is similar in chronological setting to Averbuch and the latter part of Rose et al.'s Mississippian sequence. In the absence of skeletal samples of large size from the Cahokia site, this series is the paleopopulation from the largest Mississippian community available for study. Estimates for population density at the site during the mid-fourteenth century reach 3,000.

Using ethnographic information, as well as other bioarchaeological data, Powell generates a set of expectations for the physical effects of differences in diet and in certain behavior patterns between elite individuals and those of lower status in the ranked system defined by Peebles on the basis of grave location and funerary goods (Peebles and Kus 1977). Prior trace element study by Schoeninger and Peebles (1981) had suggested differential access to animal protein by ranked status and by gender, with the elite and the masculine eating relatively greater amounts of meat. Powell examined adult skeletal dimensions, developmental and diet-related features such as dental hypoplasia, and skeletal evidence of anemia, trauma, and infectious disease across status groups. Results are compared to those previously reported for four other Mississippian sites from the Deep South: Chucalissa, Dallas, Hixon, and Etowah.

The only differences apparent between ranked status groups are for adult body size, trauma, and anemia. Elite Moundville males tend to be larger than nonelite males, thus mirroring the situation at Dallas/Hixon and Chucalissa. However, unlike the Chucalissa and Etowah samples, the elite males at Moundville show less evidence of trauma than nonelites. This unexpected finding, given the expectation that males of high rank were more commonly engaged in raiding, Powell attributes to two aspects of sample bias: the unfortunate absence of individuals of paramount rank and the serious underrepresentation in the elite subsample of the skeletal elements most often traumatized in the series as a whole. A lower frequency of cribra orbitalia in elite remains, though not statistically significant, provides the one skeletal indicator that may reflect an association between advantaged access to animal protein by persons of elite status and superior health. The subadult cribra orbitalia rate of 21 percent and a range of 2.5 to 9.9 percent overall (with no reported cases of porotic hyperostosis) suggest advantaged health for elite juveniles. Unfortunately, this finding could not be tested against mortality data due to the incomplete nature of the available skeletal series from which the sample was selected. An observed tibial periostitis rate of 50.7 percent, including numerous examples of chronic, healed pathology, is appropriately interpreted by Powell as evidence of an endemic pathology that "afflicted many members of each generation but was rarely a direct cause of death." Powell also argues for the presence of treponemal and tuberculosis-like pathology in the series, not unexpected in Mississippian samples.

Powell's analysis is a strong example of bioarchaeological study, sensitive to both the strengths and the weaknesses of archaeologically recovered samples, including careful evaluation of the biases introduced by transformational processes. Her comparisons across status groups for the health indicators are age and sex controlled, thus providing a rigorous, statistical treatment of the data. Her conclusion—that although ranked status may have covaried with behavior and diet at Moundville, health was little affected—thus makes a convincing case for at least one Mississippian community of large size that was, in general, relatively well adapted.

Rose et al. also make an excellent case for the use of skeletal biology in archaeological investigations. Noting that the degree of dietary dependence upon maize in the central and lower Mississippi Valley remains a controversial issue, they reinterpret the development of maize agriculture basing their scenario upon recent assays of stable carbon isotope ratios and dental data. Beginning with baseline preagricultural populations with low caries frequencies and distinctive dental attrition and microwear patterns, they report that certain more recent populations, formerly assumed to be heavily dependent on maize due to presence of caries and increased dental attrition, were apparently not consuming significant amounts of this high-carbohydrate resource. Among these high-caries, high-attrition populations are series from Coles Creek in the lower Mississippi Valley, where maize is not conspicuous in the archaeological record, as well as remains recovered from central Mississippi Valley contexts where paleobotanical evidence of maize is relatively early. With one exception, which they cite as an example of ceremonial utilization of maize, isotopic evidence for significant maize dependence does not occur until Middle Mississippian times.

Borrowing a model from west-central Illinois (Asch and Asch 1985), they suggest that the Early Mississippian folks previously thought to be consuming maize were actually relying upon high-carbohydrate local seed resources such as knotweed, goosefoot, and maygrass. In addition, they present a provocative scenario whereby maize is first introduced into the central and lower valley as a status food item from the American Bottom region during Early Mississippian times. They agree with Lynott et al. (1986) that only when "population nucleation reached a critical level" did maize become a dietary staple.

Rose et al.'s argument for the relative recency of maize dependence is convincing and serves to clarify the relationship between intensification of food production and Mississippianization in the central and lower Mississippi Valley. Unfortunately the strength of Rose et al.'s arguments, which are based on a strong, problem-oriented research design and technical/methodological sophistication, is limited somewhat by the absence of diachronic sequences of skeletal series of large size. The researchers are forced to skip back and forth between the central and lower portions of the central Mississippi Valley due to a paucity of Baytown remains in the former and Mississippian materials in the latter. Age-specific comparisons of caries, infectious disease, and porotic hyperostosis are therefore not attempted, and the authors are led to make much of summary statistics for samples where very few individuals could be observed. As illustrated in Table 2-4, frequencies of infection vary widely, especially between contemporaneous sites with very small sample sizes. While the authors are to be commended in attempting to extract the maximum amount of information from reports of contexts characterized only by fragmented and imperfectly preserved remains, their interpretations of health status must be approached conservatively.

The analysis of stable carbon ratios has clearly revolutionized our ability to identify maize in the diet of North American paleopopulations. As with any new, experimental technique, there remain unresolved issues that affect the strength of our behavioral interpretations. Variation in δ C13 values can derive from factors other than diet—notably age, sex, health status, individual metabolism, measurement, and preparations technique (Bumsted 1984, 1985). Bumsted (1985) provides a review of these concerns and argues conservatively that differences of less than 50/00 may not reflect truly distinct diets. In this case, the differences between the Early Mississippian and Middle/Late Mississippian samples reported by Rose et al. would indeed indicate a shift to maize consumption. Likewise, the − 15.7 C13 δ value for the youth from Little Cypress Bayou is significantly different from the values for the adults from the same site. Whether this distinction represents a different and maize-replete diet for local high-status individuals, as has been suggested by Bender et al. (1981) for Cahokia, or the presence of a nonlocal youth in the central Mississippi Valley must remain a point at issue. Given the possibility that δ C13 values covary metabolically with age and gender, it is important that bioarchaeological interpretations be appropriately conservative.

In closing this section, I will underscore the evident variation in health status among those Mississippian populations. Unfortunately, differences in the reporting of data among the studies considered here make direct comparisons between all data categories impossible. One of the major methodological problems in modern paleoepidemiology is the much-needed standardization of observations of skeletal pathology. This is a difficult matter, but it is essential if researchers are to be certain that generalizations about differences in local Mississippian adaptations are not primarily an artifact of observational technique.

Milner, Powell, and Eisenberg all differentiate between healed and active cribra orbitalia and report frequencies by age. They likewise also distinguish between healed and active periostitis, but Milner and Eisenberg focus their discussions of the condition upon tibiae alone, whereas Powell presents prevalence rates for the entire skeleton. Rose et al.'s strategy for distinguishing between treponematosis and "other infections" is nowhere specified, and because they include data reported by a variety of other researchers, they could not separate healed from active cases of skeletal response. Despite the problems in direct comparisons noted above, it seems apparent that not all Mississippian peoples at all times in all locales had achieved identical levels of adaptation to their ecological and social environments, not a surprising situation by any means.

Activity Patterns

> As children grow up, the fathers and mothers take care each to accustom those of their own sex to the labours and exercises suited to them, and they have no great trouble to keep them employed; but it must be confessed that the girls and the women work more than the men and the boys. These last go hunting and fishing, cut the wood, the smallest bits of which are carried home by the women; they clear the fields for corn and hoe it. . . . The women on the other hand have their children to bring up, have to pound the maiz[e] for the subsistence of the family, have to keep up the fire, and to make a great many utensils, which require a good deal of work, and last but a short time, such as their earthen ware, their matts, their clothes and a thousand things of that kind. (Du Pratz 1972:325)

> When the boys are about twelve years of age, they give them a bow and arrows proportioned to their strength. (Du Pratz 1972:324)

A variety of strategies exists for reconstructing activity patterns in adults through the investigation of skeletal morphology and pathology. Most commonly investigated is osteoarthritis or degenerative joint disease, used for example by Angel (1966a) to identify "atl atl elbow" among prehistoric peoples from Tranquility site, California. More recently developed, and potentially more sensitive, is the use of biomechanical and engineering principles (Lovejoy et al. 1976; Ruff and Hayes 1983a, 1983b; Ruff and Hayes 1984) as applied here by Bridges and by Larsen and Ruff. Both studies examine external long bone dimensions in concert with the amount and distribution of bone within cortices to reconstruct the forces placed upon these bones in life. Activity patterns are then inferred.

In the first of these studies, Bridges uses direct measurement and noninvasive CAT scans to generate comparisons of bone mass distribution and size in limb long bones from hunting/gathering and agricultural populations from northwest Alabama. Her samples are large, and her interpretative arguments, based on ethnographic and ethnohistoric materials, are convincing. The discovery of increased external dimensions and strength in Mississippian long bones is explained as a response to the increasingly demanding life-style of agricultural peoples. That the arms of females are particularly and symmetrically stressed among maize cultivators is not surprising, given the division of labor in contemporary and ethnographically documented hoe agriculturalists. This biomechanical argument is likely relevant to the decreased sexual dimorphism noted by Hamilton (1976) for Illinois agriculturalists. The significant expansion and increased strength in the legs of Mississippian males are more problematic, with speculation here concerning activities not directly related to subsistence.

It will be useful to investigate the age-specificity and ontogeny of this pattern, as well as the relationship of changes in bone mass to the development of arthritis. Robert Pickering (1984) conducted a thorough study of degenerative joint disease, comparing agricultural with pre-maize folk in Illinois. The major significant difference discovered when contrasting subsistence groups by gender was in the female back, with earlier onset of arthritis in agricultural females. Males, even though apparently shifting from the spear to the bow and arrow, displayed no significant change in arthritis at the major joint surfaces. This finding underscores the fact that repetitive stresses, rather than those that are rare and extreme, mold these developmental and aging processes.

Larsen and Ruff describe a diachronic trend in adult body size reduction for the north Georgia coast that is the opposite of that described by Bridges for northwest Alabama. They suggest that the decreased bone strength and size, particularly notable in females, of these coastal agricultural peoples are due to reduced activity among agriculturalists compounded by poor nutrition for females. These data are further interpreted to indicate less dimorphism in activity among agriculturalists than in hunter-gatherers, as seen from femoral observations.

Larsen and Ruff emphasize the region-specific nature of their Georgia coast results, when compared to Bridges's Alabama perspective. Furthermore, it must be noted that they use small samples from both sides of the body, femora only, summed over centuries. Bridges's interpretations, for instance, would have been different and certainly less rich if limited to one long bone. Asymmetry in human lower limbs bones, such as that reported by Ruff and Hayes (1983b) for Pecos Pueblo, could confound analyses where sides are pooled. In addition, given the broad temporal span of the remains, there is the issue of genetic growth potential and dimorphism in agricultural and preagricultural populations. The authors of these chapters note bioarchaeological evidence for population continuity through time in their study regions, but specific biological analyses of this particular dimension are not available.

Case Studies

When the body is in the trench all those taking part throw their lighted torches into it in the same way, after which it is covered with earth. This is what the entire ceremony is confined to. It is true that it continues more than six months longer for the relations of the dead and for his friends, who during all that time go almost every night to utter howls over the grave. . . . These ceremonies, as I have said, are common to the chiefs and people. The only difference which marks the first is that at their head is planted a post on which is cut with the point of a knife the figure they have worn painted on the body during life. (L. F. B. Dumont, reported in Swanton 1911:334)

Mires's study of the Late Archaic Cowpen Slough site in Louisiana explores the implications of a differentiated mortuary program for a relatively unknown period of prehistory. Mires and her colleagues are to be congratulated for completing what was doubtless a most arduous job of excavation and osteological analysis. Radiocarbon dating is combined with stratigraphic and sediment analysis to define two temporally sequential occupations between 4500 and 2800 B.P. The cemetery area of the site is apparently associated only with the earlier, pre–Poverty Point component. The lower level of the cemetery contains both primary and secondary interments. In the upper cemetery level, cremation was added to the range of body treatments. Some of the burials were placed in pits and others placed on the ground surface and covered over with midden.

Mires considers such factors as location and season of death, population mobility, and social interactions, as she raises a number of important points in her interpretation of the diversity of burial treatments. First, the cemetery appears demographically inclusive, which would suggest that this may indeed be the interment facility for a corporate group that ritually reaffirmed its ties to the ancestors through mortuary ritual, including disposal of the dead in a formally bounded burial area. The simplest explanation for the presence of both primary and secondary burials would invoke population mobility, though a certain element of territoriality and resource control is suggested by the designated burial location, as is apparently the case for the central Mississippi Valley by 6000 B.P. (Charles and Buikstra 1983). That other, more elaborate rituals may occur as part of an annual or supra-annual cycle of mortuary events is possible, though no signals from the archaeological record confirm this suggestion. Clearly, through careful and painstaking excavation and osteological analysis, Mires's contribution provides an excellent initiative for understanding the social and economic conditions characteristic of the Late Archaic in the lower Mississippi Valley.

Miller-Shaivitz and İşcan report on the A.D. 200 to 600/800 component of the Fort Center site. Prior archaeological interpretations had identified the residents of the site as high-ranking individuals who specialized in mortuary ritual. The extended burial program followed at Fort Center included at least two distinctive stages: (1) maceration in association with a charnel structure, followed by (2) placement upon a platform that was subsequently burned. The platform was located in an artificial pond (Figure 9-2). An argument was also made for maize dependence (W. H. Sears 1982).

A bioarchaeological perspective holds excellent potential for examining the propositions raised by Sears for Fort Center. A sample of these are addressed in the chapter in this volume by Miller-Shaivitz and İşcan, such as maceration and health status of the community. Such observations are rendered much more challenging by the total disarticulation of the skeletal sample. (For a more extensive report on this series, see Miller-Shaivitz 1986.) Miller-Shaivitz and İşcan suggest that the almost total absence of cut marks from maceration of bodies may indicate the use of tools that did not cut into the bone (e.g., the fingernails of the morticians). Ancillary information could be gained through the investigation of body part representation, both from the platform and from the site of the charnel house. Consistent absence of small bones of the hands and feet would support the concept of a staged maceration sequence. Likewise, one would expect the shallow-rooted incisors to be underrepresented in the dental sample.

The paleodemographic analysis of the Fort Center site identifies age groups clearly underrepresented in the sample, though without formal reference to mortality statistics set against expectations developed from other contexts (e.g., Weiss 1973). Miller-Shaivitz and İşcan argue that juveniles are underenumerated due to the fragility of their bones, but they also note the possibility that juveniles were seldom accorded this form of elaborate burial treatment. If infants and children had been included in the burial areas, it would seem likely that primary teeth along with relatively unworn secondary incisors/molars and tooth crowns should have been present and recovered in some frequency. In sum, because a great deal of the interpretation of the site hinges upon identifying just who was and was not accorded this form of mortuary treatment, further extensive effort to identify biases in the sample (and their source) is warranted.

Based upon a caries frequency of 3 percent, the authors argue for a "mixed economy." Elevated caries frequencies should not necessarily be used to support Sears's argument for maize dependence, however, because relatively high caries rates can develop in the absence of maize intensification (Rose et al., Chapter 2, this volume). Biochemical analysis, if the nature of the sample will permit, would clarify the issue. The presence of porotic hyperostosis in the sample is of interest, given its absence at the Mississippian Moundville (Powell, Chapter 3, this volume) and American Bottom (Milner, Chapter 4, this volume) sites. Even though the rate of porotic change does not seem high when compared to Mississippian samples, the fact that only 7 percent of the sample is below eighteen years of age suggests that the health status for the population may be similar to that reported by Eisenberg for Averbuch. Interpretation of hypoplasia frequencies is difficult without knowing how these are patterned in individual teeth, given the documented differential suspectibility by tooth type (Rose, Condon, and Goodman 1985). The fact that 10.3 percent of the male skulls show evidence of healed fractures is important and matches the order of magnitude predicted for Mississippian populations. This is one behavioral parameter that should be emphasized in comparison with other population samples.

In sum, Miller-Shaivitz and İşcan have made an important first effort in providing a bioarchaeological understanding of the Fort Center site. Further comparative study will clearly be crucial in assessing Sears's contention that the sample is a special status group. Especially significant in this effort will be the generation of data sets large enough for statistical testing. In the present study, such comparative information is scanty and the authors are forced to base their determinations of significance upon intuition.

Rathbun's and Scurry's analysis of a Colonial period cemetery from South Carolina represents an exciting new focus for bioarchaeological research: the study of historic mortuary sites and skeletal remains. Pioneered by Angel, who developed general comparisons of Colonial and post-Colonial whites and blacks from across North America (1976), this form of study is now assuming greater visibility in the Southeast (e.g., Rose 1985). Much of Rathbun's and Scurry's report is descriptive, as is appropriate with the small sample size and relative paucity of comparative data. An organizing theme of the work is similar to that upon which Powell focuses: the degree to which advantaged status—plantation owner vs. slave in the Rathbun and Scurry example—is associated with better health. Rathbun's and Scurry's conclusion is that no evidence exists in their data to indicate inferior health status for slave populations. The family of Belleview Plantation owner Edward Croft suffered recurrent bouts of childhood illnesses and in fact, if the evidence concerning skeletal lead burden, antemortem tooth loss, and adult mortality is representative, appear to be somewhat disadvantaged when compared to the slaves. Unfortunately, it is impossible in this sample to evaluate juvenile mortality, an exceedingly sensitive measure of health for the elite and nonelite communities. As with many of the studies of prehistoric remains, larger samples are desirable if bioarchaeological methodology is to be fully applied to the study of historic populations.

I would urge, however, that historical bioarchaeology not limit its comparative domain solely to other historic samples. Valuable dia-chronic insights would be gained, for instance, through comparisons of pathology patterns for periostitis in Colonial and more recent samples with the "treponematosis" presented by our prehistoric Native Amer-icans. Likewise, patterns of degenerative change and activity-related re-modeling that characterize agricultural blacks and whites could be usefully compared to those reported for prehistoric agriculturalists.

This concludes my commentary on this excellent, stimulating series of papers. We see here the maturation of an earlier descriptive human osteology to a truly anthropological bioarchaeology where sophisti-cated models are developed, expectations are formally derived, and tests are statistically rigorous. As noted above, and reinforced directly by several authors in this volume, the major limiting factor would seem to be sample size and the quality of contextual data. The potential con-tributions of bioarchaeological research to archaeology in the Southeast are obvious, as abundantly illustrated here. What remains necessary now is the development and execution of truly integrative problem-oriented research designs where priority is given to identifying and sampling mortuary components.

✳ References Cited

Acheson, R. M.
1960 Effects of Nutrition and Disease on Human Growth. In *Human Growth,* edited by J. M. Tanner, pp. 73–92. Pergamon Press, Oxford.

Acsadi, G., and J. Nemeskeri
1970 *History of Human Life Span and Mortality,* Akademiai Kiado, Budapest.

Adair, J.
1930 *History of the American Indians.* Reprinted. Edited by S. C. Williams. Watauga Press, Johnson City, Tennessee. Originally published 1775, London.

Adams, W. H. (editor)
1985 *Aboriginal Subsistence and Settlement Archaeology of the Kings Bay Locality.* Reports of Investigations No. 1. University of Florida, Department of Anthropology, Gainesville.

Aegerter, A., and J. A. Kirkpatrick (editors)
1975 *Orthopedic Diseases.* 4th ed. W. B. Saunders, Philadelphia.

Albanese, A. A., and G. A. Orto
1964 The Proteins and Amino Acids. In *Modern Nutrition in Health and Disease,* edited by M. G. Wohl and R. S. Goodhart, pp. 125–93, 3d ed. Lea and Febiger, Philadelphia.

Allison, M. J., D. Mendoza, and A. Pezzia
1973 Documentation of a Case of Tuberculosis in Pre-Columbian America. *American Review of Respiratory Diseases* 17:985–91.

Anderson, D. G., and J. Schuldenrein
1985 *Prehistoric Human Ecology Along the Upper Savannah River: Excavations at the Rucker's Bottom, Abbeville and Bullard Site Groups.* Vols. 1 and 2. U.S. Department of the Interior, National Park Service Branch—Atlanta.

Angel, J. L.
1966a *Early Skeletons from Tranquility, California.* Smithsonian Contributions to Anthropology, vol. 2, no. 1. Smithsonian Institution, Washington, D.C.
1966b Porotic Hyperostosis, Anemias, Malarias, and Marshes in the Prehistoric Eastern Mediterranean. *Science* 153:760–63.

1967 Porotic Hyperostosis, or Osteoporosis Symmetrica. In *Diseases in Antiquity, A Survey of the Diseases, Injuries, and Surgery of Early Populations,* edited by D. R. Brothwell and A. T. Sandison, pp. 379–89. C. C. Thomas, Springfield, Illinois.

1971 *The People of Lerna: An Analysis of a Prehistoric Aegean Population.* Smithsonian Institution Press, Washington, D.C.

1976 Colonial to Modern Skeletal Change in the U.S.A. *American Journal of Physical Anthropology* 45:723–35.

1977 Appendix II-1. In *Historical Archaeology and Salvage Archaeological Excavations at College Landing. An Interim Report,* by C. L. Hudgins, pp. 95–96. Virginia Research Center for Archaeology, Yorktown.

1979 Osteoarthritis in Prehistoric Turkey and Medieval Byzantium. *Henry Ford Hospital Medical Journal* 27:38–43.

1980 Appendix 2. Physical Anthropological Report. In *Archaeological Investigations at Catoctin Furnace, Frederick County, Maryland,* by R. A. Thomas et al., pp. 11–14. Mid-Atlantic Archaeological Research, Newark.

Angel, J. L., and J. O. Kelley

1983 Health and Status of Colonial Iron-worker Slaves. *American Journal of Physical Anthropology* 60:170.

Asch, D. L., and N. E. Asch

1985 Prehistoric Plant Cultivation in West-central Illinois. In *Prehistoric Food Production in North America,* edited by R. I. Ford, pp. 149–203. Anthropological Papers No. 75. Museum of Anthropology, University of Michigan, Ann Arbor.

Aufderheide, A. C., G. Rapp, and L. E. Lorentz

1982 Skeletal Lead Analysis: Catoctin Furnace, Governor's Land, College Landing, Kingsmill on the James, Irene Mound. Ms. on file, Archaeometry Laboratory and Department of Pathology, University of Minnesota, Duluth.

Aufderheide, A. C., F. D. Neiman, L. E. Wittmers, and G. Rapp

1981 Lead in Bone II: Skeletal-lead Content as an Indicator of Lifetime Lead Ingestion and the Social Correlates in an Archaeological Population. *American Journal of Physical Anthropology* 55:285–91.

Aufderheide, A. C., J. L. Angel, J. O. Kelley, A. C. Outlaw, M. A. Outlaw, G. Rapp, and L. E. Wittmers

1985 Lead in Bone III. Prediction of Social Correlates from Skeletal Lead Content in Four Colonial American Populations (Catoctin Furnace, College Landing, Governor's Land, and Irene Mound). *American Journal of Physical Anthropology* 66:353–61.

Baby, R. S.

1954 Hopewell Cremation Practices. *Ohio Historical Society Papers in Archeology,* No. 1.

Bareis, C. J.

1976 *The Knoebel Site, St. Clair County, Illinois.* Circular 1. Illinois Archaeological Survey, Urbana.

Bartram, W.

1853 Observations on the Creek and Cherokee Indians. *Transactions of the American Ethnological Society* 3:1–81.

1928 *The Travels of William Bartram.* Reprinted. Edited by M. Van Doren. Macy-Masius, Philadelphia. Originally published 1791, Philadelphia.

Bass, W. M.

1971 *Human Osteology: A Laboratory and Field Manual of the Human Skeleton.* Special Publication No. 2, Missouri Archaeological Society, Columbia.

1987 *Human Osteology: A Laboratory and Field Manual of the Human Skeleton.* 3d ed. Special Publication No. 2, Missouri Archaeological Society, Columbia.

Beavers, R. C.

1982 *Archaeological Site Inventory, Barataria Basin Marsh Unit—Core Area, Jean Lafitte National Historical Park, Jefferson Parish, Louisiana.* Archaeological and Cultural Research Program of the University of New Orleans. Contract No. PX J7530-1-0096. Submitted to National Park Service, Jean Lafitte National Historical Park, New Orleans.

Behar, M.

1968 Food and Nutrition of the Maya Before the Conquest and at the Present Time. In *Biomedical Challenges Presented by the American Indian,* pp. 114–19. Scientific Publication 165. Pan American Health Organization, Washington, D.C.

Belmont, J. S.

1967 The Development of Agriculture in the Lower Valley. *Southeastern Archaeological Conference Bulletin* 5:16–18.

Bender, B.

1985 Emergent Tribal Formations in the American Midcontinent. *American Antiquity* 50:52–62.

Bender, M. M., D. A. Baerreis, and R. L. Steventon

1981 Further Light on Carbon Isotopes and Hopewell Agriculture. *American Antiquity* 46:346–54.

Bennett, K. A.

1973a *The Indians of Point of Pines, Arizona: A Comparative Study of their Physical Characteristics.* Anthropological Papers No. 23. University of Arizona, Tucson.

1973b On the Estimation of Some Demographic Characteristics of a Prehistoric Population from the American Southwest. *American Journal of Physical Anthropology* 39:223–32.

Berg, R.

1984 Osteological Analysis of Selected Long Bones from the Gold Mine Site, 16Rl13, Richland Parish, Louisiana. Master's thesis, Department of Anthropology, University of Arkansas, Fayetteville.

Berryman, H. E.

1980 Mouse Creek, Dallas and Middle Cumberland: A Multivariate Approach. In *The Skeletal Biology of Aboriginal Populations in the Southeastern United States,* edited by P. Willey and F. H. Smith, pp. 1–14. Miscellaneous Paper 5. Tennessee Anthropological Association, Knoxville.

1981 *The Averbuch Skeletal Series: A Study of Biological and Social Stress at a Late Mississippian Period Site from Middle Tennessee.* Ph.D. dissertation, University of Tennessee. University Microfilms, Ann Arbor.

Bettinger, R. L.

1980 Explanatory/Predictive Models of Hunter-Gatherer Adaptation. In *Advances in Archaeological Method and Theory,* vol. 3, edited by M. B. Schiffer, pp. 189–255. Academic Press, New York.

Binford, L. R.

1971 Mortuary Practices: Their Study and Their Potential. In *Approaches to the Social Dimensions of Mortuary Practices,* edited by J. A. Brown. Society for American Archaeology, *Memoirs* 25:6–29.

1972 An Analysis of Cremations from Three Michigan Sites. In *An Archaeological Perspective,* edited by L. R. Binford, pp. 373–84. Seminar Press, New York.

Black, T. K., III

1978 A New Method for Assessing the Sex of Fragmentary Skeletal Remains: Femoral Shaft Circumference. *American Journal of Physical Anthropology* 48:227–31.

1979 *The Biological and Social Analysis of a Mississippian Cemetery from Southeast Missouri: The Turner Site 23BU21a.* Anthropological Papers No. 68. Museum of Anthropology, University of Michigan, Ann Arbor.

Blaeuer, M. W., and J. C. Rose

1982 Bioarchaeology of the Powell Canal Site. In *Powell Canal: Baytown Period Occupation on Bayou Macon in Southeast Arkansas,* by J. H. House, pp. 72–81. Research Series No. 19. Arkansas Archeological Survey, Fayetteville.

Blakely, R. L.

1977a Introduction: Changing Strategies for the Biological Anthropologist. In *Biocultural Adaptation in Prehistoric America,* edited by R. L. Blakely, pp. 1–9. Proceedings No. 11. Southern Anthropological Society, University of Georgia Press, Athens.

1977b Sociocultural Implications of Demographic Data from Etowah, Georgia. In *Biocultural Adaptation in Prehistoric America,* edited by R. L. Blakely, pp. 45–66. Proceedings No. 11. Southern Anthropological Society, University of Georgia Press, Athens.

1980 Sociocultural Implications of Pathology Between the Village Area and Mound C Skeletal Remains from Etowah, Georgia. In *The Skeletal Biology of Aboriginal Populations in the Southeastern United States,* edited by P. Willey and F. H. Smith, pp. 28–38. Miscellaneous Paper 5. Tennessee Anthropological Association, Knoxville.

Blakely, R. L. (editor)

1977 *Biocultural Adaptation in Prehistoric America.* Proceedings No. 11. Southern Anthropological Society, University of Georgia Press, Athens.

Blakely, R. L., and L. A. Beck

1981 Trace Elements, Nutritional States and Social Stratification at Etowah, Georgia. In *The Research Potential of Anthropological Museum Collections,* edited by A.-M. Cantwell, J. B. Griffin, and N. A. Rothschild. Annals of the New York Academy of Sciences 376:417–31.

Blakeman, C. H., Jr.

1974 *The Late Prehistoric Paleoethnobotany of the Black Bottom, Pope and Massac Counties, Illinois,* Ph.D. dissertation, Southern Illinois University. University Microfilms, Ann Arbor.

Bleiberg, F. M., T. A. Brun, and S. Goihman
1980 Duration of Activities and Energy Expenditure of Female Farmers in Dry and Rainy Seasons in Upper-Volta. *British Journal of Nutrition* 43:71–82.
Boesch, E. J.
1984 Dissertation proposal submitted to the Department of Anthropology, New York University. Ms. in possession of the author.
Bolling, P.
1786 Plat to Capt. Paul Pritchard, Map 22 x 22 in., Scale 1:3960, Post-revolutionary, extra-large plats, bdle. 150, plat 79. South Carolina Archives, Columbia.
Boserup, E.
1970 *Women's Role in Economic Development.* Allen and Unwin, London.
Bossu, J.
1962 *Travels in the Interior of North America 1751–1762.* Translated and edited by S. Feiler. University of Oklahoma Press, Norman.
Bourdieu, P.
1976 *Outline of a Theory of Practice.* Cambridge University Press, New York.
Bourne, E. G. (editor)
1904 *Narratives of the Career of Hernando deSoto in the Conquest of Florida.* A. S. Barnes, New York.
Boyd, C. C., Jr., P. A. Driscoll, and S. A. Symes
1983 An Analysis of the Skeletal Remains from the Brown Site (40MR260), Maury County, Tennessee. *Tennessee Anthropologist* 8:50–66.
Boyd, D. C. M.
1984 A Biological Investigation of Skeletal Remains from the Mouse Creek Phase and a Comparison with Two Late Mississippian Skeletal Populations from Middle and East Tennessee. Master's thesis, Department of Anthropology, University of Tennessee, Knoxville.
Bradtmiller, B.
1983 The Biological Effects of European Contact Among the Arikara. *American Journal of Physical Anthropology* 60:176.
Brain, J. P.
1971 The Lower Mississippi Valley in North American Prehistory. Ms. on file, Arkansas Archeological Survey, Fayetteville.
1976 The Question of Corn Agriculture in the Lower Mississippi Valley. *Southeastern Archaeological Conference Bulletin* 19:57–60.
Bridges, P. S.
1983 Subsistence Activities and Biomechanical Properties of Long Bones in Two Amerindian Populations. *American Journal of Physical Anthropology* 60:177.
1985 *Changes in Long Bone Structure with the Transition to Agriculture: Implications for Prehistoric Activities.* Ph.D. dissertation, University of Michigan.
1989 Changes in Activities with the Shift to Agriculture in the Southeastern United States. *Current Anthropology* 30(3):385–94.
Brock. S. L.
1986 Differences in Bone Remodeling in "Resilient" Compared to "Stable-based" Populations: An Example from Middle-range Research. Paper presented at the 51st meeting of the Society for American Archaeology, New Orleans.

Brock. S. L., and C. B. Ruff
1988 Diachronic Patterns of Change in Structural Properties of the Femur in the Prehistoric American Southwest. *American Journal of Physical Anthropology* 75:113–27.

Brothwell, D. R.
1981 *Digging up Bones.* 3d ed. Cornell University Press, Ithaca.

Brown, J. A.
1971 The Dimensions of Status in the Burials at Spiro. In *Approaches to the Social Dimensions of Mortuary Practices,* edited by J. A. Brown. Society for American Archaeology, *Memoirs* 25:92–112.
1976 A Reconsideration of the Southern Cult. *Midcontinental Journal of Archaeology* 1:115–35.
1981 The Search for Rank in Prehistoric Burials. In *The Archaeology of Death,* edited by R. C. Chapman, I. Kinnes, and K. Randsborg, pp. 25–37. Cambridge University Press, Cambridge.

Brown, J. K.
1970 A Note on the Division of Labor by Sex. *American Anthropologist* 72:1073–78.

Brues, A.
1960 The Spearman and the Archer—An Essay on Selection in Body Build. *American Anthropologist* 62:457–69.

Buikstra, J. E.
1976a The Caribou Eskimo: General and Specific Disease. *American Journal of Physical Anthropology* 45:351–67.
1976b Differential Diagnosis: An Epidemiological Model. *Yearbook of Physical Anthropology* 20:316–28.
1976c *Hopewell in the Lower Illinois Valley: A Regional Approach to the Study of Human Biological Variability and Prehistoric Behavior.* Scientific Papers 2. Northwestern University Archaeological Program, Evanston.
1977 Biocultural Dimensions of Archaeological Study: A Regional Perspective. In *Biocultural Adaptation in Prehistoric America,* edited by R. L. Blakely, pp. 67–84. Proceedings No. 11. Southern Anthropological Society, University of Georgia Press, Athens.
1984 The Lower Illinois River Region: A Prehistoric Context for the Study of Ancient Diet and Health. In *Paleopathology at the Origins of Agriculture,* edited by M. N. Cohen and G. J. Armelagos, pp. 217–36. Academic Press, Orlando.

Buikstra, J. E. (editor)
1981 *Prehistoric Tuberculosis in the Americas.* Scientific Papers 5. Northwestern University Archaeological Program, Evanston.

Buikstra, J. E., and D. C. Cook
1978 Pre-Columbian Tuberculosis: An Epidemiological Approach. *Medical College of Virginia Quarterly* 14:32–44.
1981 Pre-Columbian Tuberculosis in West-Central Illinois. In *Prehistoric Tuberculosis in the Americas,* edited by J. E. Buikstra, pp. 115–39. Scientific Papers 5. Northwestern University Archaeological Program, Evanston.

Buikstra, J. E., and L. W. Konigsberg
1985 Paleodemography: Critiques and Controversies. *American Anthropologist* 87:316–33.
Buikstra, J. E., and J. H. Mielke
1985 Demography, Diet, and Health. In *The Analysis of Prehistoric Diets,* edited by R. I. Gilbert, Jr., and J. H. Mielke, pp. 359–422. Academic Press, Orlando.
Buikstra, J. E., and M. Swegle
1980 Cremated Bone: Experimental Evidence. Paper presented at the annual meeting of the American Association of Forensic Sciences, New Orleans.
Buikstra, J. E., W. Autry, E. Breitburg, L. E. Eisenberg, and N. J. van der Merwe
1988 Diet and Health in the Nashville Basin: Human Adaptation and Maize Agriculture in Middle Tennessee. In *Diet and Subsistence: Current Archaeological Perspectives,* edited by B. V. Kennedy and G. M. LeMoine, pp. 243–59. Proceedings of the 19th annual Chacmool Conference, Calgary.
Bullen, A. K.
1972 Paleoepidemiology and Distribution of Prehistoric Treponemiasis (Syphilis) in Florida. *Florida Anthropologist* 25:133–75.
Bumsted, M. P.
1984 Human Variation: $C^{13}C$. In *Adult Bone Collagen and the Relation to Diet in an Isochronous C_4 (Maize) Archaeological Population.* Los Alamos National Laboratory Report LA-10259-T. Los Alamos.
1985 Past Human Behavior from Bone Chemical Analysis—Respects and Prospects. *Journal of Human Evolution* 14:539–51.
Burton, M. L., and D. R. White
1984 Sexual Division of Labor in Agriculture. *American Anthropologist* 86:568–83.
Bushnell, D. I.
1920 *Native Cemeteries and Forms of Burial East of the Mississippi.* Bureau of American Ethnology Bulletin No. 71. Smithsonian Institution, Washington, D.C.
Buxton, L. H. D.
1938 Platymeria and Platycnemia. *Journal of Anatomy* 73:31–36.
Byrd, K. M., and R. W. Neuman
1978 Archaeological Data Relative to Prehistoric Subsistence in the Lower Mississippi Alluvial Valley. *Geoscience and Man* 19:9–21.
CCROPJIAS: Charleston County, Records of the Ordinary/Probate Judge, Inventories, Appraisements, Sales. Charleston, South Carolina.
CCRRMC: Charleston County Records of the Register of Mesne Conveyance. Charleston, South Carolina.
Campillo, D.
1977 *Paleopatologia del Cranio.* Montblanc-Martin, Barcelona.
Carr, R. S., M. Y. İşcan, and R. S. Johnson
1984 A Late Archaic Cemetery in South Florida. *Florida Anthropologist* 37:172–88.
Carrier, N. H.
1958 A Note on the Estimation of Mortality and Other Population Characteristics Given Deaths by Age. *Population Studies* 12:149–63.

Cassidy, C. M.
1972 *Comparison of Nutrition and Health in Pre-agricultural and Agricultural Amerindian Skeletal Populations.* Ph.D. dissertation, University of Wisconsin. University Microfilms, Ann Arbor.

Chapman, R. C., I. Kinnes, and K. Randsborg
1981 *The Archaeology of Death.* Cambridge University Press, Cambridge.

Charles, D. K., and J. E. Buikstra
1983 Archaic Mortuary Sites in the Central Mississippi Drainage: Distribution, Structure, and Behavioral Implications. In *Archaic Hunters and Gatherers in the American Midwest,* edited by J. L. Phillips and J. A. Brown, pp. 117–45. Academic Press, New York.

Clark. W. M.
1878 Antiquities of Tennessee. *Annual Report for 1877,* pp. 269–76. Smithsonian Institution, Washington, D.C.

Clarke, S. K.
1977 Mortality Trends in Prehistoric Populations. *Human Biology* 49:181–86.

Clayton, W. W.
1880 *History of Davidson County, Tennessee.* J. W. Lewis, Philadelphia.

Cohen, M. N.
1977 *The Food Crisis in Prehistory: Overpopulation and the Origins of Agriculture.* Yale University Press, New Haven.

Cohen, M. N., and G. J. Armelagos (editors)
1984 *Paleopathology at the Origins of Agriculture.* Academic Press, Orlando.

Condon, K. W.
1981 Correspondence of Developmental Enamel Defects Between the Mandibular Canine and First Premolar. Master's thesis, Department of Anthropology, University of Arkansas, Fayetteville.

Condon, K. W., and J. C. Rose
1979 Osteological Analysis of the Burris Site (3CG218). Ms. on file, Arkansas Archeological Survey, Fayetteville.

Cook, D. C.
1976 Pathologic States and Disease Process in Illinois Woodland Populations: An Epidemiological Approach. Ph.D. dissertation, Department of Anthropology, University of Chicago, Chicago.

1981 Mortality, Age Structure, and Status in the Interpretation of Stress Indicators in Prehistoric Skeletons: A Dental Example from the Lower Illinois Valley. In *The Archaeology of Death,* edited by R. C. Chapman, I. Kinnes, and K. Randsborg, pp. 133–44. Cambridge University Press, Cambridge.

1983 Social Status and Health: A Comparison of Middle Woodland and Mississippian Population from West Central Illinois. *American Journal of Physical Anthropology* 60:184.

1984 Subsistence and Health in the Lower Illinois Valley: Osteological Evidence. In *Paleopathology at the Origins of Agriculture,* edited by M. N. Cohen and G. J. Armelagos, pp. 237–70. Academic Press, Orlando.

Corruccini, R. S., J. S. Handler, R. J. Mutaw, and F. W. Lange

1982 Osteology of a Slave Burial Population from Barbados, West Indies. *American Journal of Physical Anthropology* 59:443–59.

Crites, G. D.

1984 Late Mississippian Paleoethnobotany in the Nashville Basin: The Evidence from Averbuch. In *Averbuch: A Late Mississippian Manifestation in the Nashville Basin, Volume 1, Observations,* edited by W. E. Klippel and W. M. Bass, pp. 12.1–23. Contract No. C-5943(79). Report submitted to the National Park Service, Southeast Regional Office, Atlanta.

Crook, M. R., Jr.

1980 Spatial Associations and Distribution of Aggregate Village Sites in a Southeastern Atlantic Coastal Area. *West Georgia College Studies in the Social Sciences* 19:77–88.

Crook, Morgan R.

1984 Evolving Community Organization on the Georgia Coast. *Journal of Field Archaeology* 11:247–63.

Culbert, T. P. (editor)

1973 *The Classic Maya Collapse.* University of New Mexico Press, Albuquerque.

Cybulski, J. S.

1977 Cribra Orbitalia, a Possible Sign of Anemia in Early Historic Native Populations of the British Columbia Coast. *American Journal of Physical Anthropology* 47:31–39.

Dailey, R. C., and D. Morse

1984 The Sowell Mound, A Weeden Island Period Burial Site (8Hi998), Tampa, Florida. *Florida Anthropologist* 37:165–71.

Dean, J. S., R. C. Euler, G. J. Gummerman, F. Plog, R. H. Hevly, and T N. V. Karlstrom

1985 Human Behavior, Demography, and Paleoenvironment on the Colorado Plateaus. *American Antiquity* 50:537–54.

Denny, S. G., W. I. Woods, and B. Koldehoff

1983 Upland and Mississippian Settlement/Subsistence Systems in the Cahokia Region. Paper presented at the 48th annual meeting of the Society for American Archaeology, Pittsburgh.

Deo, M. G.

1978 Cell Biology of Protein-calorie Malnutrition. *World Review of Nutrition and Dietetics* 32:49–95.

DePratter, C. B.

1979 Shellmound Archaic on the Georgia Coast. *South Carolina Antiquities* 11:1–69.

DesJean, T., I. R. Quitmyer, and K. J. Walker

1985 A Coastal Swift Creek Community at Kings Bay, Georgia. In *Indians, Colonists, and Slaves: Essays in Memory of Charles H. Fairbanks,* pp. 155–77. Special Publication No. 4. *Florida Journal of Anthropology.*

DiBennardo, R., and J. V. Taylor

1979 Sex Assessment of the Femur: A Test of a New Method. *American Journal of Physical Anthropology* 50:635–37.

Dickie, D. L., S. A. Goldstein, M. J. Flynn, and P. S. Bridges
1984 Analysis of the Geometric Properties of Human Long Bones Using Computer Axial Tomography. *Journal of Biomechanics* 17:868.

Dicks, A. M., and C. S. Weed (editors)
1985 *Archaeological Investigations of the Little Cypress Bayou Site (3CT50), Crittenden County, Arkansas.* New World Research Report of Investigations No. 82-21. Contract No. DACW66-82-R-0064.1. Submitted to U.S. Army Corps of Engineers, Memphis District.

Dragoo, D. W.
1976 Some Aspects of Eastern North American Prehistory: A Review, 1975. *American Antiquity* 41:3–27.

Droessler, J.
1981 *Craniometry and Biological Distance. Biocultural Continuity and Change at the Late-Woodland–Mississippian Interface.* Research Series No. 1. Center for American Archaeology, Evanston.

Dubos, R.
1965 *Man Adapting.* Yale University Press, New Haven.

Dufour, D. L.
1984 The Time and Energy Expenditure of Indigenous Women Horticulturalists in the Northwest Amazon. *American Journal of Physical Anthropology* 65:37–46.

Du Pratz, M.
1972 *The History of Louisiana.* Reprinted. Translated and edited by J. G. Tregle, Jr. Louisiana State University Press, Baton Rouge. Originally published 1774, London.

Edeiken, J., and P. J. Hodes
1973 *Roentgen Diagnosis of Diseases of Bone.* 2d ed. Williams and Wilkins, Baltimore.

Edgar, W. B., and L. Bailey
1977 *Biographical Directory of the South Carolina House of Representatives, Volume 2: The Commons House of Assembly, 1692–1775.* University of South Carolina Press, Columbia.

Egnatz, D. G.
1983 Analysis of Human Skeletal Materials from Mound C. Appendix A. In *Excavations at the Lake George Site, Yazoo County, Mississippi, 1958–1960,* by S. Williams and J. P. Brain, pp. 421–41. Papers of the Peabody Museum of Archaeology and Ethnology, vol. 74. Harvard University, Cambridge.

Eisenberg, L. E.
1985a Bioarchaeological Perspectives on Disease in a "Marginal" Mississippian Population. *American Journal of Physical Anthropology* 66:166–67.

1985b Possible Evidence for Mycotic Disease in a Late Prehistoric Population from Middle Tennessee. Paper presented at the 12th annual meeting of the Paleopathology Association, Knoxville.

1986a *Adaptation in a "Marginal" Mississippian Population from Middle Tennessee: Biocultural Insights from Paleopathology.* Ph.D. dissertation, New York University. University Microfilms, Ann Arbor.

1986b The Patterning of Trauma at Averbuch: Activity Levels and Conflict During the late Mississippian Period. *American Journal of Physical Anthropology* 69:197 (abstract).

El-Najjar, M. Y.

1979 Human Treponematosis and Tuberculosis: Evidence from the New World. *American Journal of Physical Anthropology* 51:599–618.

El-Najjar, M. Y., D. J. Ryan, C. G. Turner II, and B. Lozoff

1976 The Etiology of Porotic Hyperostosis Among the Prehistoric and Historic Anasazi Indians of the Southwestern United States. *American Journal of Physical Anthropology* 44:447–87.

Ember, C. R.

1983 The Relative Decline in Women's Contribution to Agriculture with Intensification. *American Anthropologist* 85:285–304.

Emerson, T. E., and D. K. Jackson

1984 *The BBB Motor Site.* University of Illinois Press, Urbana.

Esarey, D., and T. W. Good

1981 *Final Report of FAI-270 and Illinois Route 460 Related Excavations at the Lohmann Site (11-S-49), St. Clair County, Illinois.* FAI-270 Archaeological Mitigation Project Report 39. Department of Sociology and Anthropology, Western Illinois University, Macomb.

Ferguson, R. B.

1972 The Arnold Village Site Excavations of 1965–1966. In *The Middle Cumberland Culture,* edited by R. B. Ferguson, pp. 1–49. Vanderbilt University Publications in Anthropology No. 3, Nashville.

Fiske, M.

1820 Conjectures Respecting the Ancient Inhabitants of North America. *Transactions of the American Antiquity Society* 1:300–307.

Folkow B., and E. Neil

1971 *Circulation.* Oxford University Press, New York.

Ford, J. A.

1963 *Hopewell Culture Burial Mounds Near Helena, Arkansas.* Anthropological Papers of the American Museum of Natural History 50:1–55.

Fowler, M. L.

1974 *Cahokia: Ancient Capital of the Midwest.* Addison-Wesler Module in Anthropology 48:3–38.

1978 Cahokia and the American Bottom: Settlement Archaeology. In *Mississippian Settlement Patterns,* edited by B. D. Smith, pp. 455–78. Academic Press, New York.

Fowler, M. L., and R. L. Hall

1972 *Archaeological Phases at Cahokia.* Papers in Anthropology No. 1. Illinois State Museum, Springfield.

Frayer, D. W.

1981 Body Size, Weapon Use, and Natural Selection in the European Upper Paleolithic and Mesolithic. *American Anthropologist* 83:57–73.

Garcilaso de la Vega, G. S.

1951 *The Florida of the Inca.* Translated and edited by J. G. Varner and J. J. Varner. University of Texas Press, Austin.

Garn, S. M.
1966 Malnutrition and Skeletal Development in the Pre-school Child. In *Preschool Child Malnutrition*, pp. 43–62. National Research Council, Washington, D.C.

Garn, S. M., and M. A. Solomon
1981 Do the Obese Have Better Bones? *Ecology of Food and Nutrition* 10:195–97.

Genovés, S.
1967 Proportionality of the Long Bones and Their Relation to Stature among Mesoamericans. *American Journal of Physical Anthropology* 26:67–77.

Giardino, M. J.
1977 An Osteological Analysis of the Human Population from the Mount Nebo Site, Madison Parish, Louisiana. Master's thesis, Department of Anthropology, Tulane University, New Orleans.

Gibbs, T., K. Cargill, L. S. Lieberman, and E. J. Reitz
1980 Nutrition in a Slave Population: An Anthropological Examination. *Medical Anthropology* 4:175–262.

Gibson, J. L.
1970 Archaeological Checklist of Edible Flora in the Lower Mississippi Valley. *Southeastern Archaeological Conference Bulletin* 12:90–98.

Gilbert, B. M.
1976 Anterior Femoral Curvature: Its Probable Basis and Utility as a Criterion of Racial Assessment. *American Journal of Physical Anthropology* 45:601–04.

Gilbert, R. I., Jr.
1977 Applications of Trace Element Research to Problems in Archaeology. In *Biocultural Adaptation in Prehistoric America*, edited by R. L. Blakely, pp. 85–100. Proceedings No. 11. Southern Anthropological Society, University of Georgia Press, Athens.

Gilbert, R. I., Jr., and J. H. Mielke (editors)
1985 *The Analysis of Prehistoric Diets.* Academic Press, Orlando.

Goldstein, L. G.
1980 *Mississippian Mortuary Practices: A Case Study of Two Cemeteries in the Lower Illinois Valley.* Scientific Papers 4. Northwestern University Archaeological Program, Evanston.

Goodman, A. H., and G. J. Armelagos
1985 Disease and Death at Dr. Dickson's Mounds. *Natural History* 94(9):12–18.

Goodman, A. H., G. J. Armelagos, and J. C. Rose
1980 Enamel Hypoplasias as Indicators of Stress in Three Prehistoric Populations from Illinois. *Human Biology* 56:515–28.

Goodman, A. H., N. Rothschild, and G. J. Armelagos
1983 Childhood Stress, Age at Death and Social Status at Dickson Mound (A.D. 950–1300). *American Journal of Physical Anthropology* 60:199.

Goodman, A. H., J. W. Lallo, G. J. Armelagos, and J. C. Rose
1984 Health Changes at Dickson Mounds, Illinois (A.D. 950–1300). In *Paleopathology at the Origins of Agriculture*, edited by M. N. Cohen and G. J. Armelagos, pp. 271–305. Academic Press, Orlando.

Gordon, J. E., J. B. Wyon, and W. Ascoli
1967 The Second Year Death Rate in Less Developed Countries. *American Journal of the Medical Sciences* 254:357–80.

Gray, L. C.
1958 *History of Agriculture in the Southern United States to 1860.* 2 vols. Reprinted. Peter Smith, Gloucester, Massachusetts. Originally published 1932, Washington, D.C.

Gregg, M. L.
1975 A Population Estimate for Cahokia. In *Perspectives in Cahokia Archaeology,* pp. 126–36. Bulletin 10. Illinois Archaeological Survey, Urbana.

Griffin, J. B.
1960 Climatic Change: A Contributory Cause of the Growth and Decline of Northern Hopewellian Culture. *Wisconsin Archaeologist* 41:2.
1967 Eastern North American Archaeology: A Summary. *Science* 156:175–91.

Gross, D. L.
1984 Time Allocation: A Tool for the Study of Cultural Behavior. *Annual Review of Anthropology* 13:519–58.

Haag, W. G.
1978 A Prehistory of the Lower Mississippi Valley. *Geoscience and Man* 19:1–8.

Hackett, C. J.
1976 *Diagnostic Criteria of Syphilis, Yaws, and Treponarid (Treponematoses) and of Some Other Diseases in Dry Bones.* Springer-Verlag, New York.

Hale, H. S.
1984 Prehistoric Environmental Explorations Around Lake Okeechobee. *Southeastern Archaeology* 3:173–87.

Haltom, W. L., and A. R. Shands
1938 Evidences of Syphilis in Mound Builders' Bones. *Archives of Pathology* 25:228–42.

Hamilton, M.
1976 *Variation among Five Groups of Amerindians in the Magnitude of Sexual Dimorphism.* Ph.D. dissertation, University of Michigan. University Microfilms, Ann Arbor.

Harmon, A. M.
1984 Bioarchaeology of the Wapanocca Site (3CT9), Crittenden County Arkansas. Ms. on file, Department of Anthropology, University of Arkansas, Fayetteville.

Hassan, F. A.
1981 *Demographic Archaeology.* Academic Press, New York.

Hatch, J. W.
1976 *Status in Death: Principles of Ranking in Dallas Culture Mortuary Remains.* Ph.D. dissertation, Pennsylvania State University. University Microfilms, Ann Arbor.

Hatch, J. W., and R. A. Geidel
1983 Tracing Status and Diet in Prehistoric Tennessee. *Archaeology* 36:56–59.

Hatch, J. W., and P. S. Willey
1974 Stature and Status in Dallas Society. *Tennessee Archaeologist* 30:107–31.
Hatch, J. W., P. S. Wllley, and E. E. Hunt, Jr.
1983 Indicators of Status-related Stress in Dallas Society: Transverse Lines and Cortical Thickness in Long Bones. *Midcontinental Journal of Archaeology* 8:49–71.
Haywood, J.
1959 *The Natural and Aboriginal History of Tennessee Up to the First Settlements Therein by the White People in the Year 1768.* Reprinted. Edited by M. U. Rothrock. N. P., Jackson, Tennessee. Originally published 1823, Nashville.
Heckel, A. B.
1966 Osteological Analysis. In *Archaeological Excavation of the Womack Mound,* by T. H. Koehler, pp. 65–79. Mississippi Archaeological Association Bulletin No. 1.
Hengen, O. P.
1971 Cribra Orbitalia: Pathogenesis and Probably Etiology. *Homo* 22:57–76.
Hill-Clark, C.
1981 The Mississippian Decline in Alabama: A Biological Analysis. Paper presented at the 50th annual meeting of the American Association of Physical Anthropologists, Detroit.
Hodge, A. T.
1981 Vitruvivus, Lead Pipes and Lead Poisoning. *American Journal of Archaeology* 85:486–91.
Hoeprich, P. D. (editor)
1977 *Infectious Diseases, A Modern Treatise on Infectious Processes.* 2d ed. Harper and Row, Philadelphia.
Hooton, E. A.
1930 *The Indians of Pecos Pueblo: A Study of Their Skeletal Remains.* Papers of the Southwestern Expedition No. 4. Yale University Press, New Haven.
House, J. H.
1982 *Powell Canal: Baytown Period Occupation on Bayou Macon in Southeast Arkansas.* Research Series No. 19. Arkansas Archaeological Survey, Fayetteville.
Hoyme, L. E., and W. M. Bass
1962 *Human Skeletal Remains from the Tollifero (Ha6) and Clarksville (Mc14) Sites, John H. Kerr Reservoir Basin, Virginia.* Bureau of American Ethnology Bulletin 182:329–400. Smithsonian Institution, Washington, D.C.
Hrdlička, A.
1909 Report on an Additional Collection of Skeletal Remains from Arkansas and Louisiana. *Journal of the Academy of Natural Sciences of Philadelphia* 14:171–249.
1922 *The Anthropology of Florida.* Florida State Historical Society, Deland.
Hudson, C.
1976 *The Southeastern Indians.* University of Tennessee Press, Knoxville.
Hudson, E. H.
1958 *Non-venereal Syphilis, a Sociological and Medical Study of Bejel.* E. and S. Livingstone, Edinburgh.

Huss-Ashmore, R., A. H. Goodman, and G. J. Armelagos
1982 Nutritional Inference from Paleopathology. In *Advances in Archaeological Method and Theory,* vol. 5, edited by M. B. Schiffer, pp. 395–474. Academic Press, New York.

İşcan, M. Y.
1983 Skeletal Biology of the Margate-Blount Population. *Florida Anthropologist* 36:154–66.

İşcan, M. Y., and W. J. Kennedy
1987 Osteological Analysis of Human Remains from the Nebot Site. *Florida Scientist* 50:147–55.

İşcan, M. Y., and M. H. Kessel
1988 Osteology of the Prehistoric Boynton Beach Indians. *Florida Scientist* 51:12–18.

İşcan, M. Y., and P. Miller-Shaivitz
1984 Determination of Sex from the Tibia. *American Journal of Physical Anthropology* 64:53–57.
1985 Prehistoric Syphilis in Florida. *Journal of the Florida Medical Association* 72:109–13.

İşcan, M. Y., M. H. Kessel, and S. Marits
1989 Spectrographic Analysis of Trace Elements in Archaeological Skeletal Material from Florida: A Preliminary Report. *American Journal of Physical Anthropology* (in press).

Isler, R., and M. Y. İşcan
1986 Dental Pathological Comparison of Prehistoric Inland and Coastal Florida Populations. *American Journal of Physical Anthropology* 69:217–18 (abstract).

Isler, R., J. Schoen, and M. Y. İşcan
1985 Dental Pathology of a Prehistoric Human Population in Florida. *Florida Scientist* 48:139–46.

Jacobsen, T. W., and T. Cullen
1981 A Consideration of Mortuary Practices in Neolithic Greece: Burials from Franchthi Cave. In *Mortality and Immortality: The Anthropology and Archaeology of Death,* edited by S. C. King and H. King, pp. 79–101. Academic Press, London.

Jefferson, T.
1954 *Notes on the State of Virginia.* Reprinted. W. W. Norton, New York. Originally published 1787, London.

Johannessen, S.
1984 Paleoethnobotany. In *American Bottom Archaeology,* edited by C. J. Bareis and J. W. Porter, pp. 197–214. University of Illinois Press, Urbana.

Johansson, S. R., and S. Horowitz
1986 Estimating Mortality in Skeletal Populations: Influence of the Growth Rate on the Interpretation of Levels and Trends During the Transition to Agriculture. *American Journal of Physical Anthropology* 71:233–50.

Jolley, R. L.
1980 An Archaeological Survey of the Lower Duck and Middle Cumberland Rivers in Middle Tennessee. Ms. on file, Tennessee Division of Archaeology, Nashville.

Jones, C. E.
1958 Charles Woodmason as a Poet. *South Carolina Historical Magazine* 59:189–94.

Jones, G. D.
1978 The Ethnohistory of the Guale Coast Through 1684. In *The Anthropology of St. Catherines Island: 1. Natural and Cultural History,* by D. H. Thomas, G. D. Jones, R. S. Durham, and C. S. Larsen. Anthropological Papers of the American Museum of Natural History 55:178–210.

Jones, J.
1876 *Explorations of the Aboriginal Remains of Tennessee.* Smithsonian Contributions to Knowledge 22:1–171. Smithsonian Institution, Washington, D.C.

Kelley, M. A.
1980 *Disease and Environment: A Comparative Analysis of Three Early American Indian Skeletal Populations.* Ph.D. dissertation, Case Western Reserve University. University Microfilms, Ann Arbor.

Kelley, M. A., and L. E. Eisenberg
1987 Blastomycosis and Tuberculosis in Early American Indians: A Biocultural View. *Midcontinental Journal of Archaeology* 11:89–116.

Kelly, J. E.
1980 Formative Developments at Cahokia and the Adjacent American Bottom: A Merrell Tract Perspective. Ph.D. dissertation, Department of Anthropology, University of Wisconsin, Madison.

Kelly, J. E., S. J. Ozuk, D. K. Jackson, D. L. McElrath, F. A. Finney, and D. Esarey
1984 Emergent Mississippian Period. In *American Bottom Archaeology,* edited by C. J. Bareis and J. W. Porter, pp. 128–57. University of Illinois Press, Urbana.

Kelly, L. S., and P. G. Cross
1984 Zooarchaeology. In *American Bottom Archaeology,* edited by C. J. Bareis and J. W. Porter, pp. 215–32. University of Illinois Press, Urbana.

Kennedy, W. J., and M. Y. İşcan
1987 Archaeological Investigations of the Nebot Site (8Pb219), Palm Beach, Florida. *Florida Scientist* 50:136–46.

Kent, S.
1986 The Influence of Sedentism and Aggregation on Porotic Hyperostosis and Anaemia: A Case Study. *Man* (n.s.) 21:605–36.

Kidwell, C. S., and C. Roberts
1980 *The Choctaws.* University of Indiana Press, Bloomington.

King, F. B.
1985 Presettlement Vegetation and Plant Remains. In *The Alexander Site, Conway County, Arkansas,* by E. T. Hemmings and J. H. House, pp. 49–57. Research Series No. 24. Arkansas Archeological Survey, Fayetteville.

King, F. B., and D. C. Roper
1976 Floral Remains from Two Middle to Early Late Woodland Sites in Central Illinois and Their Implications. *Wisconsin Archaeologist* 57:142–51.

Kline, G. W.
1984a The Averbuch Lithic Assemblage Interpretation and Discussion. In *Averbuch: A Late Mississippian Manifestation in the Nashville Basin, Volume 1, Ob-*

servations, edited by W. E. Klippel and W. M. Bass, pp. 11.1–15. Contract No. C-5943(79). Report submitted to the National Park Service, Southeast Regional Office, Atlanta.

1984b Descriptive Framework of the Averbuch Lithic Analysis. In *Averbuch: A Late Mississippian Manifestation in the Nashville Basin, Volume 2, Description,* edited by W. E. Klippel and W. M. Bass, pp. 8.1–43. Contract No. C-5943(79). Report submitted to the National Park Service, Southeast Regional Office, Atlanta.

Kline, G. W., and G. D. Crites

1979 Paleoethnobotany of the Ducks Nest Site: Early Mississippi Plant Utilization in the Eastern Highland Rim. *Tennessee Anthropologist* 4:82–100.

Klinger, T. C., S. M. Imhoff, and R. J. Cochran, Jr.

1983 *Brougham Lake: Archaeological Mitigation of 3CT98 Along the Big Creek Enlargement and Diversion, Item 1, Crittenden County, Arkansas.* Historic Preservation Associates Fayetteville. Contract No. DACW66-80-C0082. Submitted to U.S. Army Corps of Engineers, Memphis District.

Klippel, W. E., and W. M. Bass

1984 *Averbuch: A Late Mississippian Manifestation in the Nashville Basin, Volume 1, Observations,* edited by W. E. Klippel and W. M. Bass, p. iii. Contract No. C-5943(79). Report submitted to the National Park Service, Southeast Regional Office, Atlanta.

Krogman, W. M., and M. Y. İşcan

1986 *The Human Skeleton in Forensic Medicine.* C. C. Thomas, Springfield, Illinois.

Lahren, C. H., and H. E. Berryman

1984 Fracture Patterns and Status at Chucalissa (40SY1): A Biocultural Approach. *Tennessee Anthropologist* 9:15–21.

Lallo, J. W.

1973 *The Skeletal Biology of Three Prehistoric American Indian Societies from Dickson Mounds.* Ph.D. dissertation, University of Massachusetts. University Microfilms, Ann Arbor.

Lanyon, L. E., and C. T. Rubin

1985 Functional Adaptation in Skeletal Structures. In *Functional Vertebrate Morphology,* edited by M. Hildebrand, D. M. Bramble, K. F. Liem, and D. B. Wake, pp. 1–25. Harvard University Press, Cambridge.

Larsen, C. S.

1981 Functional Implications of Postcranial Size Reduction on the Prehistoric Georgia Coast, U.S.A. *Journal of Human Evolution* 10:489–502.

1982 *The Anthropology of St. Catherines Island. 3. Prehistoric Human Biological Adaptation.* Anthropological Papers of the American Museum of Natural History 57:159–207.

1983a Behavioral Implications of Temporal Change in Cariogenesis. *Journal of Archaeological Science* 10:1–8.

1983b Subsistence Role Behavior and the Infectious Disease Experience on the Prehistoric Georgia Coast. *American Journal of Physical Anthropology* 60:216 (abstract).

1984 Health and Disease in Prehistoric Georgia: The Transition to Agriculture. In *Paleopathology at the Origins of Agriculture,* edited by M. N. Cohen and G. J. Armelagos, pp. 367–92. Academic Press, Orlando.
1987 Bioarchaeological Interpretations of Subsistence Economy and Behavior from Human Skeletal Remains. In *Advances in Archaeological Method and Theory,* vol. 10, edited by M. B. Schiffer, pp. 339–445. Academic Press, Orlando.

Larson, L. H., Jr.
1971 Archaeological Implications of Social Stratification at the Etowah Site, Georgia. In *Approaches to the Social Dimensions of Mortuary Practices,* edited by J. A. Brown. Society for American Archaeology, *Memoirs* 25:58–67.
1980 *Aboriginal Subsistence Technology on the Southeastern Coastal Plain During the Late Prehistoric Period.* University Presses of Florida, Gainesville.

Lee, R., and I. DeVore (editors)
1968 *Man the Hunter.* Aldine, Chicago.

Le Page du Pratz, A. S.
1947 *The History of Louisiana.* Pelican Press, New Orleans.

Lewis, T. M. N., and M. Kneberg
1946 *Hiwassee Island.* University of Tennessee Press, Knoxville.
1955 *The First Tennesseans: An Interpretation of Tennessee Prehistory.* Department of Anthropology, University of Tennessee, Knoxville.

Lovejoy, C. O., A. H. Burstein, and K. G. Heiple
1976 The Biomechanical Analysis of Bone Strength: A Method and Its Application to Platycnemia. *American Journal of Physical Anthropology* 44:489–505.

Lynott, M. J., T. W. Boutton, J. E. Price, and D. E. Nelson
1986 Stable Carbon Isotopic Evidence for Maize Agriculture in Southeast Missouri and Northeast Arkansas. *American Antiquity* 51:51–65.

Magennis, A. L., D. L. Martin, and G. J. Armelagos
1985 Patterns of Disease in a Marginal Environment: The Black Mesa Anasazi. *American Journal of Physical Anthropology* 66:201 (abstract).

Manhein, M. H.
1985 Louisiana Human Skeletal Material: Anthropology's Responsibility to the Past. Master's thesis, Department of Geography and Anthropology, Louisiana State University, Baton Rouge.

Marrinan, R.
1975 Ceramics, Molluscs, and Sedentism: The Late Archaic Period on the Georgia Coast. Ph.D. dissertation, Department of Anthropology, University of Florida, Gainesville.

Martin, D. J., A. H. Goodman, and G. J. Armelagos
1985 Skeletal Pathologies as Indicators of Quality and Quantity of Diet. In *The Analysis of Prehistoric Diets,* edited by R. I. Gilbert, Jr., and J. H. Mielke, pp. 227–79. Academic Press, Orlando.

Martin, R. B., D. B. Burr, and M. B. Schaffler
1985 Effects of Age and Sex on the Amount and Distribution of Mineral in the Eskimo Tibia. *American Journal of Physical Anthropology* 67:371–80.

Martin, T. J.

1977 The Natural Resources Significant to Prehistoric Culture Adaptations in the Nashville Basin of Tennessee. Master's thesis, Department of Anthropology, University of Tennessee, Knoxville.

Martischig, E.

1952 Die Tuberculose in Sauglingsalter. *Weiner Beitrage Sur Kinderheikunde,* vol. 4.

May, J. A.

1983 Fallen Tree Revisited: Preliminary Results from Test Excavations at 9LB8, St. Catherines Island. Paper presented at the 40th Southeastern Archaeological Conference, Columbia, South Carolina.

Mead, M. (editor)

1955 *Cultural Patterns and Technological Change.* New American Library, New York.

Mehrer, M. W.

1982 *A Mississippian Community at the Range Site (11-S-47), St. Clair County, Illinois.* FAI–270 Archaeological Mitigation Project Report 52. Department of Anthropology, University of Illinois, Urbana.

Mensforth, R. P.

1985 Relative Tibia Long Bone Growth in the Libben and Bt–5 Prehistoric Skeletal Populations. *American Journal of Physical Anthropology* 68:247–62.

Mensforth, R. P., C. O. Lovejoy, J. W. Lallo, and G. J. Armelagos

1978 The Role of Constitutional Factors, Diet, and Infectious Disease in the Etiology of Porotic Hyperostosis and Periosteal Reactions in Prehistoric Infants and Children. *Medical Anthropology* 2:1–59.

Merbs, C. F.

1980 The Pathology of a La Jollan Skeleton from Punta Minitas, Baja California. *Pacific Coast Archaeological Society Quarterly* 16:37–43.

1983 *Patterns of Activity-Induced Pathology in a Canadian Inuit Population.* Archaeological Survey of Canada Paper 119. National Museum of Man, Ottawa.

Milanich, J. T., and C. H. Fairbanks

1980 *Florida Archaeology.* Academic Press, New York.

Miller, R. J.

1982 Manos, Metates, and Tennis Elbow: Degenerative Joint Disease in the Prehistoric Southwest. *American Journal of Physical Anthropology* 57:210 (abstract).

Miller-Shaivitz, P. M.

1986 Physical and Health Characteristics of the Prehistoric People from the Fort Center Site. Master's thesis, Department of Anthropology, Florida Atlantic University, Boca Raton.

Milner, G. R.

1982 *Measuring Prehistoric Levels of Health: A Study of Mississippian Period Skeletal Remains from the American Bottom, Illinois.* Ph.D. dissertation, Northwestern University. University Microfilms, Ann Arbor.

1983a The Cultural Determinants of Mississippian Community Health: An Examination of Populations from Two Areas of Western Illinois. *American Journal of Physical Anthropology* 60:227.

1983b *The East St. Louis Stone Quarry Site Cemetery.* University of Illinois Press, Urbana.

1983c *The Turner and DeMange Sites.* University of Illinois Press, Urbana.

1984 Social and Temporal Implications of Variation among American Bottom Mississippian Cemeteries. *American Antiquity* 49:468–88.

1986 Mississippian Period Population Density in a Segment of the Central Mississippi River Valley. *American Antiquity* 51:227–38.

1987 The Development and Dissolution of an Organizationally Complex Mississippian Period Culture in the American Bottom, Illinois. Paper presented at the 44th Southeastern Archaeological Conference, Charleston, South Carolina.

Milner, G. R., and V. G. Smith

1990 Oneota Human Skeletal Remains. *Archaeological Investigations at the Morton Village (11Fu19) and Norris Farms 36 (11Fu2167), Fulton County, Illinois.* Reports of Investigations. Illinois State Museum.

Milner, G. R., V. G. Smith, and E. Anderson

1988 Conflict, Mortality, and Community Health in an Illinois Oneota Population. Paper presented at the Center for Archaeological Investigations Conference, "Between Bands and States: Sedentism, Subsistence, and Interaction in Small-Scale Societies," Southern Illinois University, Carbondale.

Milner, G. R., T. E. Emerson, M. W. Mehrer, J. A. Williams, and D. Esarey

1984 Mississippian and Oneota. In *American Bottom Archaeology,* edited by C. J. Bareis and J. W. Porter, pp. 158–86. University of Illinois Press, Urbana.

Minnis, P. E.

1985 *Social Adaptation to Food Stress.* University of Chicago Press, Chicago.

Moore, C. B.

1906 Certain Aboriginal Remains of the Black Warrior River. *Journal of the Academy of Natural Sciences of Philadelphia* 13:123–224.

1907 Moundville Revisited. *Journal of the Academy of Natural Sciences of Philadelphia* 13:337–405.

Moore, J. A., A. C. Swedlund, and G. J. Armelagos

1975 The Use of Life Tables in Paleodemography. In *Population Studies in Archaeology and Biological Anthropology: A Symposium,* edited by A. C. Swedlund. Society for American Archaeology, *Memoirs* 30:57–70.

Moorrees, C. F. A., E. A. Fanning, and E. E. Hunt, Jr.

1963a Age Variation of Formation Stages for Ten Permanent Teeth. *Journal of Dental Research* 42:1490–1502.

1963b Formation and Resorption of Three Deciduous Teeth in Children. *American Journal of Physical Anthropology* 21:205–13.

Morse, D.

1983 The Skeletal Pathology of Trauma. In *Handbook of Forensic Archaeology and Anthropology,* edited by D. Morse, J. Duncan, and J. Stoutamire, pp. 145–85. Bill's Book Store, Tallahassee.

Morse, D. F., and P. A. Morse

1983 *Archaeology of the Central Mississippi Valley.* Academic Press, New York.

Morse, D. F., and P. A. Morse (editors)
1976 *A Preliminary Report of the Zebree Project: New Approaches in Contract Archaeology in Arkansas.* Research Report No. 8. Arkansas Archeological Survey, Fayetteville.

Murdock, G. P., and C. Provost
1973 Factors in the Division of Labor by Sex: A Cross-cultural Analysis. *Ethnology* 12:203–25.

Murphy, T.
1959 Gradients of Dentine Exposure in Human Molar Tooth Attrition. *American Journal of Physical Anthropology* 17:179–86.

Murray, K. A.
1985 Bioarchaeology of the Parkin Site. Master's thesis, Department of Anthropology, University of Arkansas, Fayetteville.

Neuman, R. W.
1984 *An Introduction to Louisiana Archaeology.* Louisiana State University Press, Baton Rouge.

Newman, M. T., and C. E. Snow
1942 Preliminary Report on the Skeletal Material from Pickwick Basin, Alabama. In *An Archaeological Survey of Pickwick Basin in the Adjacent Portions of the States of Alabama, Mississippi and Tennessee,* edited by W. S. Webb and D. L. DeJarnette, pp. 393–507. Bureau of American Ethnology Bulletin No. 129. Smithsonian Institution, Washington, D.C.

Noel-Hume, I.
1969 *Historical Archaeology.* Alfred Knopf, New York.

Nordin, M., and V. H. Frankel
1980 Biomechanics of Whole Bones and Bone Tissue. In *Basic Biomechanics of the Skeletal System,* edited by V. H. Frankel and M. Nordin, pp. 15–60. Lea and Febiger, Philadelphia.

Nriagu, J. O.
1983 Saturnine Gout Among Roman Aristocrats. *New England Journal of Medicine* 308:660–63.

Ortner, D. J.
1968 Description and Classification of Degenerative Bone Changes in the Distal Joint Surfaces of the Humerus. *American Journal of Physical Anthropology* 28:139–56.

Ortner, D. J., and S. Hunter
1981 Hematogenous Osteomyelitis in a Precolumbian Child's Skeleton from Maryland. *MASCA Journal* 1:236–38.

Ortner, D. J., and W. G. J. Putschar
1981 *Identification of Pathological Conditions in Human Skeletal Remains.* Smithsonian Contributions to Anthropology No. 28. Smithsonian Institution, Washington, D.C.

O'Shea, J. M.
1984 *Mortuary Variability: An Archaeological Investigation.* Academic Press, New York.

Owsley, D. W.
1975 A Demographic Analysis of Skeletons from the Larson Site (39WW2) Wal-

worth County, South Dakota. Master's thesis, Department of Anthropology, University of Tennessee, Knoxville.

Palerm, A., and E. R. Wolf

1960 Ecological Potential and Cultural Development in Mesoamerica. *Social Science Monographs* 3:1–38.

Palkovich, A. M.

1978 A Model of the Dimensions of Mortality and Its Application to Paleodemography. Ph.D. dissertation, Department of Anthropology, Northwestern University, Evanston.

1980 *Pueblo Population and Society: The Arroyo Hondo Skeletal and Mortuary Remains.* Arroyo Hondo Archaeological Series 3. School of American Research Press, Santa Fe.

1983 A Biological Perspective on Prehistoric Social Status. *American Journal of Physical Anthropology* 60:236 (abstract).

1987 Endemic Disease Patterns in Paleopathology: Porotic Hyperostosis. *American Journal of Physical Anthropology* 74:527–37.

Patterson, D. K., Jr.

1984 *A Diachronic Study of Dental Paleopathology and Attritional Status of Prehistoric Ontario Pre-Iroquois and Iroquois Populations.* National Museum of Canada, Ottawa.

Payne, R.

1843 Plat of three tracts of land known as "Lebby's Point," "Linn's Shipyard," and "Peas' tract" in Christ Church Parish and recorded in the records of Mesne Conveyance. Charleston, South Carolina.

Pearson, M. P.

1983 Mortuary Practices, Society, and Ideology: An Ethnoarchaeological Study. In *Structural Archaeology,* edited by I. Hodder, pp. 99–113. Cambridge University Press, New York.

Peebles, C. S.

1971 Moundville and Surrounding Sites: Some Structural Considerations of Mortuary Practices. In *Approaches to the Social Dimensions of Mortuary Practices,* edited by J. A. Brown. Society for American Archaeology, *Memoirs* 25:68–91.

1974 *Moundville: The Organization of a Prehistoric Community and Culture.* Ph.D. dissertation, University of California, Santa Barbara. University Microfilms, Ann Arbor.

1977 Biocultural Adaptation in Prehistoric America: An Archaeologist's Perspective. In *Biocultural Adaptation in Prehistoric America,* edited by R. L. Blakely, pp. 115–30. Proceedings No. 11. Southern Anthropological Society, University of Georgia Press, Athens.

1978 Determinants of Settlement Size and Location in the Moundville Phase. In *Mississippian Settlement Patterns,* edited by B. D. Smith, pp. 369–416. Academic Press, New York.

1979 *Excavations at Moundville: 1905–1951.* University Microfilms, Ann Arbor (microfiche).

1983 Moundville: Late Prehistoric Sociopolitical Organization in the Southeastern United States. In *The Development of Political Organization in Native*

North America, edited by E. Tooker, pp. 183–201. American Ethnological Society, Washington, D.C.

Peebles, C. S., and S. M. Kus

1977 Some Archaeological Correlates of Ranked Societies. *American Antiquity* 42:471–84.

Perzigian, A. J.

1977 Teeth as Tools for Prehistoric Studies. In *Biocultural Adaptation in Prehistoric America,* edited by R. L. Blakely, pp. 101–14. Proceedings No. 11. Southern Anthropological Society, University of Georgia Press, Athens.

Perzigian, A. J., P. A. Tench, and D. J. Braun

1984 Prehistoric Health in the Ohio River Valley. In *Paleopathology at the Origins of Agriculture,* edited by M. N. Cohen and G. J. Armelagos, pp. 347–66. Academic Press, Orlando.

Phillips, J. L., R. L. Hall, and R. W. Yerkes

1980 *Investigations of the Labras Lake Site. Volume 1, Archaeology, Part 1.* Department of Anthropology, University of Illinois, Chicago Circle.

Pickering, R. B.

1984 *Patterns of Degenerative Joint Disease in Middle Woodland, Late Woodland, and Mississippian Skeletal Series from the Lower Illinois Valley.* Ph.D. dissertation, Northwestern University. University Microfilms, Ann Arbor.

Pollitzer, W. S.

1958 The Negroes of Charleston, (S.C.): A Study of Hemoglobin Types, Serology, and Morphology. *American Journal of Physical Anthropology* 16:241–63.

Popkin, B. M., R. E. Bilsborrow, and J. S. Akin

1982 Breast-Feeding Patterns in Low-Income Countries. *Science* 218:1088–93.

Powell, J. W.

1880 Introduction. In *The Study of Mortuary Customs Among North American Indians,* pp. iii–vi. Government Printing Office, Washington, D.C.

Powell, M. L.

1977 Bioarchaeological Research Potential of Human Skeletal Material: A Case Study from Northeast Arkansas. Master's thesis, Department of Anthropology, University of Arkansas, Fayetteville.

1983 Biocultural Analysis of Human Skeletal Remains from the Lubbub Creek Archaeological Locality. In *Prehistoric Agricultural Communities in West Central Alabama,* vol. 2, edited by C. S. Peebles, pp. 430–77. (AD–A155048/2/GAR). National Technical Information Service, Washington, D.C.

1985a The Analysis of Dental Wear and Caries for Dietary Reconstruction. In *The Analysis of Prehistoric Diets,* edited by R. I. Gilbert, Jr., and J. H. Mielke, pp. 307–38. Academic Press, Orlando.

1985b *Health and Disease and Social Organization in the Mississippian Community at Moundville.* Ph.D. dissertation, Northwestern University. University Microfilms, Ann Arbor.

1988 *Status and Health in Prehistory: A Case Study of the Moundville Chiefdom.* Smithsonian Institution Press, Washington, D.C.

1989 The Nodena People. In *Nodena, an Account of 90 Years of Archaeological Investigation in Southeast Mississippi County, Arkansas,* edited by D. F. Morse, pp. 65–95, 123–50. Research Series No. 30, Arkansas Archaeological Survey, Fayetteville.

Prasad, A. S.
1978 *Trace Elements and Iron in Human Metabolism.* Plenum, New York.

PSPG
n.d. Papers of the Society for the Propogation of the Gospel, Charleston, South Carolina. Typescript on file with the society, Charleston, South Carolina.

Puffer, R. R., and C. V. Serrano
1973 *Patterns of Mortality in Childhood.* Scientific Publication 262. Pan American Health Organization, Washington, D.C.

Quitmyer, I. R., H. S. Hale, and D. S. Jones
1985 Paleoseasonality Determination Based on Incremental Shell Growth in the Hard Clam, *Mercenaria mercenaria,* and Its Implications for the Analysis of Three Southeast Georgia Coastal Shell Middens. *Southeastern Archaeology* 4:27–40.

Ramenofsky, A. F.
1986 The Persistence of Late Archaic Subsistence-Settlement in Louisiana. In *Foraging, Collecting and Harvesting: Archaic Period Subsistence and Settlement in the Eastern Woodlands,* edited by S. Neusius, pp. 289–312. Occasional Papers No. 6. Center for Archaeological Investigations, Southern Illinois University, Carbondale.

Ramenofsky, A. F., and A. M. Mires
1985 Archaeology of Cowpen Slough, 16CT147. Partially funded by the United States Department of the Interior and administered by the Division of Archaeology, Office of Cultural Development, Department of Culture, Recreation, and Tourism, State of Louisiana. Contract No. 84–A–2.

Rathbun, T. A.
1981 Human Remains as an Archaeological Resource. *South Carolina Antiquities* 13:17–39.

Reed, A.
1984a The Averbuch Ceramic Assemblage: Description and Interpretation. In *Averbuch: A Late Mississippian Manifestation in the Nashville Basin, Volume 2, Description,* edited by W. E. Klippel and W. M. Bass, pp. 1.1–10. Contract No. C–5943(79). Report submitted to the National Park Service, Southeast Regional Office, Atlanta.

1984b Environmental Setting. In *Averbuch: A Late Mississippian Manifestation in the Nashville Basin, Volume 1, Observations,* edited by W. E. Klippel and W. M. Bass, pp. 1–10. Contract No. C–5943(79). Report submitted to the National Park Service, Southeast Regional Office, Atlanta.

Reinhard, K. J.
1988 Cultural Ecology of Prehistoric Parasitism on the Colorado Plateau as Evidenced by Coprology. *American Journal of Physical Anthropology* 77:355–66.

Reitz, E. J.
1978 Report on the Faunal Material Excavated by West Georgia College from Colonel's Island, Georgia, 1977. In *Cultural Evolution and Environment of Colonel's Island, Georgia,* by K. T. Steinen, pp. 135–62. West Georgia College, Carrollton.

1982a Availability and Use of Fish along Coastal Georgia and Florida. *Southeastern Archaeology* 1:65–88.

1982b Vertebrate Fauna from Four Coastal Mississippian Sites. *Journal of Ethnobiology* 2:39–61.

1988 Evidence for Coastal Adaptations in Georgia and South Carolina. *Archaeology of Eastern North America* 16:137–58.

Reitz, E. J., and C. M. Scarry

1985 *Reconstructing Historic Subsistence, with an Example from Sixteenth-century Spanish Florida.* Special Publication No. 3. Society for Historical Archaeology.

Rindos, D.

1984 *The Origins of Agriculture.* Academic Press, Orlando.

Robbins, L. M.

1977 The Story of Life Revealed by the Dead. In *Biocultural Adaptation in Prehistoric America,* edited by R. L. Blakely, pp. 10–26. Proceedings No. 11. Southern Anthropological Society, University of Georgia Press, Athens.

1978 Yawslike Disease Process in a Louisiana Shell Mound Population. *Medical College of Virginia Quarterly* 14:24–31.

Robinson, R. K.

1976 Social Status, Stature, and Pathology at Chucalissa (40SY1), Shelby County, Tennessee. Master's thesis, Department of Anthropology, University of Tennessee, Knoxville.

Romanoski, S. M.

1984a Analysis of the Faunal Remains from the Averbuch Site. In *Averbuch: A Late Mississippian Manifestation in the Nashville Basin, Volume 1, Observations,* edited by W. E. Klippel and W. M. Bass, pp. 13.1–27. Contract No. C–5943(79). Report submitted to the National Park Service, Southeast Regional Office, Atlanta.

1984b Fauna from the Averbuch Site. In *Averbuch: A Late Mississippian Manifestation in the Nashville Basin, Volume 2, Description,* edited by W. E. Klippel and W. M. Bass, pp. 1.1–46. Contract No. C–5943(79). Report submitted to the National Park Service, Southeast Regional Office, Atlanta.

Romans, B.

1962 *A Concise Natural History of East and West Florida.* Facsimile reproduction of the 1775 edition. University of Florida Press, Gainesville.

Roosevelt, A. C.

1984 Population, Health, and the Evolution of Subsistence. In *Paleopathology at the Origins of Agriculture,* edited by M. N. Cohen and G. J. Armelagos, pp. 559–83. Academic Press, Orlando.

Rose, J. C. (editor)

1985 *Gone to a Better Land.* Research Series No. 25. Arkansas Archaeological Survey, Fayetteville.

Rose, J. C., and B. A. Burnett

1985 Bioarchaeology of the Owls Bend Site. Ms. on file, National Park Service, Midwest Archaeological Center, Lincoln, Nebraska.

Rose, J. C., and A. M. Harmon

1986 Enamel Microwear and Prehistoric North American Diets. *American Jour-*

nal of Physical Anthropology 69:257 (abstract).

Rose, J. C., and M. K. Marks

1985 Bioarchaeology of the Alexander Site. In *The Alexander Site, Conway County, Arkansas,* by E. T. Hemmings and J. H. House, pp. 76–98. Research Series No. 24. Arkansas Archeological Survey, Fayetteville.

Rose, J. C., K. W. Condon, and A. H. Goodman

1985 Diet and Dentition: Developmental Disturbances. In *The Analysis of Prehistoric Diets,* edited by R. I. Gilbert, Jr., and J. H. Mielke, pp. 281–305. Academic Press, Orlando.

Rose, J. C., M. K. Marks, and L. L. Tieszen

1985 Bioarchaeology of the Little Cypress Bayou Site. Appendix IV. In *Archaeological Investigations of the Little Cypress Bayou Site (3CT50), Crittenden County, Arkansas, Volume 2. Appendices,* edited by A. M. Dicks and C. S. Weed, pp. 4.1–53. New World Research Report of Investigations No. 82–21. Contract No. DACW66–82–R–0064.1. Submitted to U.S. Army Corps of Engineers, Memphis District.

Rose, J. C., B. A. Burnett, M. S. Nassaney, and M. W. Blaeuer

1984 Paleopathology and the Origins of Maize Agriculture in the Lower Mississippi Valley and Caddoan Culture Areas. In *Paleopathology at the Origins of Agriculture,* edited by M. N. Cohen and G. J. Armelagos, pp. 393–425. Academic Press, Orlando.

Rothschild, N. A.

1979 Mortuary Behavior and Social Organization at Indian Knoll and Dickson Mounds. *American Antiquity* 44:658–75.

Ruff, C. B.

1987 Sexual Dimorphism in Human Lower Limb Bone Structure: Relationship to Subsistence Strategy and Sexual Division of Labor. *Journal of Human Evolution* 16:391–416.

Ruff, C. B., and W. C. Hayes

1983a Cross-sectional Geometry of Pecos Pueblo Femora and Tibiae—A Biomechanical Investigation: I. Method and General Patterns of Variation. *American Journal of Physical Anthropology* 60:359–81.

1983b Cross-sectional Geometry of Pecos Pueblo Femora and Tibiae—A Biomechanical Investigation: II. Sex, Age, and Side Differences. *American Journal of Physical Anthropology* 60:383–400.

Ruff, C. B., and F. L. Leo

1986 Use of Computed Tomography in Skeletal Structural Research. *Yearbook of Physical Anthropology* 29:181–96.

Ruff, C. B., C. S. Larsen, and W. C. Hayes

1984 Structural Changes in the Femur with the Transition to Agriculture on the Georgia Coast. *American Journal of Physical Anthropology* 64:125–36.

SCRSSW: South Carolina, Records of the Secretary of State, Wills. Charleston, South Carolina.

Sahlins, M. D.

1972 *Stone Age Economics.* Aldine-Atherton, Chicago.

Sattenspiel, L., and H. C. Harpending

1983 Stable Populations and Skeletal Age. *American Antiquity* 48:489–98.

Saul, F. P.
1972 *The Human Skeletal Remains of Altar de Sacrificios.* Papers of the Peabody Museum of Archaeology and Ethnology, vol. 63. Harvard University, Cambridge.

Saunders, L. P.
1972 Osteology of the Republic Groves Site. Master's thesis, Department of Anthropology, Florida Atlantic University, Boca Raton.

Saxe, A.
1970 *Social Dimensions of Mortuary Practices.* Ph.D. dissertation, University of Michigan. University Microfilms, Ann Arbor.

Schoeninger, M. J., and C. S. Peebles
1981 Notes on the Relationship Between Social Status and Diet at Moundville. *Southeastern Archaeological Conference Bulletin* 24:96–97.

Scott, E. C.
1979a Dental Wear Scoring Techniques. *American Journal of Physical Anthropology* 51:213–18.
1979b Principal Axis Analysis of Dental Attrition Data. *American Journal of Physical Anthropology* 51:203–11.

Scrimshaw, N. S.
1975 Interactions of Malnutrition and Infection: Advances in Understanding. In *Protein-Calorie Malnutrition,* edited by R. E. Olson, pp. 353–68. Academic Press, New York.

Scrimshaw, N. S., C. E. Taylor, and J. E. Gordon
1968 *Interactions of Nutrition and Infection.* World Health Organization Monograph 57. Geneva, Switzerland.

Sears, E. O.
1982 Pollen Analysis. In *Fort Center: An Archaeological Site in the Lake Okeechobee Basin,* edited by W. H. Sears, pp. 118–29. University Presses of Florida, Gainesville.

Sears, W. H. (editor)
1982 *Fort Center: An Archaeological Site in the Lake Okeechobee Basin.* University Presses of Florida, Gainesville.

Sellers, L.
1934 *Charleston Business on the Eve of the American Revolution.* University of North Carolina Press, Chapel Hill.

Shea, A.
1985 Macro Paleobotanical Analysis. Appendix III. In *Archaeological Investigations of the Little Cypress Bayou Site (3CT50), Crittenden County, Arkansas, Volume 2. Appendices,* edited by A. M. Dicks and C. S. Weed, pp. 3.1–34. New World Research Report of Investigations No. 82–21. Contract No. DACW66–82–R–0064.1. Submitted to U.S. Army Corps of Engineers, Memphis District.

Sheldon, C. T.
1974 *The Mississippian-Historic Transition in Central Alabama.* Ph.D. dissertation, University of Oregon. University Microfilms, Ann Arbor.

Smith, B. D.
1978 Variation in Mississippian Settlement Patterns. In *Mississippian Settlement*

Patterns, edited by B. D. Smith, pp. 479–503. Academic Press, New York.

Snow, C. E.

1962 *Indian Burials from St. Petersburg, Florida.* Contributions of the Florida State Museum, Social Sciences No. 8. Gainesville.

Spears, C. S.

1978 The DeRossitt Site (3SF49). Master's thesis, Department of Anthropology, University of Arkansas, Fayetteville.

Sperber, J.

1982 Analysis of Burials. In *The Magrun Site: Mitigation Through Excavation and Preservation,* by T. C. Klinger, pp. 109–22. Research Series No. 20. Arkansas Archeological Survey, Fayetteville.

Spier, R. F. G.

1955 Skeletal Remains from the Campbell Site. *Missouri Archaeologist* 17:(2, 3):121–40.

Springer, J. W.

1980 An Analysis of Prehistoric Food Remains from the Bruly St. Martin Site, Louisiana, with a Comparative Discussion of Mississippi Valley Faunal Studies. *Midcontinental Journal of Archaeology* 5:193–224.

Steinbock, R. T.

1976 *Paleopathological Diagnosis and Interpretation.* C. C. Thomas, Springfield, Illinois.

Steinen, K. T.

1982 Other Nonceramic Artifacts. In *Fort Center: An Archaeological Site in the Lake Okeechobee Basin,* edited by W. H. Sears, pp. 68–110. University Presses of Florida, Gainesville.

1984 Cultural Occupation of the Georgia Coastal Marsh. *Southeastern Archaeology* 3:164–72.

Steponaitis, V. P.

1983 *Ceramics, Chronology and Community Patterns: An Archaeological Study at Moundville.* Academic Press, New York.

Stewart, T. D.

1979 *Essentials of Forensic Anthropology.* C. C. Thomas, Springfield, Illinois.

Stuart-Macadam, P.

1985 Porotic Hyperostosis: Representative of a Childhood Condition. *American Journal of Physical Anthropology* 66:391–98.

1987 Porotic Hyperostosis: New Evidence to Support the Anemia Theory. *American Journal of Physical Anthropology* 74:521–26.

Styles, B. W.

1981 *Faunal Exploitation and Resource Selection. Early Late Woodland Subsistence in the Lower Illinois Valley.* Scientific Papers 3. Northwestern University Archaeological Program, Evanston.

Swanton, J. R.

1911 *Indian Tribes of the Lower Mississippi Valley and Adjacent Coast of the Gulf of Mexico.* Bureau of American Ethnology Bulletin No. 43. Smithsonian Institution, Washington, D.C.

1946 *The Indians of the Southeastern United States.* Bureau of American Ethnology Bulletin No. 137. Smithsonian Institution, Washington, D.C.

Tainter, J. A.

1978 Mortuary Practices and the Study of Prehistoric Social Systems. In *Advances in Archaeological Method and Theory,* vol. 1, edited by M. B. Schiffer, pp. 105–41. Academic Press, New York.

Thomas, D. H., and C. S. Larsen

1979 *The Anthropology of St. Catherines Island. 2. The Refuge-Deptford Mortuary Complex.* Anthropological Papers of the American Museum of Natural History 56:1–179.

Thruston, G. P.

1897 *The Antiquities of Tennessee.* Robert Clark, Cincinnati.

Todd, T. W., and D. W. Lyon

1925 Cranial Suture Closure, Its Progress and Age Relationship, Part II. Ectocranial Closure in Adult Males of White Stock. *American Journal of Physical Anthropology* 8:23–45.

Trinkaus, E.

1984 Western Asia. In *The Origins of Modern Humans: A World Survey of the Fossil Evidence,* edited by F. H. Smith and F. Spencer, pp. 251–93. Alan R. Liss, New York.

Trotter, M.

1970 Estimation of Stature from Intact Long Bones. In *Personal Identification in Mass Disasters,* edited by T. D. Stewart, pp. 71–83. National Museum of Natural History, Washington, D.C.

Trotter, M., and C. C. Gleser

1958 A Re-evaluation of Estimation of Stature Based on Measurements of Stature Taken During Life and of Long Bones After Death. *American Journal of Physical Anthropology* 16:79–123.

Tuggle, W. O.

1973 Shem, Ham and Japheth. In *The Papers of W. O. Tuggle,* edited by E. Current-Garcia and D. B. Hatfield. University of Georgia Press, Athens.

Turner, C. G., II

1979 Dental Anthropological Implications of Agriculture among the Jomon People of Central Japan. *American Journal of Physical Anthropology* 51:619–35.

Ubelaker, D. H.

1974 *Reconstruction of Demographic Profiles from Ossuary Skeletal Samples: A Case Study from the Tidewater Potomac.* Smithsonian Contributions to Anthropology No. 18. Smithsonian Institution, Washington, D.C.

1978 *Human Skeletal Remains: Excavation, Analysis, Interpretation.* Aldine, Chicago.

1979 Skeletal Evidence for Kneeling in Prehistoric Ecuador. *American Journal of Physical Anthropology* 51:679–86.

Upham, S.

1984 Adaptive Diversity and Southwestern Abandonment. *Journal of Anthropological Research* 40:235–56.

Vickery, K. D.
1970 Evidence Supporting the Theory of Climatic Change and the Decline of Hopewell. *Wisconsin Archaeologist* 51:57–76.

Vogel, J. C., and N. J. van der Merwe
1977 Isotopic Evidence for Early Maize Cultivation in New York State. *American Antiquity* 42:238–42.

Waldron, H. A.
1983 On the Post-mortem Accumulation of Lead by Skeletal Tissues. *Journal of Archaeological Science* 10:35–40.

Walker, P. L.
1986 Porotic Hyperostosis in a Marine-Dependent California Indian Population. *American Journal of Physical Anthropology* 69:345–54.

Walker, R.
1980 Dental Pathologies, Wear, and Sexual Dimorphism at the Gold Mine Site. B.A. Honors Thesis, Department of Anthropology, University of Arkansas, Fayetteville.

Washburn, S. L.
1952 The Strategy of Physical Anthropology. In *Anthropology Today: An Encyclopedic Inventory,* edited by A. L. Kroeber, pp. 1–14. Wenner-Gren Foundation, New York.

Webb, C. H.
1968 The Extent and Content of Poverty Point Culture. *American Antiquity* 33:297–321.
1970 Settlement patterns in the Poverty Point Cultural Complex. *Southeastern Archaeological Conference Bulletin* 12:3–12.

Webb, W. S., and D. L. DeJarnette
1942 *An Archaeological Survey of Pickwick Basin in the Adjacent Portions of the States of Alabama, Mississippi and Tennessee.* Bureau of American Ethnology Bulletin No. 129. Smithsonian Institution, Washington, D.C.
1948a *Little Bear Creek Site Ct8.* Alabama Museum of Natural History Museum Paper No. 26, University.
1948b *The Perry Site Lu25.* Alabama Museum of Natural History Museum Paper No. 25, University.

Weinberg, E. D.
1974 Iron and Susceptibility to Infectious Disease. *Science* 184:952–56.
1977 Infection and Iron Metabolism. *American Journal of Clinical Nutrition* 30:1485–90.

Weiss, K. M.
1973 *Demographic Models for Anthropology.* Society for American Archaeology, *Memoirs* 27.

Welch, P. D.
1990 *Moundville's Economy.* The University of Alabama Press, Tuscaloosa.

Wells, C.
1967 Pseudopathology. In *Diseases in Antiquity, A Survey of the Diseases, Injuries, and Surgery of Early Populations,* edited by D. R. Brothwell and A. T. Sandison, pp. 390–404. C. C. Thomas, Springfield, Illinois.

1975 Ancient Obstetric Hazards and Female Mortality. *Bulletin of the New York Academy of Medicine* 51:1235–49.

White, D. R., G. P. Murdock, and R. Scaglion
1971 Natchez Class and Rank Reconsidered. *Ethnology* 10:369–88.

Willey, G. R., and J. A. Sabloff
1980 *A History of American Archaeology.* 2d ed. W. H. Freeman, San Francisco.

Willey, G. R., and D. B. Shimkin
1973 The Maya Collapse: A Summary View. In *The Classic Maya Collapse,* edited by T. P. Culbert, pp. 457–501. University of New Mexico Press, Albuquerque.

Williams, S., and J. P. Brain
1983 *Excavations at the Lake George Site, Yazoo County, Mississippi, 1958–1960.* Papers of the Peabody Museum of Archaeology and Ethnology, vol. 74, Harvard University, Cambridge.

Wing E. S., and A. B. Brown
1979 *Paleonutriton.* Academic Press, New York.

Winters, H. D.
1974a Introduction to the new edition of *Indian Knoll,* by W. S. Webb, pp. v–xxvii. University of Tennessee Press, Knoxville.
1974b Some Unusual Grave Goods from a Mississippian Burial Mound. *Indian Notes* 10:34–46.
n.d. A Commentary on the Contents of a Mississippian Burial Mound at the Mitchell Site, Madison County, Illinois. Ms. in possession of the author.

Wittmers, L. E., A. Alich, and A. C. Aufderheide
1981 Lead in Bone. I. Direct Analysis for Lead in Milligram Quantities of Bone Ash by Graphite Furnace Atomic Absorption Spectroscopy. *American Journal of Clinical Pathology* 75:80–85.

Wittry, W. O., and J. O. Vogel
1962 Illinois State Museum Projects: October 1961 to June 1962. In *First Annual Report: American Bottoms Archaeology: July 1, 1961–June 30, 1962,* pp. 15–30. Illinois Archaeological Survey, Urbana.

Wobst, H. M.
1974 Boundary Conditions for Aeolithic Social Systems: A Simulation Approach. *American Antiquity* 39:147–78.
1976 Locational Relationships in Paleolithic Society. In *The Demographic Evolution of Human Populations,* edited by R. H. Ward and K. M. Weiss, pp. 49–58. Academic Press, London.

Wolf, D. J.
1977 Middle Mississippian: A Prehistoric Cultural System Viewed from a Biological Perspective. In *Biocultural Adaptation in Prehistoric America,* edited by R. L. Blakely, pp. 27–44. Proceedings No. 11. Southern Anthropological Society, University of Georgia Press, Athens.

Woodiel, D. K.
1980 St. Gabriel: Prehistoric Life on the Mississippi. Master's thesis, Department of Geography and Anthropology, Louisiana State University, Baton Rouge.

Woods, W. I.
1986 Prehistoric Settlement and Subsistence in the Upland Cahokia Creek

Drainage. Ph.D. dissertation, Department of Geography, University of Wisconsin, Milwaukee.

Wright, M. H., D. C. Stout, and W. M. Bass
1973 Skeletal Material from the West Site (40DV12), Davidson County, Tennessee. *Tennessee Archaeologist* 29:12–50.

Yarrow, H. C.
1880 *Study of Mortuary Customs Among the North American Indians.* Government Printing Office, Washington, D.C.

❊ Contributors

Patricia S. Bridges (Ph.D. 1985, University of Michigan) is an Assistant Professor of Anthropology at Queens College and the CUNY Graduate Center. Her primary research interest involves the assessment of physical activity levels from skeletal morphology using long bone dimensions and patterns of degenerative joint disease. She is currently working on a study utilizing diachronic skeletal collections from the comprehensive and well-known archaeological sequence in the lower Illinois valley.

Jane E. Buikstra is the Harold H. Swift Distinguished Service Professor of Anthropology at the University of Chicago. She is a Diplomate of the American Academy of Forensic Sciences, a Fellow of the National Academy of Sciences, a past president of the American Association of Physical Anthropologists, and current president of the American Anthropological Association. Her original focus of bioarchaeological research was the Woodland and Mississippian societies of the lower Illinois River valley, but her research universe now includes complex late prehistoric societies in Peru, ecclesiastical cemetery populations in Argentina, and Upper Paleolithic sites in Spain.

Leslie E. Eisenberg is an Adjunct Assistant Professor in the Department of Anthropology at New York University and a Consultant in Forensic Anthropology at the Office of Chief Medical Examiner in New York City. She is currently revising a manuscript for the University of Tennessee Press based on late prehistoric community health in Middle Tennessee.

Mehmet Yaşar İşcan is a Professor of Anthropology at Florida Atlantic University. He has written, co-written, and edited several publications on skeletal biology, forensic anthropology, and paleopathology. He is a Diplomate of the American Board of Forensic Anthropology and serves as forensic anthropology consultant to both the Palm Beach and the Broward County Medical Examiners' Offices. He is a member of the American Association of Physical Anthropologists, American Anthropological Association, and American Academy of Forensic Sciences.

Clark Spencer Larsen is Associate Professor of Anthropology at Purdue University and Research Associate in the Department of Anthropology at the American Museum of Natural History. While a graduate student at the University of Michigan, he developed an interest in human ecology and physical anthropology of southeastern U.S. native populations. Dr. Larsen is the author of articles and monographs in this area, including *The Anthropology of St. Catherines Island 3. Prehistoric Human Biological Adaptation,* published by the American Museum of Natural History. He is currently collaborating with Christopher B. Ruff on a study of biomechanical adaptation of contact-period coastal populations from Spanish Florida and the prehistoric western Great Basin.

Murray K. Marks is currently a doctoral candidate in the Department of Anthropology at the University of Tennessee, Knoxville. He has co-written a number of bioarchaeology reports, including the *Bioarcheology of Seminole Sink.*

Patricia Miller-Shaivitz is currently a doctoral candidate at the University of South Florida and an Adjunct Instructor in the Department of Anthropology at Florida Atlantic University and at Palm Beach Community College. She has co-written several articles on forensic anthropology and paleopathology. She is a member of the American Anthropological Association, American Association of Physical Anthropologists, American Academy of Forensic Sciences, and Sigma Xi.

George R. Milner is an Assistant Professor in the Department of Anthropology at The Pennsylvania State University. Much of his work focuses on the late prehistoric peoples of western Illinois, especially the American Bottom. Current areas of interest include the evolution of the complex chiefdom-level society at Cahokia and the biological and cultural correlates of differential adaptive success among the prehistoric populations of eastern North America.

Ann Marie Wagner Mires is a doctoral candidate in anthropology at the University of Massachusetts, Amherst. Although she continues to maintain her interest in prehistoric social systems and skeletal analyses, she is presently involved in current health research with living Native Americans. By contrasting clinical records with an individual's perception of his or her own health, Mires hopes to develop holistic health models for use by health care administrators that integrate traditional and western concepts of health and well-being.

Mary Lucas Powell is Director/Curator of the Museum of Anthropology at the University of Kentucky. She has published articles on bioarchaeological research on late prehistoric skeletal series from Alabama (Lubbub Creek and Moundville), Arkansas (Nodena and several Caddo sites), Georgia (Macon Plateau and Irene Mound), and Oklahoma (McCutchean-McLaughlin). Her revised Ph.D. dissertation from Northwestern University (1985) was recently published as *Status and Health in Prehistory, A Case Study of the Moundville Chiefdom* by the Smithsonian Institution Press. She is currently co-writing a book chapter (with Donald J. Ortner) on health and disease patterns in the southern United States prehistory for the volume on the Southeast in the Smithsonian Institution series, *Handbook of North American Indians.*

Ted A. Rathbun is Chairman and Professor in the Department of Anthropology at the University of South Carolina. He continues his research in health and disease conditions of past populations and in 1987 published a study of nineteenth-century slaves, "Health and Disease at a South Carolina Plantation: 1840–1870," in the *American Journal of Physical Anthropology* 74:239–53. He currently is analyzing skeletal samples from Union and Confederate troops of the American Civil War.

Jerome C. Rose is an Associate Professor in the Department of Anthropology at the University of Arkansas, Fayetteville. He has written or co-written a number of articles on dental histology, such as *Diet and Dentition: Developmental Disturbances,* as well as a number of works dealing with southeastern bioarchaeology, such as *Gone to a Better Land: A Biohistory of a Rural Black Cemetery in the Post-Reconstruction South.*

Christopher B. Ruff is an Associate Professor in the Department of Cell Biology and Anatomy at the Johns Hopkins University School of Medicine. After graduating in anthropology from the University of Pennsylvania, Dr. Ruff spent two years in the Orthopaedic Biomechanics Laboratory, Beth Israel Hospital/ Harvard University, Boston. He has used biomechanics theory to study the interface between behavior and skeletal morphology in several prehistoric North American population samples as well as in living human and nonhuman primates. He is currently applying this approach to the study of early hominid and hominoid remains from East Africa in addition to ongoing collaboration with Clark Spencer Larsen.

James D. Scurry currently is employed by the South Carolina Water Resources Commission and has just completed his master's thesis in geography. He received a B.A. in anthropology at the University of South Carolina in 1976 and has combined his interests in archaeology with mapping, remote sensing, and computer analysis. Excavation of the Belleview Plantation materials occurred when he was employed by the South Carolina Institute of Anthropology and Archaeology.

Bruce D. Smith, educated at Cranbrook School and the University of Michigan, is a curator of North American Archaeology in the National Museum of Natural History, Smithsonian Institution. Long an advocate of interdisciplinary research and the structure of archaeological explanation, Smith's early work in eastern North America focused on the analysis of faunal remains and the role that economies played in the landscape demography of prehistoric societies. In the 1980s one of his major interests was the long, complex history of initial development and subsequent elaboration of food-producing economies in eastern North America.

Larry L. Tieszen is a Professor in the Department of Biology at Augustana College. He has written and co-written numerous articles in the areas of stable isotopes in ecological research, prairie ecology, and paleoecology. Examples include *Estimation of Plant Biomass by Spectral Reflectance in an East African Grassland* and *Validation of Collagen Procedures for Isotopic Dietary Estimates From Present, Historic, and Fossil Consumers in the Great Plains.*

❋ Index